Queens, Concubines, and Dowagers

Pauline Stafford 👑 *Queens,*

Concubines, and Dowagers

👑 *The King's Wife in the*

Early Middle Ages

The University of Georgia Press Athens

Copyright © 1983 by the University of Georgia Press
Athens, Georgia 30602

Designed by Richard Hendel

Set in Zapf International

The paper in this book meets the guidelines for permanence and
durability of the Committee on Production Guidelines for Book
Longevity of the Council on Library Resources.
Printed in the United States of America

Library of Congress Cataloging in Publication Data

Stafford, Pauline.
    Queens, concubines, and dowagers.

    Bibliography: p.
    Includes index.
    1. Queens—Social conditions.   2. Princesses—Social con-
ditions.   3. Europe—History—392–814. 4. Middle ages—
History.   I. Title.
HQ1147.E85S73   1983   305.4'890655   82-13368
ISBN 0-8203-0639-8

For Bill, Edmund, Benjamin & Eleanor

 Contents

From the *Encomium Emmae Reginae*, by permission of the British Library.

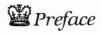 *Preface*

This book is a study of royal bedfellows and queens from about A.D. 500 to the mid-eleventh century. Its subject matter is the wives and queens of the dynasties that ruled in Frankia, Italy, and England within these date limits.

The decline and fall of the Roman Empire in the fourth, fifth, and sixth centuries left Western Europe in great turmoil. The legacy of Rome was fought over by the Germanic tribes who had contributed to that downfall, or rather by certain great families within those tribes, the greatest of whom established kingdoms and dynasties of varying duration. The idea of kingship, let alone its institutions, was far from well established in these early centuries; both kingdoms and dynasties were chronically unstable. Their raw material was provided not only by these Germanic warriors, but by the Roman and pre-Roman populations of Western Europe, and by the Christian Church, which survived the fall of the Empire to become a potent symbol of all things Roman, an agent of cultivation as well as Christianization.

During the late fifth and sixth centuries a number of dynasties and kingdoms emerged, by no means a final pattern for the political development of Western Europe and in many ways only temporary simplifications of underlying complexities, but significant nevertheless. In what had been the northern part of Roman Gaul and the Low Countries, the Merovingians had established control, with some degree of success, by the time of the death of their first great king, Clovis, in 511. To the east and south of them many other tribes and dynasties had succeeded in carving out a territory: the Burgundians, the Thuringians, the Bavarians, the Gepids, and so on. Across the Alps in Italy, the seat of Roman civilization, the Ostrogoths had taken control under their greatest king, Theoderic, who ruled from 493 to 526. His Amal dynasty was short lived, and sixth-century Italy saw a succession of kings before the arrival during the 560s of the Lombards in northern Italy. Lombard kings were to rule northern Italy from then until the conquest by Charlemagne in 774. At the end of the sixth century the Lombards were not even convinced of the need of kings, and for a brief period lived only under the rule of their dukes. The seventh and eighth centuries in Lombard Italy certainly never saw the triumph of a single dynasty with sufficient prestige to monopolize the kingship over several generations.

The situation was rather different in Merovingian Frankia. During the sixth century the Merovingian kings extended Frankish control and won great though not always lasting victories over Thuringians, Burgundians, and Bavarians. They survived as a dynasty until 751. But before the end of the seventh century the power of the Merovingian kings was shared by the increasingly important mayors of the palace, great aristocrats whose influence was confirmed by control of the royal household and even of the king himself. During the early eighth century the Carolingian mayors of Austrasia were in all but name rulers of Frankia. In 751 they finally dispensed with the Merovingian puppet kings, and Pepin I became the first true Carolingian king. It was his son Charlemagne, who ruled from 768 until 814, who created the Carolingian Empire, extended his rule into Lombard Italy and what is now Germany, and created a name and an empire with which later rulers would long conjure.

In England by the seventh century, when historical information becomes fuller, Roman Britain had been succeeded by a series of kingdoms and dynasties. The most important Anglo-Saxon kingdoms to have arisen were those of Northumbria, Mercia, East Anglia, Kent, and Wessex. But during the seventh century and even later, these were still as much confederacies as kingdoms and the rule of particular families was far from unchallenged. By the ninth century the superior position of the kingdoms of Northumbria, Mercia, and Wessex seemed established. Of these three, the West Saxon dynasty was largely a creation of the ninth century, though it could claim royal antecedents, and both Northumbria and Mercia were torn by disputes between rival families trying to make good their claims to the throne.

By the ninth century Christianity was established, in name at least, as the religion of these kingdoms, and especially of their ruling families. The baptism of the Merovingian king Clovis in the early sixth century and of the various Anglo-Saxon kings in the first half of the seventh century, as well as the conversion of the Arian Lombard king to orthodox Western Christianity in the early seventh century marked only the beginnings of the process of Christianization. This continued to advance until the end of the period under consideration. On the fringes of Christian Europe there was still pure missionary activity as late as the tenth and eleventh centuries. The East Germans in Saxony were only technically converted in the early ninth century and the earliest stages of Christianization were still under way during the rule there of the Ottonians in the tenth century.

The ninth century was dominated in continental Europe by the history of the Carolingian Empire and by the tensions and quarrels amongst the Carolingian family over its inheritance. An empire which had never been conceived of as a political and administrative unity was soon a series of kingdoms ruled by Carolingian kings. In West Frankia (roughly what was to become France) Carolingian kings continued without break until the 880s and 890s, and the tenth century saw the last descendants of the dynasty struggling for survival until supplanted in 987 by the Capetians, a family of northern French aristocrats. The Carolingian Middle Kingdom itself split three ways. Lotharingia in the north was constantly reclaimed by the West Frankish Carolingians and became a bone of contention between them and the East Frankish rulers. From its central portion emerged in the tenth century the kingdom of Burgundy. South of the Alps the kingdom of Italy was subject to constant dispute between the death of the Carolingian Louis II in 875 and the Ottonian take over in 952. In East Frankia, descendants of the Carolingians ruled until 911, when they were replaced first by the East Frankish noble Conrad and in 919 by the Liudolfing, Henry the Fowler. He and his son Otto I created the kingdom and dynasty known as the Ottonians. In 962 Otto I had himself crowned in Rome as emperor, continuing a tradition of empire in Italy that had never died since the coronation of Charlemagne on Christmas Day A.D. 800. In Britain the late ninth and tenth centuries saw the final emergence of the West Saxon dynasty to rule, at least in name, the whole of England, a rule brought to an end by the Norman Conquest of 1066.

It is the wives of the kings of these dynasties who form the subject of this book. The time and geographical span is broad, covering kingdoms and dynasties very different in their stages of development and decay. But certain basic conditions of succession and ecclesiastical politics, of the centrality of dynastic and family politics, remain similar. The condition of royal wives is so bound up with these that they provide some justification for the broad limits adopted. Inevitably a work of synthesis and generalization may do violence to the complexities of individual situations. Each marriage, each succession, each queenly action was a specific event with its own particular context. I have tried not to lose sight of this in presenting the material, but since each case could be the subject of a study in its own right some distortion is unavoidable. The advantages of synthesis lie in the light that comparable situations throw one upon another and upon the underlying conditions determining the role of queens throughout the period.

I have chosen to present these queens through the stages of their lives, not simply dynasty by dynasty. The chronicle and narrative sources that provide almost all the detail pose such problems that I have considered them specifically in the first chapter. I have tried to examine not only the distortions in their accounts that arise from the prejudices and situation of the authors, but also to consider the views of women and female action which determined their picture at the most fundamental level. In the second chapter I have dealt with the factors that influenced the king's choice of wife, how free that choice was, and what sort of bride he sought; I have also looked at the technical side of wooing and choosing wives. Marriage for kings, as for nobles, was a family concern, and in Chapter Three I have looked at the marital practices of kings, the numbers of wives they had, their reasons for divorce and remarriage, and the interaction between royal needs and ecclesiastical theory. Chapters Four and Five are concerned with the activities of queens during their husbands' lifetimes: Chapter Four with their role in the royal household, their domestic position and politics, and Chapter Five with the wider political role they were sometimes able to play as well as the formal making of a queen. Chapters Six and Seven cover the queen's dowagerhood, examining the fates which repudiated or widowed wives suffered. In Chapter Six I have looked at queens who attempted to control the succession (usually in favor of their own sons), what they hoped to gain from such control, and how far they were successful. Chapter Seven deals with the retirement of widows, with their final years and death.

Throughout I have tried to examine not only the general social and political issues raised by the activities of these women, but also to give some picture of the life of an early medieval queen. The sources are so sparse and so different from those of a later age that we may never be able to gain a vivid impression of any individual queen, but we may be able to discover *something* of the way they lived, acted, and even felt.

My thanks are due to the inter-library loan staff at Huddersfield Polytechnic, without whose efforts to track down continental publications this book would be immeasurably impoverished, and to the staff of the Brotherton Library, Leeds, especially those of the history section, for their unfailing help and courtesy. My colleagues in the Department of History and Political Studies at Huddersfield Polytechnic carried the burden of my light timetable in 1979–80, during which much of the work for this book was completed. I am grateful to them and especially to Keith Dockray, who has always encouraged my interest in these areas of history. I owe an especial debt of gratitude to Janet Nelson for much encouragement, advice, and discussion over several years and for reading this book in manuscript, giving me the benefit of her knowledge, and saving what follows from many errors. I was fortunate in having in Sandra Lewis a typist of great accuracy and intelligence. My deepest debt is to my husband and children, who created conditions in which I could work and who were both sympathetic and long suffering. I hope that this book may seem worth their efforts.

Queens, Concubines, and Dowagers

Chapter 1 ♜ *Sources and Images*

Women have usually stood half hidden in the wings of the historical pageant. This is true of all periods, but is an acute problem in the early Middle Ages, when even the men of the house are rarely well illuminated. Although royal women fared better than their sisters in this respect, they have often been hauled under the spotlight only to be vilified, to be depicted in ways that tell as much about their detractors as about themselves. To bring the queens of the early Middle Ages into the light of day, let alone to give them life or comprehend their actions, is a task which our sources never make easy, often render impossible.

From 984 to 991 the Ottonian Empire was ruled by a woman. The dowager empress Theophanu controlled a vast agglomeration of territories stretching from Italy to the Baltic, from Lorraine to the Slavonic marches. As regent for her infant son Otto III she granted land, made war and peace, received ambassadors, appointed bishops. She enjoyed power matched only by a handful of tenth-century kings, surpassed by none. Yet Theophanu's life is a series of questions. Her feelings, thoughts and motives are as obscure as those of any tenth-century man. The most fundamental details of her biography are lacking: her date of birth is unknown, her parentage fiercely debated; the dates, even the order, of the births of her children, especially her four daughters, is only tentatively established. Theophanu was a Greek princess, which helps account for doubt over her antecedents, and medieval sources frequently lack our interest in births, know little of our passion for precise dating. But the problems are not confined to Theophanu nor to such minor issues. Long stretches of early history, especially in England, are shrouded in mystery. The very identity of the elusive Osyth escapes us: was she a queen, wife of King Sighere of East Anglia, repudiated by him for her failure to consummate their marriage and thus incarcerated in the nunnery of Crich near Clacton where she was murdered by pirates; or was she the abbess of Aylesbury, daughter of King Penda of Mercia? We shall never know. Even in the better-documented England of the late tenth century, the parentage of the first wife of Æthelred the Unready is unknown. Was she the daughter of the shadowy ealdorman Ordmaer, or of the obscure Thored of York? How many of Æthelred's many children did she bear? When was she born? How, why, and where did she die? The only fact which has survived to give her a place in history is her name, Ælfgifu. There at least she has the edge on her husband's ancestor, the wife of his forebear, King Ecgberht, whose existence can be surmised only from the fact of her son.

Ninth- and tenth-century Europe is better illuminated, though its royal women often lurk in dark places. Of the descendants of Charlemagne, 359 born before A.D. 1000 have been traced: 229 are men, 130 are women. The slight numerical advantage enjoyed by boys at birth could not account for such an imbalance, especially since higher rates of male infant mortality and violent death favor girls. The figures merely indicate the difficulties of tracing women. Women who married kings may fare better than most, but still tend to remain obscure. Queen Adelaide was the second wife of the late ninth-century Carolingian king Louis the Stammerer. She was the mother of a daughter and of his posthumous son, Charles the Simple. She salvaged the infant from the clutches of his half brothers, kept him safe until circumstances favored his accession to the throne, and was rewarded with influence at his court. Yet only long debate has settled the question of her origins, while the date of her marriage—875 or 877—remains undecided. In this case a normal obscurity has been compounded by a deliberate contemporary ambiguity. The major source of information for the 870s in West Frankia is the *Annals of St. Bertin*, written by Archbishop Hincmar of Rheims. Hincmar will come to our notice again as a great champion of the Christian view of marriage and monogamy, also as a chief counsellor of Louis's father, the emperor Charles the Bald. It seems likely that Charles forced his son Louis to divorce his first wife and marry this same Adelaide. Hincmar, as Charles's courtier, found himself tacitly assenting to the double offense of adultery compounded with incest: Louis and Adelaide were distant cousins. The archbishop's desire to draw a veil over the affair in his *Annals* has complicated all subsequent enquiry.

When the doings of kings were retailed, the activities of their queens were normally considered unimportant; when these activities are chronicled, the emerging picture cannot be accepted unquestioned. Every possible form of bias and distortion enters in: malicious gossip, political propaganda, deliberate suppression of facts, inadequate knowledge, blatant antifeminism, even simple lies. It is too easily forgotten that the remote men of the early Middle Ages were political animals, and that their political battles were fought as fervently as our own, though sometimes with weapons unfamiliar to us. Character assassination was a perennial weapon in their armory: great men, or would-be great men, could always be attacked through their wives and mothers. As easy targets, royal women became scapegoats for the actions of their men. More subtle were the distortions produced by the images of women and of female action available to their contemporaries. Only as we begin to understand the palettes these authors used can reality be reconstructed from the pictures they have left.

Contemporary Biographies of Queens

A handful of near-contemporary lives of individual queens have survived. From sixth- and seventh-century Frankia there are two lives of Saint Radegund and one of Balthild. Briefly the queen of Clothar I, Radegund, after repudiation, became the founder and abbess of the nunnery of Poitiers. Balthild was an Anglo-Saxon slave girl who became the wife of Clovis II and was mother and regent for her son Clothar III before her enforced retirement from political life took her into the nunnery at Chelles. Tenth-century Germany produced three lives of saintly queens. Mathilda, wife of Henry the Fowler and mother of Otto the Great, like Radegund, boasts two lives: the so-called *Vita Mahthildis reginae antiquior*, written for her grandson Otto II, and the *Vita Mahthildis reginae posterior* for her great-grandson Henry II. Mathilda's daughter-in-law, the empress Adelaide, second wife of Otto the Great, was the subject of a biography written by Abbot Odilo of Cluny, the *Epitaphium Adelaidae*. Two other works, both from eleventh-century England, deserve consideration here, though strictly speaking neither is the biography of a queen. The *Encomium Emmae Reginae* was written for and at the request of Emma, wife and widow successively of Æthelred the Un-

3

ready and his Danish supplanter, King Cnut; she was mother both of Harthacnut and Edward the Confessor. The work is a selective history of the early eleventh century, in which Emma's doings are justified even if she is not always its central figure. Emma's daughter-in-law Queen Edith, wife of Edward the Confessor, commissioned a work in the mid-1060s, now known as the *Life of King Edward Who Rests at Westminster*. This title reflects a change in the author's intentions during the composition of the work. His original brief was praise of Edith and her influential family—her father, Earl Godwin of Wessex, and her brothers, Harold and Tostig. While never intended as a biography of Edith, it has much to say of her, especially in its original, unmutilated form. Eight lives of queens from a period of five centuries is a scanty haul, especially when they are so concentrated in date and areas, and when two of them do not focus on the queen herself.

The *Encomium Emmae* was written in praise of Emma: at the same time its writer was demonstrating that her son Harthacnut had been the right choice as king. The death of the Danish conqueror Cnut in 1035 had left the English throne open to dispute. The major contenders were his two sons: Harold Harefoot, son of his first wife, Ælfgifu of Northampton, and Harthacnut, son of his second wife, Emma. There were two additional claimants in Edward and Alfred, Emma's sons by her first marriage to the English king, Æthelred the Unready. From 1035 to 1037 these four struggled over the succession, though Edward and Alfred, in exile on the continent in 1035, were late entrants in the field. Emma's primary support was for Harthacnut, though she may have flirted with an encouragement of Edward and Alfred, who arrived in England in 1036. Harold's success in 1037 drove Emma into exile in Flanders, where she remained until Harthacnut's accession in 1040. It was only after this date that the *Encomium* was commissioned, probably from a Flemish monk. The work claims that Cnut had promised the English throne to Harthacnut. In his desire to emphasize Harthacnut's throneworthiness the author completely suppresses Emma's first marriage to Æthelred; her sons by that marriage, Edward and Alfred, with their excellent claims to the English throne, are tacitly treated as sons of Cnut. Emma's actions are systematically excused. She had given full support to neither Edward nor Alfred in their attempts to claim inheritance, attempts in which Alfred had met a cruel death by blinding.

The author claims as a forgery a letter supposedly sent by Emma summoning these sons to England; in fact, it was a deliberate lure by Harold Harefoot. The author of the *Encomium* defends Emma against criticism that she had failed to die with Alfred, "since it would have appeared wrong . . . if a matron of such reputation had died for worldly power." Edward himself is made to discount his own claims in favor of Harthacnut, instructing his mother to support this half brother to whom the English nobility had taken an oath. The author has complicated still further an obscure political crisis. He has left us uncertain how Emma reacted to each of her sons between 1035 and 1037. A source that suppresses the very marriage that gave Emma her place in English life and denies the paternity of a future king has indulged in more than marginal trimming of the truth. Yet it leaves us in no doubt of Emma's central involvement in the crisis of 1035–37 nor of the importance she attached to the question of succession.

The *Life of Edward* was written at the request of Queen Edith during the troubled years 1065–66. Although he probably began writing before the death of the childless Edward the Confessor, the author's work spanned the usurpation of the English throne by Edith's brother, Harold son of Godwin, and his subsequent removal at Hastings by the conquering Duke William of Normandy. The author was overtaken by events that have probably obscured his original purpose. His book lavishes praise on the family of Earl Godwin, especially on Edith herself, while her brothers Harold and Tostig are paragons among men. Only the quarrel between these brothers in 1066 clouds the writer's view of the house of Godwin. The work may have been intended to groom the family for kingship: it certainly could be used to suggest the house's crucial importance to a new king, even its rights as king maker. Edith like Emma feared for her own future on the death of her royal husband and sought to salvage some security. The picture that the life gives of the aged, holy Edward, for whom the troubles of politics were a distraction, is matched by that of the devoted Edith, a daughter rather than wife to a saintly king, who took upon herself the care for his worldly image and the running of his court.

The *Encomium Emmae* and the *Life of King Edward* were commissioned by and dedicated to living queens. They offer a rare opportunity to examine these women and their purposes from their own viewpoint, and reveal an obsession with the succession to the throne that we shall explore more fully later. Most queenly biographies were post-mortem products, describing women whose fame is largely a measure of their utility to a religious house or a dynasty. The lives of Radegund, Balthild, Mathilda, and Adelaide all extolled the virtues of dead queens; all but the last were written in nunneries founded by those queens. Both lives of Radegund were produced at Poitiers, the first by Venantius Fortunatus, who served Radegund in the abbey and knew her well, the second written a generation later by the nun Baudonivia. Both recensions of the life of Balthild come from her nunnery at Chelles. The two lives of Mathilda were written in Nordhausen, the favored house where she spent much of her retirement. It is therefore no surprise that all present their subjects as holy women and saints. Not only was this, as we shall see, an image of the female with which writers at this date felt at ease, but attributions of holiness also brought to the nunnery concerned all the benefits of the possession of the memory and cult of a royal saint. These lives are products of two societies, sixth- and seventh-century Frankia and tenth-century Germany, widely separated in time but similar in important respects. Both were still in the early stages of conversion to Christianity, in which the royal dynasty played a central role; both had a vigorous monastic life in which nunneries grew wealthy and important as the havens for daughters and wives of kings and nobles. Women were able to achieve prominence as abbesses of nunneries which themselves helped to shape contemporary culture. Thus when in tenth-century Germany Otto II and Henry II wished to have historical works lauding their dynasty and ancestry, they turned to a nunnery at Nordhausen for the life of a female saint and prophet, their forebear, Queen Mathilda. In such societies the lives of saintly queens may rival if not exceed those of holy kings.

A saintly ancestor was an earnest of divine favor beloved of kings. The desire to possess them was impeded in later centuries by the due processes of canonization. In earlier times saints were local products, their cults more easily encouraged. Ottonian writers rarely missed an opportunity of casting an additional aura of sanctity over the dynasty. Hroswitha, a Gandersheim nun who wrote a work on Otto the Great, claimed that Otto's Anglo-Saxon wife Eadgyth was descended from the great English martyr-king, Saint Oswald, a dubious piece of genealogy. Mathilda, wife of Henry the Fowler, the first king of the dynasty, became the favored Ottonian family saint. Mathilda's biographers are emphatic as regards her beauty and her virtues. She was descended from the Saxon hero Widukind, who had led the resistance to Charlemagne, a descent that probably mattered to Otto II and Henry II as much as it had ever done to Henry the Fowler when he chose his bride. Mathilda's first biography was fashioned in part on the model of Fortunatus's *Life of Radegund*. Radegund had been presented as a great ascetic, and her garment does not always fit Mathilda, a queen who never lost her taste for luxurious ornament and who produced five children in the course of her married life. Mathilda was primarily a political saint, short on miracles but strong in the gifts of prophecy conveniently exercised in favor of those who later proved successful in gaining the throne. In the older life, written for Otto II, his grandmother shows more than normal delight on the occasion of his birth, remarking portentously that the child will be a great credit to his parents.

The second life was written during the early and insecure years of Henry II, her great-grandson through the cadet line. Mathilda's gifts of political prophecy were deployed in his favor. His father, Henry the Wrangler, had been Mathilda's favorite grandchild. On the occasion of a delightfully informal family gathering Mathilda and her daughter-in-law Empress Adelaide are surrounded by playing and laughing children. The young Henry comes up to his grandmother for a kiss and lays his head on her lap. As she strokes his hair, Mathilda foretells that this beloved name Henry, that of her own dead husband, will not pass from the dynasty: some future Henry will be a great king. This same second life is the source of Mathilda's alleged preference for her younger son Henry, Henry II's own grandfather. It is claimed that she attempted to gain the throne for him rather than for his elder brother Otto the Great. A statement of such utility to Henry II, the beneficiary of this life, would have to be dismissed were it not borne out by more neutral evidence. Its inclusion in the second life, like its omission from the first, dedicated to Otto's son, reminds us of the prime purposes of these biographies. The two lives of Mathilda are not simple portraits of the queen but mixtures of accepted norms of female sanctity and political requirements. They belong to a spate of family histories in Ottonian Germany, to be numbered with those other products of royal nunneries, the *Annals of Quedlinburg* and Hroswitha's *Gesta Ottonis*. Both inside the family circle and on a wider scale the Ottonian dynasty was beset by the problems arising from the recent acquisition of kingship. When the security of the family, its unity, and its past mattered, women were given a more prominent place in history.

The empress Adelaide, Mathilda's daughter-in-law, attracted a biographer in the person of Abbot Odilo of Cluny. Odilo knew Adelaide in her old age; he was her regular companion during the later 990s, when she had already turned sixty. His *Epitaph*, written soon after her death in 999, is the account of a personal friend, who apparently stood in some awe of this grand old lady. Especially in his lengthy description of her final years, the mist that shrouds all these women as people is often pierced by flashes of intimate detail. Odilo's Adelaide is not the child-bride of King Lothar, nor the determined woman who fled in disguise from the prisons of King Berengar. She is not the empress who sat beside Otto I, nor the regent for her grandson Otto III, although stereotyped shadows of all these women flit across his pages. Odilo's Adelaide is preeminently an old woman approaching death, nostalgically reminiscing about her past, encountering old friends with tears in her eyes. Adelaide's strong personality, which impressed Odilo in old age, has left us many glimpses of the woman herself. She was remembered at Quedlinburg for the vigor of her almsgiving, hitching up her long skirts like a peasant woman the more easily to minister to the poor, distributing alms with both hands until she collapsed with fatigue. It is an echo of the vigor and determination of the young queen who escaped the prisons of Berengar of Italy in 951. According to Hroswitha, Adelaide and her servant tunneled out of the prison, hiding in caves and out-of-the-way places as they journeyed toward safety at Reggio. On one occasion, when Berengar and his men were hard on her heels, Adelaide hid in the tall ripe corn while Berengar passed within yards of her, parting the grass with his sword. Odilo tells of the flight in disguise, the wandering in the marshland. Tired and hungry, Adelaide and her maid met a fisherman with his catch. He failed to recognize a queen divested of her outward rank, but offered to share his fish, which Adelaide cooked like any servant girl. The flight of the later empress in disguise appealed to the tenth-century imagination as it does to ours, and may have been embellished in the telling. Yet there is something of the woman herself in these stories.

But Odilo's *Epitaph* is in no sense a modern biography; it is partisan, uncritical, and much influenced by the models—especially from the Church fathers—that Odilo used. It is heavily biased towards her last years and her religious works, diverting attention from her long political life. Adelaide had been a lifelong friend and patron of the Abbey of Cluny, whether in her Burgundian homeland, in Italy, or in Germany: Odilo was the second abbot of that monastery to be bound closely to her. The work was dedicated to Andreas, the abbot of San Salvatore in Pavia, one of Adelaide's favored foundations. Odilo was providing a model for empresses and queens, yet, although he stresses at the outset Adelaide's domestic role and her strength in government, the latter remains shadowy. Her virtues are faith, hope, and charity, but also justice, strength, and prudence, assumed to be male attributes. Where we might wish for some detail of her practice of these virtues, Odilo passes into stereotypes. In early life she played Leah and Martha, active women: in old age she prefers the contemplative parts of Rachel and Mary. She is worthy to see her sons' sons to the third generation. There is a hint of her reluctance to relinquish power to her daughter-in-law, "that Greek woman" (the strength of Adelaide's feeling is echoed by Odilo, who consistently refuses to name Theophanu) but the precious detail, even the self-justification, are missing.

Odilo, like other biographers, preferred to draw a religious rather than a political picture of Adelaide: it was a picture which his sources and preconceptions favored. The holy woman par excellence was presented in one of the most influential queenly biographies of the early Middle Ages, Fortunatus's *Life of Radegund*. This is a sustained picture of ascetic athleticism. Radegund's life at Poitiers was a prolonged round of prayers, fasting, and self-mortification. As a queen she had shunned her royal tasks, arriving late at meals because she would not curtail her vigils, spurning the royal bed for the king's chapel, until the king in anger protested that he had a nun for a wife and sent her to fulfil her true vocation. As a nun she delighted in menial tasks: cleaning the shoes of her sister nuns, washing the foul sores of the poor (though confining her more intimate ablutions to the women), brushing out the darkest corners, carrying wood for the fire. Her constant fasts reached their height in Lent, when she ate scarcely at all and drank so little that she was almost too parched to say the psalms. Her flesh was mortified by iron bands that became embedded in her skin; on one occasion she had a brazier of hot coals prepared in the shape of a cross and lay upon it until the sisters could smell her flesh burning. Fortunatus's portrait is repellent to the modern eye, but exercised a powerful appeal in the Middle Ages as a type of consecrated womanhood. How accurate a description it is of Radegund is a more difficult question. We should be wary of outright dismissal of medieval asceticism from a modern, rationalist standpoint. Yet Fortunatus's ascetic Radegund is sometimes difficult to reconcile with the abbess to whom he dedicated charming classical poems when presenting her with a bunch of flowers or some other small gift. Fortunatus was a sixth-century Italian; he and Radegund were products of a culture that united the literature and life of early Christian asceticism with that of Rome.

It is a different though not necessarily more accurate picture of Radegund that emerges from the pages of Baudonivia's later *Life*. Admittedly Baudonivia takes Fortunatus as read and claims to concentrate on other aspects of her subject's life, but her Radegund is a fearless, proud, and intensely royal woman who excites admiration among the Franks for her brave personal attack on pagan idols. She treats with bishops and nobles, never loses interest in the affairs of the kingdom, writes to kings, prays for peace. Her prayers, vigils, and insatiable lust for relics have a practical aim; as she writes to King Sigibert, they are to ensure the stability of the kingdom. Here is not the menial queen turned servant, but a royal abbess aware of her dignity. When a servant girl dares to sit on Radegund's chair in church, she is riveted there for three days while the seat burns her until the smoke rises. Only after this due punishment does the queen and abbess deign to hear her pleas and remit her punishment, exercising the royal virtues of severity and mercy. The force of Radegund's character did not make her a comfortable neighbor; at her death a protracted dispute with the local bishop was unresolved and he refused to bury her. If Fortunatus belongs to the thought-world of late antiquity and the Christian fathers, the Frankish nun Baudonivia sits firmly in the religious world of the emergent Germanic kingdoms, a world not untouched by that of Fortunatus, but with its own sense of what became kings and their queens, of the purpose of the religious vocation and its quasi-noble style of living. Her ideal of sanctity is active; it is involved, through prayers and the collection of relics, with the safety of the kingdom and the advance of Christianity.

Yet other aspects of Radegund and her Poitiers are highlighted by her sister abbess, Caesaria of Arles, and by Gregory of Tours. Caesaria wrote to Radegund expressing her concern at the familiarity of the Poitiers nuns with men, urging her to pursue divine reading, perhaps wooing her from the secular aspects of Fortunatus's culture. Poitiers was no great center of sacred studies in the sixth century. The troubles that broke out there after Radegund's death—with the nuns playing dice, admitting men, and taking frequent baths—suggest that her rule there was relaxed. Any attempt to discover the real Radegund founders between conflicting images. It would certainly be unwise to accept Fortunatus's picture without quibble.

Yet that picture became a model for later queens' lives and in its presentation of an image of female action may even have influenced their practices. Both the seventh-century life of Balthild and the older tenth-century life of Mathilda used Fortunatus, though both are only shadows of the original. Cultural patterns and saintly requirements had changed. Mathilda may be described rising from the king's bed by night to pray, but only after Henry has fallen asleep; she returns in the morning before he awakes. Her prayers, in other words, did not interfere with her conjugal duties. The later life of Mathilda introduces a reference to the continence of Henry and Mathilda, reflecting a further shift of ideas by the early eleventh century. Like Radegund, Mathilda washed the poor, but the later life indicates that this was done only on Sundays, to commemorate the day of her husband Henry's death. Mathilda is a family saint and her biographers show her as wife, mother, and grandmother. Balthild had similarly been cast in Radegund's mold, performing servants' duties and cleaning out lavatories at Chelles, but again her biographer is eager to remind us that Chelles had a queen for a founder. Her religious works were less ascetic than political: the reforming of monastic discipline and the bringing of religious houses more firmly into the royal orbit.

Most of these lives were written in religious houses founded by queens and set out to glorify their founders. If they stress their good works, their piety, their ecclesiastical benefactions, this reflects the milieu of their production, the acceptability of such images in the ecclesiastically dominated culture and the fact that most were written from the perspective of a retired or repudiated queen. Propa-

11

ganda purposes in several cases complicate the interpretation. Their failure to provide the picture desired by a modern reader may prompt their dismissal, or at best their acceptance as stereotypes. Did Radegund, Balthild, and Mathilda *all* wash the feet of the poor? Arguably the answer might be yes. There is the ring of circumstantial truth to the detail that Mathilda performed the ritual on Sundays, to the story of Adelaide hitching up her skirts to free her actions. Queens cannot have been immune from the ideals presented to them; it would be the supreme irony if only Radegund, whose life so powerfully reinforced this model of Christian humility, should have failed to conform to the type. The major problem with all these lives is their cursory treatment of all but the religious roles of their subjects; neither the ideal nor the reality of other activities is presented. Yet through these writings we begin to understand how queens were *encouraged* to act, even if we do not get a rounded picture of how they actually behaved.

Chronicles, Narratives, and Tracts

The motives of their authors make the lives of queens adulatory. They give insight into the virtues that contemporaries admired in queens, especially in monastic founders and dynastic saints. The lives of kings and the chronicles of their doings present us with portraits of royal women that suffer from all the problems of images, stereotypes, and bias. In addition, these accounts are rarely flattering. The difficulty ceases to be that of skirting compliments; the challenge is to make any sense out of the actions of women systematically vilified.

No one can make even a passing acquaintance with Merovingian history without taking away a vivid impression of two formidable women, Brunhild and her archenemy, Fredegund. The wives respectively of two brothers, kings Sigibert and Chilperic, their actions fill the pages of the chronicles of late sixth- and early seventh-century Frankia. Their importance is beyond doubt: Brunhild, for example, was wife of one king, regent for her son and grandsons. The reputations they have left in the sources is tribute to the impression they made. The violence of Merovingian political passions has distorted the accounts of their actions. Gregory of Tours, the chief chronicler of sixth-century Frankia, identified Chilperic as the Nero and Herod of his day, and his third wife Fredegund as his evil abettor. Gregory's Fredegund is a scheming and murderous woman, locked in implacable hatred against her stepsons but especially against Brunhild, the avenging sister of Chilperic's second and murdered wife Galswinth. His Brunhild is thrown in a favorable light by contrast. Her probable role in Gregory's appointment to the bishopric of Tours and her patronage of the cult of its saint, Martin, can only have endeared Brunhild to Gregory.

For Gregory, as a sixth-century writer, Brunhild had a legitimate part as an avenger of her murdered sister. For Fredegar, writing in Burgundy more than a generation later, Brunhild had become a bloodthirsty and unscrupulous woman. Unlike Gregory, Fredegar knew the end of her career; her horrific murder at the hands of her nephew, Fredegund's son Clothar, and the feud that rent Merovingian politics under her grandsons and nephew. Fredegar also had access to the powerful representations of Brunhild as the queen pitted against Columbanus in Jonas's life of that saint, and against Desiderius in Sisebut's life. Both lives subsume Brunhild into the character of the biblical Jezebel, wife of Ahab, who caused the death of prophets and holy men and who fell in old age into the hands of King Jehu. Jezebel's attempt to seduce him with her faded charms failed miserably; he threw her from a window to be trampled to death by horses and torn apart by dogs until little remained of that once-seductive body. The story was ideal for adaptation to describe a queen who found herself in conflict with a latter-day prophet like Columbanus. It has deeply colored the seventh-century view of Brunhild and her later career. It informs the descriptions of her violent end, tied to the tail of an unbroken horse and trampled until only shreds of her body remained to be burned; it is discernible in the later story (in the early eighth-century *Liber historiae Francorum*) of this sixty-year-old great-grandmother who set out her charms to woo her young nephew Clothar III. If Gregory found the vengeance motif useful in his representation of Brunhild against Fredegund, Fredegar used the equally strong idea of women as peacemakers against her when he retailed the catalogue of Brunhild's supposed murders, recounted the discord she stirred. Brunhild is partly a victim of the perennial need for scapegoats; her undoubted influence

13

and her clash with Columbanus set her up for the part. The power of such images prolonged their life in the propagandist legends of the seventh century. When these came to be committed to writing in the unfriendly Neustrian *Liber historiae Francorum*, Brunhild had become fixed as the utterly evil genius of Merovingian politics, murderer of eleven kings, including her own grandsons and great-grandsons.

Fredegund and Brunhild pose a typical problem. Truth is distorted by bias, propaganda, gossip, and sheer antifeminism. Yet a blind defense of either would be no service to the truth. Merovingian political methods were nothing if not violent; no one involved in them could look forward confidently to a peaceful deathbed. Both women were political actors with strong motives. Fredegund, her husband's third wife, inevitably saw her brace of stepsons standing in her way. Brunhild, a widow seeking vengeance and fearing for her own safety in a shifting situation, had to be ready to dispose of her enemies. Some of the crimes imputed to them are fantastic, such as Fredegar's suggestion that Brunhild incited Sigibert, immediately after their marriage, to murder his mayor of the palace, Gogo; Gregory informs us that Gogo died some fifteen years later of natural causes. The multiple murders of her descendants imputed to Brunhild by the *Liber historiae* say much about Neustrian propaganda, little about Brunhild's career. In other cases, motivation and circumstance must be carefully weighed if answers are to be found.

Then as now contemporaries could be genuinely ill informed of the precise details of murders. Accusations were bandied about according to bias and taste. When such murders are domestic, women are an easy target. At least five people are variously accused of the murder of King Chilperic, husband of Fredegund and brother-in-law of Brunhild, at his hunting lodge at Chelles in 584. With his customary impartiality, Fredegar arraigns Brunhild. She certainly had the motive to avenge the murders of husband and sister, not to mention the control of the resources of a Frankish court as a means to hire and deploy assassins. Fredegar has a telling detail in the name of the assassin she used. Gregory of Tours tells how Fredegund accused Eberulf, King Chilperic's treasurer, because he refused her advances. Here Gregory was indulging his own bias against Fredegund, using the common motif of liaison between queen and court official. The same theme occurs in the story of Chilperic's death in the *Liber historiae Francorum*, where Fredegund herself is accused of committing the crime in order to cover her own adulteries with the mayor of the palace. The story tells how Chilperic discovered their adultery when he returned early and unexpected from his hunting. He found Fredegund with her head over a bucket washing her hair; a playful slap across the buttocks drew a retort addressed not to him but to her expected lover. Fredegund together with that same mayor of the palace then plotted the death of Chilperic, so that both could rule for her infant son. The story is not entirely improbable. If, as has been argued, Chilperic had been planning to adopt as his heir Childebert, son of Fredegund's enemy Brunhild, a motive would have existed for Fredegund's desperate action. Even at the time the case was obscure; at least two other people were accused of or confessed to Chilperic's murder. Gregory of Tours, closest in time to the events, withholds an opinion, merely using the opportunity of Chilperic's death to expand on the moral shortcomings of a king whose practice of vice and debauchery exhausted the capacity of the imagination. Nevertheless the wild accusations give a little insight into the political issues of the day.

Brunhild's historical image was badly tarnished by her misfortune in crossing swords with Columbanus, that torchbearer of morality who doubtless enjoyed his role as outspoken prophet confronting the latter-day Jezebel. She is not the only queen whose reputation has suffered as a result of a brush with the forces of virtue. Balthild was cultivated as a saint at Chelles; for Eddius, the Northumbrian biographer of Bishop Wilfrid, she was a Jezebel. Her involvement in the disputed episcopal election at Lyons that resulted in the murder of Aunemundus, a friend of Wilfrid, marked her out. Eddius had his native Jezebel in Iurminburg, wife of King Ecgfryth of Northumbria. He tells how the Devil used this weak vessel of woman to overthrow the holy bishop: she objected to Wilfrid's avid acquisition of secular glory, his great buildings, his royal finery, and his host of armed followers. Iurminburg connived with Archbishop Theodore at Wilfrid's deposition. Both she and Ecgfryth were later to suffer for the saint's discomfiture; yet after her husband's death even Iurminburg became for Eddius a perfect abbess, a mother of her community, a queen in ecclesiastical retirement from the political battleground.

Ecclesiastical writers continued to cast the queens and kings who opposed their heroes in the guise of villains, agents of the Devil and

15

vessels of debauchery. At the end of the tenth century an anonymous writer produced a life of Archbishop Dunstan, a man whose forceful personality had involved him in almost every conflict in tenth-century England. His ascendancy under King Eadred was destroyed by a palace revolution on the death of that king, when Eadred's nephew Eadwig came to power and exiled Dunstan. There may be room for skepticism in accepting Dunstan's biographer's assessment of Eadwig: young in age and endowed with scant wisdom in government. The king allowed himself to be led astray by a certain elderly noblewoman, foolish and wicked, who attempted first to ensnare him in matrimony with herself and then to foist her daughter upon him. The anonymous writer informs us how their wanton behavior, their disgraceful and indecent caresses culminated in an orgy of lust after the consecration banquet. The king left the banquet early, put aside his crown, and gave himself up to the arms of these loose women. There the intrepid Dunstan found him, wallowing between them like a pig in a sty. Nothing daunted, he reminded the king of his dignity and dragged him away. This was the direct cause of Dunstan's exile. One might be forgiven for failing to recognize these women as members of a prominent noble family of southwest England, descendants of King Æthelred I, in fact the king's lawful wife and her mother. Eadwig's marriage, intended to secure his power in southern England, did not please Dunstan and those of his allies who fell from grace in the new reign. Later, when the tide was turning against Eadwig, they lost no time in forcibly separating him from his wife on the grounds of consanguinity. Dunstan was later to make an enemy of another queen, Ælfthryth, the third wife of King Edgar, when he accused her and Edgar of adultery. Dunstan is presented as a guardian of virtue, but his actions were at least partly motivated by pursuit of his own interests and influence. The characters of the women concerned are the victims.

The story of Dunstan and Ælfthryth does not occur in the earliest life of Dunstan but in the twelfth-century chronicle of Gaimar. Later chronicles were frequently concerned with the lives of early kings and their queens; in their pages gossip, legend, and truth have become inextricably entwined. Queen Cynethryth of Mercia, wife of Offa, has fared badly at their hands. The *Life of Offa* was written at St. Albans, a house which kept green the memory of its founder. In it Cynethryth is the evil queen who tried to poison Offa's mind against

King Æthelberht of East Anglia, suitor to their daughter. When Offa refused to be drawn into violence against Æthelberht, she encompassed the murder herself, exhibiting a scrupulous attention to detail. She had a pit dug in a bedchamber, poised a chair above it and then enticed Æthelberht with the prospect of a sight of his bride to be. When Æthelberht sat on the chair he was precipitated into the pit, where the queen's servants suffocated him with cushions and hangings. The story is late and from a source with a vested interest in exonerating Offa; yet the earliest laconic reference in the *Anglo-Saxon Chronicle* imputes the murder to him. Between the late eighth century and the twelfth, blame shifted to Offa's wife and exculpated the king. St. Albans is the likeliest source of this change, though the general growth of antifeminism in the eleventh and twelfth centuries made the shift easier.

A similar late story of dubious credibility concerns the empress Angelberga, wife of the ninth-century Carolingian ruler of Italy, Louis II. It is preserved in the *Epitome chronicorum Casinensium*. While Louis was on campaign in the south, Angelberga turned lustful eyes on Hucbald, count of the palace. Finding him handsome and nobly born she attempted to seduce him with promises of power. She lured him to her bedchamber, where he barely escaped her clutches, leaving his mantle in her libidinous grasp. Angelberga now denounced Hucbald to Louis, claiming he had attempted to seduce her; Louis condemned him to death. Hucbald's distraught wife begged the aid of the pope, proving her husband's innocence by walking unharmed over burning coals. Overcome by sorrow, Louis granted the son of Hucbald the duchies of Liguria and Tuscany, all the Camerino, and the county of Costanza, throwing in lands in Alemannia and nine other counties for good measure. By the time of its recording, the story had clearly been reworked in the interests of Hucbald's descendants. At some stage it was influenced by biblical models, in this case the narrow escape of Joseph from Potiphar's wife. Accusations of liaisons between queens and court officials are common, and in 872 Louis II briefly divorced Angelberga, for which action he would have needed an excuse. If any truth lies behind the garbled tale, it may be a version of a story originally used against Angelberga by a husband eager to be rid of her for other reasons.

Most slander against queens naturally involves their role in the household, since this was their major sphere of activity. Eadburh, the daughter of Offa and wife of King Beorhtric of Wessex, became the subject of a story current in ninth-century Wessex, recorded in Asser's *Life of King Alfred*. Eadburh attempted to dominate Beorhtric's court in the tyrannical fashion that she had learnt from her father. Those she could not woo, she poisoned, until with lamentable carelessness she accidentally poisoned the king himself. Her position was now untenable, so she snatched part of the royal treasure and fled to West Frankia. There she impressed Charlemagne sufficiently for him to offer her the choice of himself or his son in marriage. Miscalculation based on personal preference led her to choose the son; as a result she lost both and received a nunnery instead. Not content with this quiet life, she wandered on to Italy where she died in poverty in Pavia. This, Asser tells us, is why the West Saxons no longer had queens.

Many details of the story ring true. The change of dynasty on the death of Beorhtric would have left Eadburh with little alternative other than flight. Mercia was uninviting, since her own father and brother were dead. Charlemagne's court was an obvious refuge; she was not the only potentially useful royal widow to whom the Carolingians offered asylum and a nunnery. A final pilgrimage to Rome and Italy would be in keeping for a ninth-century Anglo-Saxon queen. Alfred's own sister, Queen Æthelswith of Mercia, died in exile at Pavia ca. A.D. 888. But these credible details have been woven into a story which has anti-Mercian overtones and denigrates Eadburh. Such a story would be useful to the king who replaced Beorhtric, Alfred's grandfather Ecgberht, who fought against Mercia. Ecgberht would have been especially eager to discredit the wife of his predecessor, particularly if she had sons who could claim his throne. Even after the new dynasty was established, the story had a continued utility in justifying the fact that West Saxon wives were not raised to the status of queen, a practice followed, as we shall see, for other reasons. Propaganda soon after the event may have done more to distort the picture of many queens than the elaborations of later chroniclers.

Few queens stood nearer to the storm-center of a propaganda war than Judith, second wife of Louis the Pious. Judith's role in Louis's reign centered in the household. She aimed at securing an inheritance for her son, Charles the Bald, in the face of his three adult stepbrothers. Therefore she became the prime target of those stepsons during her lifetime and even after her death. The educational results of the Carolingian Renaissance ensured that the war was fought with words as well as swords; the court of Lothar I king of Italy and eldest of the three stepsons was its chief armory. In the second book of his life of Wala, an ecclesiastic whose court career under Louis the Pious suffered premature eclipse, Paschasius Radbertus delivered a blistering attack on Judith and the court over which she presided. Paschasius was a partisan of Lothar and the abbot of Wala's abbey of Corbie. His bitterness against Judith outlived her death as useful propaganda against her son Charles. For him, the power of woman had ended all virtue; the palace was a brothel where adultery was queen, a den of sorcery and witchcraft in which Judith and her incestuous lover, Louis's godson Bernard, turned the king's mind. According to Paschasius Louis's true instincts were good, and when they triumphed—that is, when he listened to his sons—good resulted; too often these instincts were perverted by Judith's urging of wicked plans. When his sons, acting from loyalty, imposed deposition on their father, it was she who made Louis fight back. Like Adam, our first parent, Louis was misled by feminine persuasion. Judith was Eve the temptress, a second Brunhild, jealous and intolerant of holy men.

Agobard of Lyons, another of Lothar's supporters, wrote two tracts in the summer and autumn of 833 whose title, *Two Books in Favor of the Sons and against Judith the Wife of Louis*, leave little doubt of his stance. Judith has the mind and bearing of a child, disporting herself in the palace even with the priests. She does not know how to govern herself, let alone the palace and the kingdom. She is soft and yielding, she gains her way by subtle arts rather than argument. His sons fear for Louis. Judith is the cause of all the evil which has come upon him. She poisons his mind and they worry lest Louis go the way of Ahab, who did evil in the sight of the Lord with Jezebel and had to be called to penance by the prophet. Wicked wives ruin their husbands; Samson, though he was a just man, lost his eyes for believing in an untrue woman. Every antifeminist image in the early ninth-century repertoire was hurled at Judith. The virulence of the abuse is a tribute to her importance.

Yet is this the same Judith whom we meet in the court poets? Is this Walahfrid Strabo's beautiful Rachel, leading her infant Benjamin by the hand, a second biblical Judith, a Mary sister of Aaron in her musical abilities, a Sappho, a prophetess, cultivated, chaste, intelligent, pious, strong in spirit, and sweet in conversation? Judith had another verbal champion in Hrabanus Maurus, who dedicated his commentaries on the books of Judith and Esther to her, reminding her that by imitating these great biblical women who overcame their enemies with spiritual weapons, she too could triumph. The suave tongue of the courtier raises as many problems as the barbs of enemies. In later years, when Hrabanus was seeking favor at the court of Judith's erstwhile enemy Lothar I, he sent these same commentaries with a changed dedication to Lothar's own queen, Ermengard.

The courtly compliment would be a welcome foil to the almost uniformly scurrilous portraits of late ninth- and tenth-century Italian queens and countesses. Most of them survive from the witty but venomous pen of Liudprand of Cremona; their vices might be held as pure figments of his fevered imagination did they not find occasional echoes in the sober pages of Flodoard of Rheims. Liberally mixed with his own prejudices, Liudprand has preserved the gutter politics of his day, where character assassination was a crude but effective weapon. Liudprand wrote between 958 and 962, by which date he had firmly attached himself to the rising Italian political star of the Ottonians. He had a violent hatred for his former master King Berengar II and his wife Willa, who was for Liudprand yet another Jezebel. Liudprand had deserted the memory of another former patron, King Hugh. Add to this his dislike of the Romans, and the wide area over which he scattered his venom becomes comprehensible. Chivalry was no inhibition for a man who could castigate the Alps themselves for failing to hinder the flight of the heavily pregnant Willa. For Liudprand the alliances and advances of Italian life were forged and cemented in bed; Italy was a realm of female and sexual politics. Thus Marozia, mistress of Rome and third wife of King Hugh, is a lascivious whore for whom Roman politics meant papal caresses. Bertha of Tuscany, Hugh's mother, secured supporters for herself and her son after the death of her husband Adalbert of Tuscany "by cunning, lavish gifts and the pleasant exercises of the nuptial couch." Her daughter Ermengard, wife of Adalbert of Ivrea, was a strong rival in the "sweet delights of Aphrodite." Indeed the strife of early tenth-century Italy largely resulted from Ermengard's arousal of desire in all, coupled with a selectivity in the bestowal of her favors.

Many of Liudprand's stories had grown and matured for almost a century before he committed them to writing. He embellished the slanders of political propaganda from an age when power in the peninsula was fiercely disputed. He relates, for example, that Bertha's sons were not her own, but procured from another woman to meet her own desperate need after Adalbert's death, precisely the rumors of paternity that a question of succession would start. Liudprand's was a jaundiced, one-sided view, yet he was aware of some of the facts of political life, even if he heightened and distorted them. He appreciated that marriage was a question of power. When Rudolf of Burgundy married Bertha of Swabia it was "for the augmenting of his power"; Rudolf's supposed dalliance with Ermengard was really an attempt to gain an important ally in his Italian endeavors. Liudprand's stories are further colored by his abomination of female rule. Like Benedict of Mont Soracte, the thought of a woman controlling the holy city of Rome filled Liudprand with horror, fulfilling the prophecy that the effeminate would rule in Jerusalem. The undoubted power of women in tenth-century Italy could not fail to draw a strong reaction from such men.

By the twelfth century new ideals of chivalry and romantic love had evolved, and few lives of kings committed to writing after A.D. 1000 have escaped their molding influence. The tales of Edgar's wooing of Ælfthryth, although set in late tenth-century England, survive in the twelfth-century chronicles of Gaimar and William of Malmesbury. In William's account, Edgar sent his ealdorman and follower Æthelwold to bring Ælfthryth. Æthelwold went, inspected the lady, fell in love with her, and reported back to the king that she was "small, vulgar, and common," then marrying her himself. When Edgar later visited the couple, Ælfthryth dressed herself to best advantage to seduce him. Fired by passion, Edgar slew Æthelwold in a hunt in Wherwell Forest. Gaimar repeats the story, with minor variations: Ælfthryth is now reported by Æthelwold, as "ugly, dark, and misshapen"; when the king realizes he has been fooled, he sends Æthelwold to rule at York and the ealdorman mysteriously dies en route.

There are parallels with the other twelfth-century romance of royal passion, the affair of Philip I and Bertrada de Montfort. The queen is cast in the role of seductress; there is love, intrigue, perfidy, murder, a wronged husband and lord betraying his vassal—all the elements that would appeal to a twelfth-century knightly audience. These have been grafted on to an earlier literary motif, found in the stories of Clovis and Clotild, of Henry and Mathilda, namely, the king's vicarious wooing of his bride. The tales of Bertrada and Philip were elaborated by the followers of Bertrada's stepson and enemy, Louis VI. Those of Edgar and Ælfthryth may have originated in the succession struggle on the death of Edgar, though they have undergone subsequent elaboration in the chivalric tradition. When Edgar's sons fought over the throne in 975, the opponents of Ælf-thryth and her son Æthelred would have found any slander concerning her marriage useful. Gaimar's version contains the story of Dunstan's accusations of adultery against Edgar's Ælfthryth, another argument perhaps from the opposition camp in 975.

Strong partisan attitudes combined with new ideals of kingship to produce the unflattering portrait of Ælfthryth's near contemporary, the French queen Constance, third wife of the Capetian Robert the Pious. For several years Constance had a living rival at court in the shape of Robert's former wife Bertha, whose divorce did not see her immediate eclipse in the king's affections. Constance had a second misfortune when her sons grew to maturity and lost all feelings of loyalty to their mother. The early Capetian world was notoriously treacherous, and with so many cards stacked against her, only decisive action could preserve Constance. There is little doubt that she took such action, but she has been unfortunate in that her moves were reported only in unsympathetic sources: in the letters of her enemy, Fulbert of Chartres, or the pages of her husband's biographer Helgaud. Helgaud's *Life of Robert the Pious* was a new picture of a "monk's king." His pious king is generous to the Church and openhanded to the point of absurdity, allowing himself to be robbed before his own eyes at table or in the royal chapel. Robert's continual plea is, "Don't tell Constance": his queen, constant, strong, never joking (if Helgaud's portrait of her husband has any truth, she had little cause for levity), is the antithesis of Robert's generosity. She stays his best impulses, prevents him from bestowing his last buttons on beggars and churchmen. The picture of Robert, which has echoes in the later eleventh-century portrait of the pious Edward the

Confessor, may not be entirely accurate. But Edward's wife Edith was fortunate that his biography was written at her behest; instead of avarice and domination she provides the necessary practical aid for an otherworldly husband. Helgaud has little room for a "monk's queen" except as a benefactress; he reserves his sole words of praise for Constance for the list of her gifts to the Church. For enemies like Fulbert, Constance was a wicked fomentor of dissension and revolt in the royal family, a fearsome woman whose threats were never idle. To whitewash Constance would bring us little nearer to the truth; nevertheless her actions require explanations which go further than simple evil.

The role of queens in individual events may prove a problem as intractable as their general characters. In 871, for example, the nobility of Benevento and Campania in central Italy rebelled against Louis II. The accounts of the revolt isolate a range of motives that include the activities of Louis's empress, Angelberga. Writers like Erchanpert and Regino of Prum point to the vexations of the Franks and the ambitions of Adelchis duke of Benevento. The north Italian chronicler Andrea of Bergamo brings in the Devil and the desire of the nobility of southern Italy for independence. The West Frankish Hincmar in the *Annals of St. Bertin* lays sole blame on the empress Angelberga and her machinations against Adelchis. His involvement of Angelberga is echoed in the southern Italian, anonymous chronicler of Salerno, who claims that it was her arrogance and especially her insulting behavior toward the Beneventan women that sparked trouble. The revolt had its origins in rival ambitions in central Italy, an area undoubtedly sensitive to treatment by Louis. Adelchis of Benevento, a powerful duke who boasted descent from former Lombard rulers, was the inevitable leader of discontent. Angelberga was an active queen; dislike of her among certain factions in central Italy contributed to Louis's divorcing her in 872 to marry a noblewoman from this area. But when Hincmar singled her out for blame he was speaking as a counsellor of Charles the Bald, no friend of his nephew's wife, since she had never supported his own interests in Italy. The southern chronicler, explaining the actions of his neighbors, could feel that Angelberga's insults were a more honorable excuse for rebellion than ambition. Angelberga was only one part of the jigsaw that some observers chose to stress at the expense of others.

Images

Chroniclers saw with the eyes of their politics and prejudices, but more insidiously with the eyes of their own culture. Particular images have already been seen to recur: biblical types, the holy woman, the witch. Not all are products of the ecclesiastical culture, though most have interacted with it. The images available to describe queens are determinants certainly of the surviving pictures, perhaps of the actions of royal women.

The sources of early medieval history leave an overriding impression of antifeminism. Women are evil geniuses; although their husbands may be castigated for their vices, the bitterest taunts are usually reserved for wives who urged them on. Liudprand vilified Berengar, but Willa takes the brunt of his most virulent attack. She is a boundless tyrant, a second Jezebel, a vampire greedy for plunder; she is the worthy daughter of an avaricious mother whose own greed led her to hide her husband's jewelled belt in her vulva rather than give it up when she was captured. Fredegund's complicity in the deaths of her stepsons Chlodovech and Merovech is emphasized even though her husband Chilperic was equally loath to allow his sons' kingly aspirations to come to fruition. Ambitious wives drive husbands to the greatest excesses: it is Ageltrudis rather than Guy of Spoleto who aims for empire in the Italy of the 880s. It is the former princess Bertha of Tuscany who urges her husband Adalbert on to attempt to gain the Italian crown. It is Ermengard who goads Boso to kingship. As Hincmar remarked, "The daughter of an emperor of Italy, the fiancée of an emperor of Greece, she did not wish to live unless her husband was king." In Gregory of Tours it is the evil Amalaberg who sows the seeds of discord and taunts her husband Hermanfrid of Thuringia, laying only half the table at meals because he controlled only half a kingdom. The unacceptable face of naked ambition is masked in the husband by appearing on his wife. Judith and Constance are made the source of all the evil done by the pious Louis and Robert. Male virtues become female vices; reward and generosity, vengeance and protection are strengths and virtues when exercised by kings, but become partiality, intrigue, and personal vindictiveness when practiced by queens. Some vices are regularly attributed to queens, the most common being avarice, of which

Willa, Angelberga, Constance, Fredegund, Brunhild, and many others stand accused.

Yet to cry "antifeminism" would be to oversimplify a complex issue. Queens were expected to counsel and aid kings; the line between counsel and domination may be fine and difficult both in reality and in the eyes of the beholder. Royal virtues do have their other face, often shown by kings as well as queens. Were queens less able to exercise these virtues fully and openly, more likely to fall into their perversions? In a system of personal monarchy contemporaries needed, wherever possible, to believe in the impartiality of kings, to set them above intrigues. Queens had no such immunity; indeed, they filled the converse need to blame on others the king's excesses. Although our sources show a deep-seated bias against the politically active woman, they also recognized ways in which women could and should act. Their opinions were shaped by models of female action.

The Bible was one of the most important sources of images, whether of male or female action. It molded the mentality of the entire period. At its peak in the "biblical kingship" of the early Carolingians, Charlemagne became David, Louis the Pious a second Moses, surrounded by his sons Joshua, sweet Jonathan, and Benjamin. From the Bible and its interpreters came the archetypal picture of Eve the temptress, specifically applied to Judith, wife of Louis the Pious, and formative of all descriptions of wives who led their husbands into sin. Woman as seductress, as author of man's evil, and active opponent of virtue was represented also by Jezebel and Delilah. Brunhild, Balthild, Iurminburg, Judith, and Willa were all Jezebels. But the Bible contained many images of women: the quiet and contemplative Rachel and Mary, whom Odilo's Adelaide imitated in old age; the active but housewifely Leah and Martha whose parts she had played earlier. Judith was like Mary, sister of Aaron, to Walahfrid Strabo; she was a Bathsheba to Freculf of Orleans. Edward the Confessor's Edith was another Susannah, accused and punished though innocent, when her husband dismissed her from the marriage bed into captivity at Wherwell. Two Old Testament women, Judith and Esther, have a particular significance, providing the strongest types of the completely political and active woman. Hrabanus Maurus dedicated commentaries on both women to the empress Judith in the 830s, and later sent the book of Esther to Queen Ermengard. Here were the images to use in the flattery of queens, as Pope John VIII knew when in 876 he wrote to Richildis, wife of Charles the Bald, calling on her to act "in the manner of the holy Esther." Judith and Esther had been queens who fought battles, ruled kingdoms, and saved their people; their images had a power far beyond simple flattery. Hrabanus's dedicatory letter to Judith shows how they offered a mode of action to queens who could overcome worldly enemies by cultivating spiritual qualities. It seems possible that the Anglo-Saxon poem *Judith* was written for or about that great Mercian queen and military leader Æthelflæd. Its stress on the warlike capacities of Judith, the reknown she won in battle, the emphasis on her execution of Holofernes, her vanquishing of the heathen and the inspiration she gave to her warriors would all fit Æthelflæd. Like Judith, she received the spoils of war from her returning armies.

Yet the Anglo-Saxon Judith is a reminder that these biblical types had already passed through Christian interpretation. In the Apocrypha, Judith was a widow. In the Anglo-Saxon poem she is a virgin, anxious to preserve her chastity. It is the celibate, desexualized woman who is most admired, the ideal of chastity influencing the Christian mind however inappropriate it might be in practice. The early Church fathers Jerome, Ambrose, and Tertullian fused antifeminism and antisexuality in their pictures of women. For some there could scarcely be an ideal woman. Tertullian saw woman as "the gate of the devil, who opened up the tree, the first deserter of divine law," who persuaded Adam to sin when the Devil's wiles had proved inadequate. Woman's fault is her sex and the temptation it poses to man. For Ambrose, Eve was a virgin before the Fall: sex and marriage are results of that Fall and redemption has been achieved only through the conception of a virgin. The ideal woman was chaste, her chastity to be preserved at all costs. In the eighth century Paul the Deacon wrote approvingly in his *History of the Lombards* of the daughters of Romilda, who kept their chastity when captured by the Avars by tying rotting chicken flesh beneath their breasts to repel the Avar warriors. The ideal woman was passive and self-effacing. For Jerome she should be humble, liberal to the poor, a student of scripture, quiet in speech, dressing always the same, spending her time weaving and spinning. "Her song is the psalms, her words the gospel, her delight constancy, her life a fast." Ambrose agreed; the picture of Mary in his *De Virginibus* is of a modest, scripture-reading ascetic, who ate only to keep herself from dying of hunger, who slept only when absolutely necessary. Only the virgin martyrs like Agnes can achieve heroic proportions, facing death in pursuit of purity with a stoicism that made her executioner tremble. There is little here to give comfort to an active wife and mother, much to show the origins of Radegund's type of femininity.

Christian thinkers have always seen in Mary the mother of Christ a type of womanhood. But Mary has had many faces. She could be the meek, self-effacing housewife of Ambrose, his antithesis of Eve, the virgin-mother who never experienced sexual pleasure, an anti-woman, idealized especially in this way in the eleventh and twelfth centuries. Yet she could receive the attributes of a fertility goddess, and was prayed to in the ninth and tenth centuries by the sterile and those who longed for children. By the tenth century she was also Maria Regina, Queen of Heaven, crowned and sceptered, ruling with her son. The iconography of Mary as queen was strong in Ottonian Germany and in late tenth-century England, illustrated in Bibles and books produced in the court circle or presented to the royal family. Where earthly queens ruled and were powerful, they could be given a heavenly model.

The Church's views on women were ambivalent and contained contradictions. In the mid-ninth century both Sedulius Scottus and Angelomo of Luxeuil likened the marriage of Lothar I and Ermengard to the union of Christ and his Church. The Church is not the virgin but the Bride of Christ, adorned with precious cloths and jewels, made worthy to share in his rule by baptism. Alongside powerful currents of antifeminism, showing woman as the weaker vessel and incarnation of feared sexuality, stood woman the spiritual equal of man, possessor of an immortal soul redeemed by Christ. Even the Church's dislike of sex brought gains to women. It expressed itself in a monogamous view of Christian marriage that in practice was normally favorable to women. It necessitated a revaluation of the humanity of women, making them worthy mates for their husbands. The ninth century, for example, saw a determined campaign in favor of Christian ideals of marriage that became for Smaragdus the only good thing Adam and Eve brought out of Paradise. Woman might have been the first temptress, but in Mary she was also the first to see the Resurrection. She should not be the object of undying hatred, since she brought the first grace as well as the first fault. At her worst she may be a seductress, charming and deceitful, but man too has his sexual vices: violence, abduction, preying on the weak.

Woman's role in marriage and the household fostered a series of favorable images, which at the same time provide grounds for the criticism of certain queens. In the economic and political world of the early Middle Ages with its domestic focus, to stress woman's role in the family and the household was in no sense derogatory. The wife, the mother, the mistress of the family's resources, was no negligible drudge. The household was not only the center of government but a model for it. Sedulius Scottus in his *Book on Christian Rulers* wrote the only theoretical picture of a queen. She is, as we might expect, chaste and endowed with the Christian virtues, but she is also skilled, rules her household, influences and counsels her husband. From her wisdom flow benefits both to her household and to the kingdom. The king and queen who rule their kingdom well will also rule their children well. The family, especially the royal family, was a model of rule. Hrabanus Maurus's *Book on the Reverence of Sons toward Their Fathers and of Subjects toward Their Kings* contains ideas that receive clear expression in the Carolingian and Ottonian periods. Charlemagne is always presented as a paterfamilias surrounded by his wives and children in the pages of Einhard and in the court poems of Theodulf of Orleans. Theodulf describes the king's homecoming: his sons rush to take his cloak and sword, his daughters bring him gifts of roses, lilies, apples, bread, and wine. The two lives of Mathilda in tenth-century Germany consistently portray queens in family life; indeed, the family and its activities are prominent in most Ottonian sources. The household imagery is diffused throughout the period. The Anglo-Saxon epic poem *Beowulf* depicts the queen in the royal court, serving at table, presiding at the feast. For Saxo Grammaticus the queen is the housewife who deals with royal domestic matters. For Paul the Deacon stability to a kingdom torn by war was brought by Queen Ansa, wife of the Lombard Desiderius, the counsellor of her husband but also the mother of children whose marriages built peace. For Odilo and Gerbert, Adelaide is the mother of her household, even the mother of kingdoms. Balthild is a mother to the great nobility, daughter to the bishops, nurse to the young men and boys. Edith is a daughter to Edward the

Confessor, responsible for the secular dignity of the palace. The images recur, stressing always the queen who counsels her husband, converts him to Christianity if necessary, produces and rears royal children, manages a family and a household that are the very center of the realm. It is here, where contemporaries point so unanimously, that we should seek the origins of the queen's power.

The familial model shapes criticism as much as praise of queens. Management of the royal estate vigorously pursued becomes avarice, maternal love feeds rivalry in complex marriage situations, and wives whose marriages are designed to cement peace between peoples bring discord and suspicion into the royal household. As in-marriers and outsiders, wives are often objects of suspicion in the family hearth, especially when domestic tragedy strikes. As intruders who are suspect, wielding power within the tensions and crosscurrents of the family but denied the expression of legitimate aggression, wives and queens are accused of domestic crimes, of encompassing their ends by covert means, by plots, poison, and witchcraft.

Witchcraft beliefs emerge in strange forms. In the infamous debate over Lothar II's attempted divorce from Theutberga, the Lotharingian bishops wrote to Hincmar of Rheims asking whether Theutberga could have conceived a child yet remained a virgin. Hincmar replied that through the use of witchcraft the female vulva was able to attract male sperm without any physical copulation. In the same case he voiced a typical view on the use of sorcery to harm an enemy: Waldrada had been Lothar's mistress, whom he had wished to marry, and who had prevented Lothar and Theutberga through sorcery from conceiving a child. Former concubines, it seems, frequently prevented their erstwhile lovers from consummating a new marriage by this means, such that Hincmar recommends exorcism and not divorce as the correct response to a husband's incapacity. Sorcery could wreak the vengeance of a discarded mistress or ensnare a lover: in the *Annals of St. Bertin* Hincmar accused Waldrada of using witchcraft to gain Lothar's affections. It could also be a way of gaining influence. Judith and Bernard used it to turn the mind of Louis the Pious; the sixth-century prefect Mummolus employed it to procure the favor of King Chilperic. Often it is a way of bringing about unexplained death. Brunhild's son Childebert constantly demanded the delivery to him of his aunt, the murdering witch Fredegund. Fredegund stood accused also as a mistress of the art of poisoning, a practice which carries the same connotations of underhand aggression. Witchcraft beliefs combined with the tensions of family politics to throw suspicion on women.

Images of queens active beyond the household sphere were rare but not unknown. If Judith, Esther, and Mary Queen of Heaven were inspirations, so was the living example of the Byzantine empress. Her power was known in western Europe, especially in Italy, throughout the period, and was a strong influence on the formation of Carolingian imperial ideas. Popes used flattering terms when addressing Byzantine empresses, while Byzantine patriarchs sent back letters likening queens such as Angelberga to Pulcheria, who on her father's death had ruled the Empire for her young brother and brought a new emperor to the throne. The Byzantine ritual praises of rulers, the *laudes*, came into use in the West in Carolingian times. They were addressed to Charlemagne and to his wife Fastrada and praised both in extravagant terms. By contrast with the Byzantine, late Roman images of politically active women failed to survive. There are echoes of the stoic ideal of the virago, the man-woman, which Liudprand uses to abuse Theodora, the shameless strumpet of Rome who exercised power in a manly fashion. But in the early eleventh century Wipo, in his *Deeds of Conrad II*, describes the emperor's wife Gisela as endowed with "manly probity," and Thietmar of Merseburg tells how Theophanu, although of the weaker sex, held the kingdom for her son "in a manly fashion." These German examples need not argue continuity of thought from the Roman world, but rather present an image arising from the fact of female rule combined with preconceptions of female incapacity. Those most virile and belligerent women of classical legend, the Amazons, who killed their own menfolk, put in brief appearances on the margins of medieval thought. Fredegar in the seventh century has a story of Belisarius and Justinian married to two Amazonian sisters; Paul the Deacon refers to a putative race of great women living in the depths of Germany. And when all other epithets had been exhausted on Constance, the *Miracles of St. Benedict* describe her as "Amazonian."

Subsuming and reinforcing many of these images, the lives of former queens became types in their own right. Stories of wicked queens could be mobilized against the dangers of female rule. Brunhild was for the Merovingians and Carolingians, Eadburh for the West Saxons, what the Empress Wu was in Chinese history, a name to be reckoned with, rendering further argument superfluous. In Norway, evil days became synonymous with the "time of Ælfgifu," Cnut's English wife who was regent there for her son Swegn. Saintly queens became models of virtue. When the *Life of Balthild* was written in the seventh century, its author could look back to three other Merovingian queens whom the Franks remembered for their "devotion to the divine cult": Clotild, who converted Clovis, Ultrogotha, the consoler of the poor and the aid of monks and priests, Radegund, who so loved God that she spurned the world. Odilo wrote his *Epitaph of Adelaide* with the instruction of queens in mind.

Incarnation of evil or unattainable perfection, great ascetic or materfamilias, mistress of the household or Jewish warrior, seductress or virgin, Queen of Heaven or Byzantine empress—the images of queens varied. Antifeminism plays a part in building the complex picture. If the type of the active queen was relatively rare, eclipsed by holy rivals, there were Old Testament examples: the mother of children and kingdom is an image it is unwise to ignore.

Chapter 2 ♛ *The Bride to Be*

According to her first biographer, Mathilda, future wife of Henry the Fowler, was reared in the nunnery of Herford by her grandmother, the abbess. When young Henry's father sought a wife for his son, this female descendant of the Saxon leader Widukind seemed a good choice. Henry's tutor Thietmar was sent to view the girl and his favorable report brought Henry and a group of his friends to visit Herford. Henry entered the church in disguise to see the lady for himself. Satisfied that he had not been misled as to her charms, he changed into royal robes, went to the abbess, and asked for Mathilda's hand. So filled was he with love that he could not take his eyes off the girl, and the thought of the lengthy procedure of betrothal seemed unbearable. With the consent of her grandmother, if not yet of her family, he carried her off immediately to Wallhausen, where they were married with full honor.

Some sixty years or so later King Edgar was seeking a second wife. His wooing is recorded only in the late eleventh-century *Life of St. Wulfhilde*. A casual visit to the abbey at Wherwell kindled a passionate desire for the nun Wulfhilde. The abbess, Wulfhilde's aunt, supported Edgar's desires and connived at his suit, arranging a meal where the couple might meet, tricking her niece into the meeting. But the king met only religious intransigence in Wulfhilde. His determined advances were repulsed and when he imprisoned Wulfhilde in her own room she fled in desperation, escaping through the abbey's sewers. Edgar was chastened by the strength of her attachment to virginity, but in any case secured Wulfthryth, Wulfhilde's own cousin, for his bride. Wulfthryth was to discover her own religious vocation later in life, when Edgar repudiated her and made her abbess of Wilton.

Another thirty years passed and Robert the Pious, the second Capetian king, became enamored of Bertha, widow of Eudes of Blois. According to Richer, the initiative was partly Bertha's, who was seeking protection for herself and her sons. The witty pen of Adalbero of Laon in his *Rythmus satiricus* accused Bertha of employing not only charm but a semiprofessional marriage broker, Landri of Nevers, whose services she never repaid. Passion drew Bertha and Robert into a liaison which was not regularized until late in 996, after the death of Robert's father Hugh Capet.

The wooing of kings was a popular subject in the chronicles and biographies of the Middle Ages—interest in the intimate lives of the great is seemingly a hardy perennial. By the twelfth century they were cast in the form of romantic seduction, but long before this they had been the object of legend. Before the end of the sixth century Gregory of Tours was describing how Childeric, founder of the Merovingian dynasty, came by his wife Basina, mother of the great king Clovis. Childeric was in exile at the court of her husband, Bisinus of Thuringia. Basina followed Childeric on his return to Frankia, giving as her reason a desire to be married to so strong and able a man. The legends covered an obvious discourtesy on Childeric's part, returning from his place of refuge with his host's wife. It also enabled Gregory and others to place in Basina's mouth praises of the father of Clovis. Stories of Clovis's own bride-getting, committed to writing in the eighth century, already contained the favored motif of secret wooing; Paul the Deacon's account of Authari's wooing of Theudelinda tells of disguise and secrecy. Legend gathered quickly around royal courtship. The tale of Edgar's wooing was recorded a century after the events, yet the story of Henry the Fowler and Mathilda, committed to writing soon after Mathilda's death by someone who had known her, is already full of inaccuracy. Henry was nearing thirty, with a repudiated wife and son, at the time of his marriage to Mathilda. Neither his father nor his tutor is likely to have played a part in arranging a match that brought land and allies to the rising duke of Saxony. The stories of Robert and Bertha were embellished by satire and propaganda by contemporary observers; in reality marriage against his father's wishes marked Robert's alliance with Blois, suiting him as much as it did Bertha.

A variety of personal motives are attributed to kings in their choice of wife. Henry the Fowler found Mathilda overwhelming, Edgar burned with desire for the virginal Wulfhilde. Edgar may have found Wulfhilde irresistible, but the involvement of her aunt and his immediate consolation with her cousin leave a suspicion that the attraction lay in her family as much as in herself. Mathilda may have

been chaste and beautiful, but she was also a member of the powerful Immeding clan, with land and followers in Westphalian Saxony
and Lower Lotharingia. She brought a dowry of lands around Engern and Osnabruck and boasted descent from Widukind, so her
charms were a bonus. When Henry the Fowler sought a bride for his
son Otto, he turned to Anglo-Saxon England. According to Hroswitha, Eadgyth the Anglo-Saxon princess had much to recommend
her—nobility, excellence, charm, queenly bearing, radiant good-
ness, and sincerity of countenance; in England she was considered
the best of all existing women. Such attributes, if true, were no dis-
advantage. But Henry was especially seeking a *royal* bride for the
son he was designating as heir, a woman whose birth would under-
score the regality of the new dynasty. When Sigibert married the
Visigothic princess Brunhild, Gregory stresses that he wanted a wife
worthy of him at a time when his brothers were sinking so low as to
marry their own slaves. Stung by his example, his brother Chilperic
asked for the hand of Galswinth, Brunhild's sister. Alliance and
friendship with the Visigothic court was not far from the mind of
either king, and at a time when treasure meant power, Chilperic can
only have been impressed by the rich dowry Brunhild as a princess
brought with her. Sexual preference must have existed, but most
kings could satisfy it in other ways. Hugh of Arles, King of Italy, took
four concubines to cater to his preferences, four wives for his politics. Marriages were matters of allies, claims, lands, treasure, and
prestige; they bound peace negotiations and marked transitions in
royal life. They were affairs between families rather than individuals, as the tales of Edgar and Henry, in spite of embellishment, reveal. They were an instrument of policy rather than passion.

Marriage and the Family

A royal dynasty was first a family, and the choice of its wives cru-
cially important. Marriage arrangements played a part in most of
the dynastic settlements that are a feature of this period. Between
928 and 930 Henry the Fowler sought to arrange his inheritance and
to cope with the problems that the acquisition of kingship had posed
for his family. He provided for the dower of his wife Mathilda; he

destined his youngest son Bruno for the Church, sending him to be educated appropriately; he married his daughter Gerberga to the duke of Lotharingia; and he designated his son Otto as his heir. To coincide with that designation, he sought a bride of adequate status for a future king and gave maximum publicity to the marriage of Otto and the Anglo-Saxon princess Eadgyth. In 806 and 817 Charlemagne and Louis the Pious produced family settlements to govern the Carolingian inheritance. These kings were concerned not only with the passing on of the kingship and property, but also attempted to regulate the marriages of their children. Charlemagne ordered that the marriages of his daughters should be controlled after his death by their brothers, the new heads of the family; they should choose only worthy men. In 817 the *Ordinatio imperii* of Louis the Pious openly attempted to manipulate the choice of his sons' wives in the interests of family unity. No son might choose a foreign wife, being enjoined rather to select their wives within the three Carolingian kingdoms to bind them together; all marriages were to be approved by the head of the family, Louis himself, or after his death the new Carolingian paterfamilias, Lothar, the eldest son. In neither case are the interests of family and kingship distinguished.

The Carolingians in 806 and 817 attempted to control marriage in the family's interests through the head of that family. Charlemagne and Louis put this into practice, personally choosing wives for their sons. The principle was strongly held in most dynasties. Between the ninth and the eleventh centuries Anglo-Saxon kings inhibited the marriages of their sons before their own deaths wherever possible, because married princes with the support of their wives' families could escape the control of their father, even becoming dangerous rivals for kingship. When Alfred married before the death of his brother, King Æthelred I, Asser associates it with the fact that he was an underking. Merovingian princes ordinarily confined themselves to concubines until the death of a father or other such opportunity provided them with a kingdom. These royal family practices were later adopted by nobility, similarly anxious to preserve the power of the paterfamilias over the family's concerns, to inhibit the rebellious aspirations of sons to premature inheritance, and to preserve the family property. Where a son was married with his father's permission, he was normally designated as heir or given an outlet for ambition by being established in a subkingdom. Merovingian princes who married before their fathers' deaths normally acquired a share in power. Charlemagne's sons received subkingdoms; Louis the Pious married off his sons and immediately dispatched them and their wives to their allotted realms. All sons of Merovingian and Carolingian kings had strong claims to inherit land and kingship, and all normally received kingdoms and brides, whether before or after their father's death. By the tenth century, impoverishment drove more and more dynasties to restrict inheritance and marriage to a single heir, excluding younger sons from the kingship. It was a step that met fierce and natural resistance. While Henry the Fowler designated Otto his heir and married him off within months, the marriage of his younger son Henry formed no part of the family settlement, and a third son, Bruno, was sent into the Church. Otto later designated his own son Liudolf as his heir and married him to Ida at the same time. Both Otto and Liudolf were paraded through the kingdom with their new wives so that every area could participate in the wedding and recognize the future king and queen. Otto the Great arranged the marriage and designation of his son Otto II, and Hugh of Arles combined the marriage of his son Lothar to Adelaide with his association in the kingship. Robert the Pious designated two sons in turn during his own lifetime, but allowed neither to marry. Fulbert of Chartres complained that Hugh, the eldest, was kept in such penury that he rebelled against his father. Straitened circumstances helped to force new practices on the royal family, but although the ground rules changed the principle remained the same. The marriage of sons and heirs to the throne should be controlled in the interests of the royal dynasty as a whole.

In the ideal world of the early Middle Ages, heads of families chose wives and even timed precisely the marriages of their sons. But fathers have many aspirations that are upset by realities. Sons inevitably aspired to the joys of manhood, even if this involved rebellion against the parent who blocked their path. Marriage against parental wishes formed a regular part of the revolt of youth. When Charles the Bald's sons Charles and Louis the Stammerer rebelled against their father in 862, each took a wife as part of his defiance. Their cousin Louis the Young betrothed himself in the course of revolt against his father Louis the German in 865. When Æthelred the Unready's eldest son, Edmund Ironside, rose in revolt in 1015 his gesture of rebellion was to take a wife. In sixth-century Frankia the rebellions of both Merovech and Chramn involved marriage.

Where parental authority was strong, this symbolic act of emancipation from parental control and entry into manhood was a powerful gesture. But it was more than ritual defiance. A son who wished to rebel and make good his claims against his father needed allies. Edmund Ironside's marriage brought him the support of a strong and disaffected noble family in the north midlands; Charles and Louis sought their wives from powerful families in their subkingdoms; Merovech married the widow of an uncle whom his father had murdered. No one will be stronger supporters of a young pretender than the family and friends of his wife, who have everything to gain from his success. Like the marriages of designated heirs or adult kings, those of pretenders emphasize the politics of matrimony. Wives were taken to bolster shaky claims or to acquire new ones, to procure allies or strengthen friendships.

Noble Women

In 806 Charlemagne insisted that his daughters marry "worthy men"; in practice he showed an equal concern for the pedigree of his sons' brides. There was strong belief that the status of a wife and her family should match those of her prospective husband, or at least should not debase him. Commenting on a notorious ninth-century marriage affair, Hincmar noted that Count Stephen had married "like a nobleman . . . to a wife equal in birth." Charles the Bald's Judith was confined at Senlis in her widowhood until she should marry "legally and worthily"; she eloped illegally but worthily with Baldwin, Count of Flanders. Charles the Simple's dowry document for his wife Frederun speaks of his choice of her as a worthy wife, from whom he could produce sons fit to rule the kingdom. A wife of the correct status maintained the dignity of the family. It was no empty thing, but indicated the treasure, land, and supporters she would bring with her. The belief was so strong that it served as a legitimate excuse to cover Hugh Capet's rejection of the last Carolingian, Charles of Lorraine. Charles had married a wife from the lesser nobility and

Hugh, the great duke of the Franks, claimed that he could not bend the knee before a queen who was the daughter of one of his own vassals. In the tenth century, when kings and great nobles were dangerously equal and status an overriding concern, the worthiness of wives was doubly important. Henry the Fowler, Hugh of Arles, Hugh Capet, all upstart kings themselves, were careful to select wives of the correct dignity for their sons.

The strength of the norm of status matching, found in virtually all highly stratified societies, makes the Merovingian marriages to servants and slaves intriguing. Such marriages were not the rule. They were outnumbered by the more normal alliances with princesses and noblewomen and rarely occurred before the mid-sixth century. Merovingian kings in taking slavegirls as wives may have been emphasizing their distinctiveness, their freedom from the rules that bound noble society. Their preeminent position may have enabled them to marry without regard for the wealth and allies a noble wife could bring. It may be, however, that we are attributing deliberate choice where pressures of expediency really applied. It was always the prerogative of kings and nobles to satisfy their appetites where they would. In the Merovingian case the difference is that kings went on, occasionally though not invariably, to marry these women. Marriage followed only if the woman bore a son, and then only in the later sixth century, when ecclesiastical censure and dynastic splits were combining to bring pressure to legitimate all sons. Many kings married servant girls when their legitimate wives proved sterile; the barren wife was divorced, the fertile mistress married. As we shall see later, these strange marriages are a product of ecclesiastical and political pressure on the sensitive area of succession to the throne. Later kings were to eschew servant girls even as mistresses until they had secured the necessary heirs to the throne.

Kings chose the majority of wives from among the daughters of great noble clans. Those clans were important, sometimes crucial to the survival of the dynasty. A series of marriage alliances might signify a clan's continuing power and at the same time bolster it. The ninth-century Carolingian rulers of Italy proved well aware of the power of the Supponide clan. Charlemagne's grandson Bernard was the first to marry into the family when he took Cunigund to wife; Bernard's successor, his cousin Lothar I, chose the Supponide Angelberga for his own son Louis II. In the turmoil of late ninth-century

Italy that followed the death of Louis II, Berengar turned to this same family for support, married Bertilla, and gained the throne with the help of her clan. Kings sometimes appear to have had little freedom of choice. Returning to England after long exile in the continent, Edward the Confessor found it necessary to come to terms with the entrenched power of Earl Godwin; their alliance was sealed by his marriage to Godwin's daughter Edith. Yet royal marriages to noble daughters are a feature of the entire period and are not to be identified as a sign of a dynasty in special difficulties. Kings could strengthen their hands through the support of a noble clan without being eclipsed by overmighty subjects. Charlemagne was seeking allies in his attempts to oust his brother, whose kingdom included Alemannia. In 771 he therefore married Hildegard, whose father, Gerold, held power in Alemannia and whose maternal grandfather, Gottfried, was its duke. In 783 Charlemagne married Fastrada, daughter of the East Frankish count Radulf, with a view to obtaining her family's aid in his Saxon campaigns. In 842 Charles the Bald married Ermentrud, daughter of Count Odo of Orleans and niece of Adalhard, to cement the support of Adalhard in his struggle against his brothers, just as in 956 the English Eadwig chose Ælfgifu to strengthen his hand against threats to his own position. Medieval politics was a dialogue, not a constant confrontation between royal and noble power. The choice of a king's wife will tell much about the state of the argument.

The Middle Kingdom, which stretched from the Low Countries to Italy, proved the most disputed and unstable portion of the Carolingian inheritance. Its would-be rulers chose their brides with care. Louis the Pious destined his son Lothar as emperor and ruler of the Middle Kingdom, and Lothar duly married Ermengard, daughter of the Etichone count Hugh of Tours, whose lands lay in Alsace. Lothar would spend time in Italy, and the marriage might fulfil Louis's purpose of binding the kingdoms together. Lothar divided the Middle Kingdom among his three sons. Louis II, who was to receive Italy, was married to the Italian noblewoman Angelberga. Lothar's second son and namesake, Lothar II, was to have Lotharingia as his share. The needs of that kingdom and especially the power of the Bosonide clan led Lothar into his unhappy and barren marriage with Theutberga. Indeed, the Bosonides remained important for anyone with aspirations in this area. Charles the Bald lusted after his nephew's inheritance here, and when Charles's first wife, Ermentrud, died he lost no time in taking another, Theutberga's niece Richildis. Lotharingia remained important to the later Carolingians. When Louis d'Outremer married Gerberga in 939 he was not only taking the daughter of the German king Henry the Fowler, but also the widow of the duke of Lotharingia, whose duchy he was struggling hard to acquire.

Royal marriages can be clear indications of changes in the direction of royal ambitions. Danish kings had usually taken wives near to home. Yet in 1016, when Cnut was fighting to gain the English throne, he contracted his first marriage with Ælfgifu of Northampton, a member of the same north midlands family from which his rival Edmund Ironside sought support. Once king, he turned to the problem of securing his position and took as second wife Emma, the widow of his predecessor and sister of the Duke of Normandy, hoping to utilize her expertise in English politics but also to divert family support from her royal English sons. During the sixth, seventh, and eighth centuries, kings of Lombards and Franks and dukes of Bavaria were involved in a three-cornered relationship. In the sixth century the Bavarian duke Garibald married a Lombard princess, Waldrada; their daughter Theudelinda in turn became the wife of Authari, a new Lombard king. In the eighth century a daughter of the Bavarian ducal house, Swanhild, became the hostage and wife of the Frank Charles Martel; Charles's own daughter married Duke Odilo of Bavaria, producing a son who married a Lombard princess—a labyrinthine nightmare of relationship created by the shifting fortunes of battle and alliance.

A noble wife brought with her the support of her family; sometimes she brought the family itself. A royal marriage secured advancement and opportunities for the father and brothers of the bride. The family of Hildegard, Charlemagne's second wife, was prominent at court after the marriage, and Hildegard's death produced a crisis in the career of her brother Udalrich. When Louis the Pious took Judith to wife, he gained her Welf brothers in the bargain. Judith's stepsons were later as anxious to be rid of them as of the queen. The fortunes of a royal wife and her family could be closely intertwined, especially where that family had enlarged its power through the marriage. An attack on one might involve, even necessitate, attack on the other: Berengar I's wife Bertilla was murdered in

911 as part of a palace revolution in which her brothers fell from grace. When Edward the Confessor moved against the family of Godwin in 1051, he sent Edith to a nunnery, but the return to power of her father and brothers brought Edith back up on the wheel of fortune. A queen's brother could dominate the court, even aspire to kingship. Edith's brothers Harold and Tostig overshadowed the last years of Edward the Confessor's reign: Harold's ill-starred acquisition of the throne in 1066 after Edward's death needs no retelling. Boso, brother of Richildis and thus brother-in-law of Charles the Bald, advanced from prominence at Charles's court to virtual regency in Italy before he married Charles's niece Ermengard, set himself up as king of Provence, and finally made a bid for Italy and the imperial title.

Where Edward the Confessor had found it expedient to marry the daughter of Godwin, Earl of Wessex, Godwin's son Harold in the anxieties of 1066 turned for his bride to a daughter of the Earl of Mercia. When kings and their great nobles pursued similar ends in the same world it is no surprise that their brides were indistinguishable. Tenth-century France saw little difference between the origins of wives chosen by the last Carolingians and those of the brides of ducal ancestors of the Capetians. These two families struggled for position in northern France, and chose their wives to outmaneuver each other. Hugh the Great and Charles the Simple married sisters, the daughters of the Anglo-Saxon king Edward the Elder. Hugh the Great's second wife was sister of Gerberga, the bride of Charles's son Louis d'Outremer; both women were daughters of Henry the Fowler. When Hugh Capet chose his wife Adelaide for her connections in Aquitaine, the Carolingian Lothar arranged a marriage for his son Louis to an Aquitainian widow. A new dynasty rising to power or an old one challenged did not necessarily turn to a particular type of bride: these Carolingians and Capetians chose royal princesses *and* noblewomen. But such periods of uncertainty see the marriages of kings and nobles run closely in parallel.

The first Capetian kings navigated the matrimonial sea with a sharp eye to advantage. When he was seeking a bride for his son Robert, Hugh Capet first aimed high. He wrote to the Byzantine emperor, requesting a princess and explaining his need to search far afield for a wife by the fact that intermarriage and the fear of incest had reduced his choices close at hand. In the search for a worthy bride a Byzantine princess would have been a prestigious catch. But the plan came to naught, in part because a preferable match became available. The death of the Count of Flanders put his widow on the marriage market, so Hugh snapped her up for his son. The wealth and power of Flanders made any leverage there highly desirable. Robert himself was to find incest no inhibition where advantage was involved. Bertha of Blois might be his cousin and mother of his godson, but wardship of such a key county in northern France overrode any doubt. When expediency demanded a son and heir and a new friendship with Anjou, Robert discarded Bertha in favor of the Angevin noblewoman Constance. Both marriages were part of the tortuous politics of the Loire valley. They enmeshed Robert still further in the bitter rivalries of northern France.

His son Henry I was betrothed or married on three occasions. In 1033 Henry's betrothal to the six-year-old Mathilda sealed friendship with her father, Emperor Conrad II. The child died before Henry met her, and he took in her stead her ten-year-old namesake, a stepdaughter of Conrad II and niece of Emperor Henry III. She was a distant relation of Agatha, wife of the exiled Anglo-Saxon prince Edward. Did Henry hope not only to renew his alliance with the emperor but gain a remote chance of embarrassing Cnut, whose conquest of England had expelled Edward? In 1051 Henry married for the third time, to Anne of Russia, sister of Sjatoslav II. This remote but learned princess from the fringes of Europe, who could sign her name in Cyrillic letters, was the sister-in-law of his previous wife's niece. This may have brought to his notice a woman who brought him little or no political advantage, save a tenuous link with a possible Russian enemy of the emperor. But all Henry's brides were chosen with another end in view; to remove him from the world of the nobles on his own doorstep. Anne of Kiev certainly had no family to help her or trouble him. After Henry's death she was driven to marry one of his close counsellors to safeguard herself. The legacy of tenth-century intermarriage was a pool of incest that enemies could easily fish to the discomfiture of kings. Henry's choices placed him beyond reproach. His foreign princesses confirmed his prestige and distanced him in every way from the nobility of his kitchen garden, thus outweighing any advantages to be gained from marriages close at hand.

Marriage to the daughter of a noble was usually a royal attempt to capture support: in the delicate chess game between king and nobles it could lead to the capture of the king himself through the queen. An already important clan gained an advocate in the most intimate court circles. Its power was enhanced, its voice in the affairs of the kingdom amplified. Political revolutions became palace revolts to replace the influence on the king's person and the removal of the queen herself—the key piece on the chessboard—paramount. Early Europe had no strict analogy to Heian Japan, where the Fujiwara family controlled puppet emperors for generations through the marriages of their sisters and daughters. But it had its Harolds and its Bosos. There were times when marriage to a royal princess seemed not only a good match but a safe one.

Royal Princesses

When status was at stake, few could match the importance of a king as well as a member of his own family. Incest was no taboo when politics required a marriage within the family. In marrying Ermentrud, Charles the Bald was taking his own cousin to wife, if the *Annals of St. Bertin*, where Ermentrud's brother is identified as Charles's cousin, is to be relied upon. Charles's desire for a marriage alliance with Adalhard could not be thwarted by degrees of kindred. When the royal dynasty itself was rent with tension over inheritance, cross-cousin marriage might be especially desirable. Late ninth-century Wessex had been ruled in turn by four brothers. When the youngest brother Alfred died in 899, descendants of at least one older brother, Æthelred I, survived to contest the throne with Alfred's own son Edward. Particularly pressing were the powerful rival claims of Edward's older cousin Æthelwold. One of Edward's earliest actions after his father's death was to discard his concubine and take a legitimate wife. In the circumstances his choice fell on Æthelwold's niece, Ælfflæd, daughter of Æthelwold's elder brother Æthelm and granddaughter of Æthelred I. Marriage with his cousin's daughter was an attempt to heal the splits which the indivisibility of kingship had set up within the royal family. The royal blood of Æthelred I continued to flow in the noble veins of tenth-century England and to fuel its dynastic politics. In the crisis of 956 Edward's grandson Eadwig himself chose a bride from this same royal line, seeking the strength it could bring him, looking for the support of a family that few tenth-century kings willingly alienated. Eadwig was to be forcibly separated from his wife on the grounds of incest, but that, as we shall see, is another political story.

Royal marriages within the immediate family were comparatively rare, but marriages between dynasties were common in the sixth, seventh, and eighth centuries in the endless war- and peacemaking among the emergent Germanic kingdoms. In the world where Lombards fought Gepids and Franks, Northumbrians fought Mercians and Welsh, Mercians fought West Saxons and East Angles, and Merovingians fought everyone, including each other, women were given and taken, sometimes forcibly, as hostages and sealers of peace. Rosamund, daughter of the Gepid king and second wife of Alboin, king of the Lombards, was taken as hostage in battle; Radegund was Clothar I's share of the booty of the Thuringians; Charles Martel brought back his future bride Swanhild and her aunt as Bavarian hostages. The method of acquisition might at other times be ostensibly more peaceful. Edwin of Northumbria married Æthelberga, daughter of the king of Kent, to seal his alliance. Eanfled, the daughter of this union, became the bride of King Oswy of Northumbria, whose family rivaled hers for possession of the Northumbrian throne. Oswy had murdered Eanfled's relative Oswin, and Eanfled was to seal peace between the families. She persuaded Oswy to build a monastery to atone for the murder. The violence of battles and murder is rarely far below the surface of such marriages. When women sealed alliances made by the sword, they became forcible reminders of defeat. Cenwalh of Wessex took a sister of Penda of Mercia when Penda's strength made Cenwalh his ally; his later repudiation of the wife was a gesture of defiance that provoked Penda to war.

In theory these women were peacemakers and peace bringers, a powerful ideal. In practice, however, their presence at a foreign court generated tensions that could end in tragedy. In the poem *Beowulf* when Hrothgar married his daughter Freawaru to Ingeld, son of his deadly enemy Froda, he planned "to settle with the woman a part of his deadly feuds and struggles." In the obscure story of

Finn, Finn had taken a Danish wife, Hildeburh, to establish peace between peoples. In Fredegar's *Chronicle* Brunhild arranged to meet her granddaughter-in-law Bilichild that the women might try to bring peace. The idea of the queen as peacemaker became a hagiographical motif. Radegund was presented as ever-solicitous for peace, Balthild made peace between Franks and Burgundians. As late as the tenth and eleventh centuries Adelaide was a peacemaker for Odilo, Gisela for Wipo, and Emma's encomiast presents her marriage to Cnut as a reconciliation between English and Dane. Yet when Brunhild and Bilichild were to meet, Bilichild failed to appear, which was perhaps as well, since the two women had conducted a letter-war of insults, contemptuous abuse, and reproaches that augured ill for the outcome. It is a fragile bond that introduces into the family a constant reminder of past injuries. Beowulf had little faith in the effectiveness of Hrothgar's actions, remarking that peace can rarely be established so soon, "even though the bride is of worth." He foresaw the trouble that the presence of Freawaru and her Danish followers would one day cause in the halls of the enemy, how they would unwittingly reopen the old sores of battle and vengeance, reminding old warriors of defeat and the death of kinfolk. In the tale of Finn, Hildeburh's brother and son were both killed in the land of Finn, vengeance was taken, and she was carried back to Denmark, a symbol of failure.

Where a woman's family had suffered defeat and death, she rarely forgot their fate and might change from peacemaker to vengeance-wreaker. After Radegund had been repudiated by Clothar I she was to ask Fortunatus to write in memory of her family and their achievements, destroyed by her former husband. Swanhild never lost contact with her Bavarian relatives. On the death of Charles Martel she fought to support her own son against his half brothers, seeking help from Bavaria, conniving at the marriage of her stepdaughter Hiltrud to Duke Odilo. Swanhild was not taking revenge, but turning naturally to her own kin for aid in her need.

Rosamund's is a simple story of a wife's vengeance. With the supposed help of her lover she plotted the death of her husband Alboin, who had taken her as wife and hostage after a Gepid defeat in which he had killed her father. With a macabre pride he had fashioned the head of the dead king into a drinking vessel. Well advanced in his cups one night, he handed the skull to Rosamund and invited her to drink with her father. Surely hers is a case where vengeance was provoked.

When vengeance was turned inward into the family it provoked fratricidal violence. Fredegar blamed Brunhild's desire to avenge her sister and husband for the family feuds that tore at the Merovingian house. When the vengeance was turned outward it produced war. Queen Clotild, wife of Clovis I, stirred up her sons to avenge the death of her parents. Her daughter Clotild herself became a subject for revenge, when she went as a foreign princess to the court of her husband Amalaric the Visigoth. She found herself an ill-treated and defenseless queen in a distant court and sent a bloodstained towel back to her brothers as earnest of her ill treatment. Childebert was moved to march to Spain to avenge his sister. Cut off from kin and protection in foreign courts, Clotild was not the only queen to be a defenseless victim; in the Anglo-Saxon poem *Wife's Lament*, a woman is persecuted by her husband's hostile kin. The seventh-century Northumbrian princess Osthryth may have suffered the ultimate persecution. She became the wife of Æthelred, King of Mercia, and was murdered by the Mercians. Her death may have been vengeance for the actions of her own sister, whom the Mercians blamed for the death of the sister's husband, King Peada. When women were passed from court to court as formal gifts to seal peace, to act as hostages, they caricatured the position of all in-marrying women, becoming objects of suspicion for their in-laws, representatives of rival families, personifications of old grievances. They were exposed, far from the best protection of their own kingroup. Fears for their fate caused many kings to refuse to marry out their daughters in this way.

Charles the Bald felt such unease when he married his daughter Judith to the West Saxon king Æthelwulf in 856. He hedged the marriage with every possible safeguard for a young girl about to cross the Channel to share a kingdom with an elderly man, who already had adult sons. Charles had personal experience. His own mother Judith had married an elderly husband and been vilified and attacked by her stepsons; the dangers of a foreign court were added for her granddaughter. Charles was contracting the first foreign marriage in the Carolingian family since Charles Martel had carried off Swanhild and Charlemagne had contracted his brief union with the Lombard princess; the projected Byzantine marriages of Charlemagne's day had all aborted. Charles expressed his apprehension by a marriage for Judith meticulous in its observation of the forms of legitimacy and accompanied by the first certain anointing of a medieval queen.

Marriages between royal dynasties were rare in Carolingian Frankia, having been actively discouraged in the family settlement of 817. Writing to Charlemagne and his brother Carloman in 768 Pope Stephen III had outlined the dangers of foreign marriage. "No man who has taken a foreign bride has remained unharmed. See how many great men have been led from the laws of God by foreign wives. Following the wishes of these same wives they have been led into enormous excesses and great crimes." Stephen's advice was not disinterested; he was alarmed at the prospect of an alliance between the hated Lombards and his new-found Carolingian friends and could cite Old Testament strictures against foreign entanglements.

It was less the thought of excesses and crimes which steered the ninth-century Carolingians from foreign marriage than an awareness of the advantages of noble alliances and the dangers of interference by foreign in-laws in domestic affairs. Charlemagne had taken as his first wife the daughter of the Lombard king Desiderius, only to repudiate her and marry again. The irate father took his vengeance by supporting Charlemagne's enemies, offering succor and shelter to the sister-in-law and nephews whom Charles had disinherited. The Carolingian conquests in Europe had in any case reduced the number of foreign brides whose prestige and Christian faith would have made them suitable consorts for the dynasty that aspired to an empire of Christendom. A projected marriage with a daughter of King Offa of Mercia came to naught when Offa presumptuously demanded one of Charlemagne's daughters for his own son.

The Carolingians dallied longest with plans for Byzantine unions. These were mooted for Charlemagne's sister and daughter, even for the king himself. There were later plans for Louis II, for his daughter Ermengard, and even for her son Louis the Blind. The prestige of the Greek Empire tempted Charlemagne, and the later Italian Carolingians saw the advantages of alliance with Byzantium against the Saracen pirates who devastated Italy. Hugh of Arles tried to arrange a Byzantine marriage for his son when he was king of Italy. But these projects foundered on distance and the finer points of negotiation. Liudprand of Cremona has left an account of his own embassy to Constantinople in quest of a Byzantine bride for Hugh. If the arrogance and lack of sympathy it shows were typical of such negotiations, their failure is not surprising. Not until Otto I successfully arranged the marriage of his son and Theophanu was a Byzantine union carried to fruition.

When Charles the Bald broke with the habits of his family in 856 he did not act lightly. The growing menace of Viking invasion forced his hand. The summer of 856 had seen campaigns in the Seine valley and ineffectual Frankish resistance. Charles married his daughter to a victorious West Saxon king who had defeated Viking armies in battle and who controlled the north bank of the Channel, which the Vikings crossed and recrossed with impunity. The Vikings engendered a sense of common purpose among the rulers of Christian Europe that was expressed in a series of marriages, that of Æthelwulf and Judith being only the first. In the early tenth century, Anglo-Saxon princesses married Carolingian and Ottonian kings, a Capetian duke, and a Flemish count. These marriages found worthy homes for Edward the Elder's numerous daughters and conferred prestige on the often upstart husbands who sought their hands. But the prestige of Edward's dynasty was largely military, its greatest fame the success of its resistance to Viking attack. It was the Vikings who drew these rulers of the North Sea kingdoms into a sense of community secured with marriage ties. Viking activity later prompted the only other continental marriage of an English king to occur between 600 and 1066, that of Æthelred II in 1002 to Emma, daughter of the Duke of Normandy. The Norman dukes boasted a Viking ancestry, and Æthelred sought to draw them more firmly into the Christian fold. Earlier Viking rulers had signaled their own entry into the Christian community by marriage. The English king Athelstan married off his sister Eadgyth to the newly baptized Viking king of York, Sihtric; the Viking lord of Frisia received Lothar II's daughter Gisela in wedlock. Neither marriage nor friendship lasted, for peace between rulers was rarely held by that fragile bond. Within ninth-century England, the Viking threat drew old antagonists together. Alfred's daughter Æthelflæd was given to Æthelred, the quasi-independent ruler of Mercia, while in 853 Alfred's sister Æthelswith had married King Burgred of Mercia. 853 sealed an alliance against the Vikings between two hitherto hostile kingdoms. As the *Anglo-Saxon Chronicle* stated, Æthelwulf gave his daughter Æthelswith to Burgred "from Wessex to Mercia," to be a peacemaker between peoples drawn together by external attack.

Widows and Sisters

In the sixth and seventh centuries royal widows were married by incoming kings or usurpers to secure through them a claim to the throne, to gain the support of their allies. The importance of such widows was grasped by rebellious sons and pretenders. Merovech, Chilperic's son, married his aunt Brunhild to gain claims to the kingdom of her dead husband, Sigibert. He failed to gain noble backing and the marriage was short lived. In 613 the *patricius* Aletheus is alleged to have planned to murder Clothar II and take his crown. His plan involved persuading Clothar's wife, Berthetrude, to marry him. Both marriage and murder aborted. In Ostrogothic and Lombard Italy a series of queen-widows married men who then became king: Amalasuntha, Theudelinda, and Gundiperga. Paul the Deacon's story of Rosamund illustrates the importance attached to an Italian royal widow: she was wooed first by an ambitious court noble and then by the Byzantine exarch, both aiming at the Lombard crown. These Lombard women have sometimes been considered as conduits of power, as women who, although they could not rule in their own right, could transmit rightful claims to their new husbands. It is more likely that Lombard Italy merely parallels Merovingian Gaul.

Pretenders to the throne married widows of their predecessors to gain what support they had and to neutralize a potentially powerful opponent. The Danish Cnut still felt it expedient to marry his predecessor's widow when he conquered England in 1016. By marrying Emma in 1017 he wooed her support away from the sons of her previous marriage, bought off her Norman kin and gained her expertise in English politics. The motives of a conqueror had not changed. Widows carried substantial influence, and especially in the early period, treasure. They and their kin were the obvious protectors and supporters of sons who could challenge the new king. After the death of Charibert, his widow Theudechild offered herself and her treasure to King Guntram. He led her on, took her treasure, and packed her off to a convent. The master plan of a sixth- or seventh-century usurper had three stages: murder the king, get the gold-hoard, marry the widow. Since the widow usually sat on the gold the two went together.

Few widows, whether of kings or nobles, remained on the shelf in the late ninth and tenth centuries. So great was the demand that church reformers felt compelled to step in and defend the right of widows to remain unmarried. Æthelbald and Judith, Otto I and Adelaide, Gerard of Lotharingia and Zwentibold's widow, Louis d'Outremer and Gerberga, Louis V and Adelaide, Robert the Pious and both Rozala and Bertha, Cnut and Emma—the list of royal marriages involving widows is a long one. Remarriage might follow so fast on the heels of bereavement that widowhood scarcely became a reality. After the fall of her husband, Gilbert of Lotharingia, Gerberga was virtually picked off the battlefield by Louis and carried back to France. The old motives still applied. Cnut neutralized the support of powerful kin; Æthelbald's marriage to his stepmother Judith gained him a prestigious mother for his children; Otto I took the widow who brought claims to the Italian throne. Æthelbald and Cnut married their predecessor's widows feeling that the alliances and prestige gained by a previous king were needful for his successor.

In the formalized world of the tenth century, marriage to a widow brought rights of wardship over her underage children. Robert the Pious secured wardship of the heirs to the county of Blois through his marriage to Bertha. A guardian could exercise lordship of the county on his heir's behalf, enjoying the opportunities to pursue his own interests. Politics, not preference for older women, made widows desirable; the tenth century did not suffer from a collective Oedipus complex. Yet disparity of age and condition could disrupt the best-planned match. The late tenth-century Carolingian king of France, Lothar, married his young son Louis V to Adelaide, widow of Count Stephen of Gevaudan and sister of Geoffrey of Anjou. Louis was fifteen or sixteen at the time, Adelaide at least twice his age. The marriage had much to recommend it. Geoffrey of Anjou favored it and it promised an Angevin alliance and influence in Aquitaine, catching Hugh Capet on his southern flank. But it failed dismally. Conjugal love was conspicuous by its absence. The couple dragged out two years of almost total estrangement: they never shared the same bedchamber, refused to inhabit the same house, and ended up meeting only in the open air to exchange the briefest of words. Divorce was the inevitable result. Adelaide fled, leaving Louis virtually penniless to abandon himself to the vices of the south. Lothar was forced to recall and rescue his son. Though politics determined the choice of bride, personal antipathy could dislocate the plans.

The predominance of politics over passion appears in the choice of sisters, even mothers and daughters, as wives of kings. In the early tenth century, Carolingian and Capetian rivals married consecutive pairs of sisters, daughters of Edward the Elder and Henry the Fowler. In the sixth century the rival brothers Sigibert and Chilperic espoused the Visigothic sisters Brunhild and Galswinth. In none of these cases could a king allow his rival to steal a march on him; each had to match, and thereby neutralize, the alliance of the other. Father and son might seek to underpin the same friendship by consecutive marriages. When Clothar II chose a wife for his son Dagobert he married him to Gomatrud, sister of Dagobert's stepmother Clothar's own queen, Sichildis. Theudebert I married Wisigard, daughter of the Lombard king; the continuing need of Lombard friendship was recognized when his own son Theudebald married Wisigard's sister, Waldrada. For their prospective husbands these women embodied the same alliances, to be doubly cemented over two generations or secured by bitter rivals.

The choice of wife never became an irrelevance to be left to personal preference. The significance of marriage politics is never clearer than in the battles for kingship in the sixth and seventh centuries and in those that dominated the tenth. Clothar I son of Clovis received his share of the Merovingian kingdom on the death of his father, together with his brothers Chlodomer and Childebert. His career was a history of wars to enlarge his kingdom, whether at the expense of foreign kings or of his brothers and their descendants. Born between 504 and 507, Clothar was first married between 517 and 523 to Ingund, a noblewoman. The death of his brother Chlodomer in 524 provided an opportunity for acquiring land and the need to take a new bride. Together with his brother Childebert, Clothar murdered Chlodomer's two elder sons, frightened the third into tonsuring himself as a monk, and then married their mother Guntheuca, taking the widow as he took the kingdom. In 531 Clo-

thar was on campaign in Thuringia. At the end of a successful battle
he brought back his share of the booty: Radegund, daughter of King
Bertacharius. She was still a child and Clothar did not immediately
marry her, preferring to have her reared and educated to his tastes.
His first wife Ingund had been pushed aside in the 520s, but not forgotten. She occupied the royal bed again by the mid-530s, if indeed
she had ever completely left it. By 537 she was replaced by her own
sister Arnegund, as Ingund had asked Clothar to find a worthy husband for her sister and with consummate irony he had replied that
he could think of no one worthier than himself. Before 540 he had
yet another mistress, Chunsina, and at some stage consummated his
marriage with Radegund. If it appears that Clothar was wiling away
his later years in passion rather than politics, the illusion is dispelled
by his last marriage. In 555 he contracted a brief union with Waldrada, a Lombard princess but also the widow of his Austrasian
grandnephew Theudebald. Desire for heirs determined some of
Clothar's unions. As for the others, his wives were taken up and put
aside as political shifts demanded rather than as passions prevailed.

Hugh of Arles in the early tenth century showed equal appreciation of the benefits of matrimony. From about 903 Hugh was count
of Provence. In 923 he was called into Italy to claim the throne, a
claim he had made good by 926. His later career was consumed by
the struggle to retain his position and to secure the elusive imperial
crown. In Provence and in Italy his rival, continuing the old enmi-
ties of the Middle Kingdom, was Rudolf II, King of Burgundy. No
ruler of Provence could ignore his close neighbor in Burgundy.
Louis the Blind, the last Carolingian king of Provence, married Adelaide, daughter of Rudolf I, and Hugh was quick to secure Rudolf's
widow, Willa, as his first wife. This first marriage was contracted
before 910 and ended before 930. By the latter date Hugh had married the unknown Alda, who became the mother of his only legitimate son, Lothar.

Alda's brief and obscure career was finished by 932, when Hugh
took as his third wife the infamous Marozia, daughter of Theophylact and virtual ruler of Rome. The marriage was one of blatant political convenience. Marozia was already twice widowed, the fact
that her second husband had been Hugh's half brother casting further doubt on the legitimacy of the new match. The loyalties of the
Roman nobility were not to be taken for granted, and Marozia

hoped that Hugh's aid, and the title of Queen and Empress, would offer greater security. Marozia's son John was pope in 932 and Hugh could feel at last that the imperial crown, hitherto denied him by the Romans, might be his. The opposition of Marozia's son Alberic shipwrecked all these plans, for Alberic feared that Hugh would cut him out of his Roman inheritance. He placed himself at the head of the discontent already grumbling against his mother. At a banquet in Castel San Angelo in 933 Alberic truculently refused to hand his mother a glass of water. Hugh accused him of insulting his mother and the incident escalated into crisis, fanned by Alberic's suspicions of his stepfather. Alleging that he feared for his personal safety, Alberic assembled his followers and his mother's enemies and led an attack. Hugh's gallantry matched his courage: he fled, leaving Marozia to be captured, imprisoned, and finally to pass into the tranquility of the nunnery, where this maligned woman spent her final days.

Hugh lived to love again. On 12 July 937 his longstanding rival Rudolf of Burgundy died, leaving a widow, Bertha of Swabia, and three underage children, Conrad, Rudolf, and Adelaide. Hugh lost no time. By August he had married Bertha and betrothed his young son Lothar to the six-year-old Adelaide. Influence in Burgundy through wardship of his stepsons seemed within his grasp. But he reckoned without the new king of Germany, Otto the Great. Otto could brook no such growth of Hugh's power. He marched into Burgundy and forcibly took the tutelage of the young Conrad. Hugh was left holding not the baby, but his mother and sister. His marriage to Bertha had been no love match. Deprived of his aim, Hugh first lost interest, then allegedly came to hate his wife. In the 940s Bertha was sent back to Burgundy, to the nunnery of Peterlingen. Hugh's need of her had been nothing but political, since the 930s and 40s saw a procession of his concubines: Wandelmoda, Pezola, Roza, and Stephanie (the three later nicknamed after the goddesses Venus, Juno, and Semele).

Four centuries after Clothar, Hugh showed himself equally prepared for divorce, adultery, even incest where his purpose required it. The changes that occurred between the sixth and tenth centuries should not be exaggerated. The tenth century certainly saw a peak in the desirability of widows as wives for kings and for nobles. In a land-hungry society faced with scarce resources, widows brought property and wardship, and kings married them in quest of counties and dukedoms as much as kingdoms. But tenth-century counts and dukes exercised powers that could equal those of sixth-century kings. When Louis d'Outremer married the widow of a duke of Lotharingia he was following rules that had governed Clothar I's choice of the widow of his nephew, King of Austrasia. By the tenth century the formal rights of wardship appear new, but control of heirs had always been an attraction of widows. Both the novelty and the formality of tenth-century "feudalism" can be overstated. Otto the Great married the widow Adelaide in 952 to take an Italian kingdom, just as Clothar had snatched at Guntheuca in 524. Situations varied, but basic similarities remained. Throughout, the choice of a king's bride was a hardheaded act of policy.

Betrothal

There could be no standard form of royal wooing when brides were sometimes betrothed unseen, sometimes carried off from the battlefield; no customary age for marriage when widows were as common as child brides. Generalization about the mechanics of choice and the age of marriage are therefore impossible, but some things can be learned of how and when kings took their brides, to add to our knowledge of why.

Queens had the childhood and education appropriate to their origins, not to their future status as king's wife. Odd exceptions like Radegund, carried off as a child, were reared with their future position in mind, but in most cases their infancy was that of the noblewoman or princess. Some families educated their daughters well. Ermengard, daughter of the Carolingian king of Italy Louis II, was educated in the nunnery at Brescia and taught by the scholar Anastasius. Italian noblewomen and princesses were often learned: Paul the Deacon wrote a history for the daughter of King Desiderius, and Berengar and Willa employed a tutor to instruct their daughters. The Visigothic court produced well-educated women in Brunhild and Galswinth, and Anne of Russia could at least sign her own name. Noble families could show an equal respect for learning. Edith, wife of Edward the Confessor, had been educated at the nunnery at Wilton, where she had become proficient in the liberal arts as well as embroidery. Queens were expected to have an education to match their status, so that wives of low birth and little learning, like Fredegund, found themselves chided for their ignorance. But no period of a queen's life is more obscure than her childhood, and knowledge of their upbringing and education is consequently thin.

Age at marriage, whether for king or queen, varied widely. The minimum age seems to have been twelve for women and fifteen for men. Judith, daughter of Charles the Bald, was about twelve when she married Æthelwulf, who must have been fifty. Hildegard, Charlemagne's second wife, was thirteen at the time of her marriage. Betrothal could occur earlier than this. Hugh of Arles betrothed Lothar and Adelaide when she was six and Lothar little more; they married in 947 at the age of sixteen. Charlemagne's sister Gisela was betrothed at eight to a Byzantine prince and at twelve to a Lombard, but remained unmarried, abbess of the convent of Chelles. His daughter Rotrud was betrothed when about nine to the even younger Constantine VI. Again marriage failed to follow; lengthy betrothals often went awry. Although few kings married before the age of fifteen, many had concubines by then. Fifteen was the minimum age for marriage in the Merovingian and Carolingian dynasties. Childebert II married Faileuba at this age, but he had already had a concubine and a son. Clovis II married Balthild at fifteen and had a son by sixteen, though she was probably his concubine before this. Eadwig was no more than fifteen when he took Ælfgifu to wife in 956, and his brother Edgar had disposed of two wives before the age of twenty-two.

Royal marriage could be delayed, often at a father's insistence. Kings whose marriages coincided with designation or the acquisition of a kingdom might have to wait beyond the minimum age. Edward the Elder may have been thirty before the death of his father Alfred allowed his marriage; before this he had taken only a concubine. Although Louis the Pious married his first wife at sixteen or seventeen, his sons had to wait longer for brides and kingdoms, Lothar I until he was twenty-six, Pepin until twenty-five, Louis the German until twenty-one. Æthelred II's eldest son, Athelstan, remained unmarried at the time of his death around 1013, although he was at least twenty-four.

The majority of kings who already controlled a kingdom married before twenty. According to his anonymous biographer, the Astronomer, Louis the Pious was betrothed and married young "for fear of being dragged into the toils of lust by the natural heats of the body." Few kings ran the risk. Charles the Bald was nineteen at his marriage, Lothar eighteen when he took Emma in 966, and his bride a similar age. Few queens, even when widows, were over twenty-five at marriage, as a more advanced age would have endangered childbearing. Gerberga had not reached this age when she married Louis d'Outremer, and Lothar's widow Adelaide was still only twenty-one when she was wedded to Otto the Great. Cnut's Emma was elderly, at least twenty-seven at her marriage in 1017. There was no upper limit on the age of kings at marriage, though Charlemagne's last marriage at fifty-seven approaches a record. Edward the Confessor was forty when he married Edith. The union was barren. His age may have been a factor, as may that of Charles the Bald, whose marriage to Richildis at forty-seven produced a series of miscarriages, though she did bear one healthy daughter. But the problem should not be exaggerated when Charlemagne and Edward the Elder could father children until well over fifty.

Where circumstances did not demand speed there was time for the leisurely niceties of wooing. Conventional elaboration has, as we have seen, made these courtships problematic. The prior inspection of the bride through an intermediary, common in the legends, is likely in practice. Prior to the marriage of Otto the Great and Eadgyth, negotiations between the Ottonian and Anglo-Saxon courts were carried out by third parties. When Chilperic wished to marry a Visigothic princess, he sent envoys to the court to arrange the marriage and pledge his good faith. The realities of royal wooing were probably as impersonal as their motives were hardheaded. The impatience of Henry the Fowler to possess the charms of Mathilda, Ælfthryth decking herself out to ensnare King Edgar, the stories of passionate attachment and even more of seduction by women, are romantic additions. Most royal brides were taken young, or unseen, or for attractions very different from those personal charms celebrated by the chronicles. The supposed bride show in which Louis the Pious chose Judith thus becomes doubly interesting. It is reported in both the *Royal Frankish Annals* and the biography by the Astronomer that Louis married Judith "after looking over many daughters of the nobility." Urged on to remarry by counsellors who feared he would become a monk, Louis had the daughters of noble houses brought before him, from whom he chose Judith, daughter of Welf, a woman, according to Thegan, noble of birth and outstandingly beautiful. Is this the Louis who cleansed his father's court of immorality, who dispatched his sisters for their loose living? A connoisseur's appreciation of female charm accords ill with Louis's other known attributes; Thegan remarked that he never bared his teeth in laughter, and alone remained serious amid the merriment of others. The bride show was a Byzantine practice, and the ceremonial of Louis's court much affected by Byzantine imperial models. Did he borrow this method of choosing a wife from Byzantium? Did his court writers borrow it for him? Or was this pious king like the later pious Robert, with an earthlier if not earthier side to his character? Otto the Great was presented with a choice of bride, admittedly more limited than that of Louis. When his father requested an Anglo-Saxon princess, Athelstan sent two from whom to choose, for he had an embarrassment of sisters and could afford to be generous. Otto, naturally, chose the prettier; the other was found a suitable match. Perhaps occasionally kings could indulge their preferences and their politics simultaneously.

Betrothal and the receipt of the bride herself were accompanied by the giving of gifts. "A king shall buy a queen with goods, with cups and with bracelets" says the Old English Gnomic poem. When Sigibert sent his palace officials to Spain to bring Brunhild, they went with presents and he received them back with feasts and poems. The story of the betrothal of Clovis and Clotild in the *Liber historiae Francorum* shows brides as part of a system of gift and exchange, and graphically portrays the obligations created by betrothal gifts. The tale may contain legendary elements, but its spirit belongs to the world of the sixth century. Clovis sought a bride from the Burgundians who were loath to comply with his wishes. They duly refused the betrothal gifts his envoys took them, but Clotild accepted a ring, which she placed in her uncle Gundobad's treasury. In the following year Clovis claimed his bride as a rightful return for the gift that had been accepted. The Burgundians knew nothing of the ring and feared a trick, suspecting that Clovis's messengers might secretly have planted a gift on them. A search was made and the ring found in the treasury. Gundobad was angry, but still recognized the obligation that the gift had created. The girl was given up.

Betrothal gifts were completed at the wedding by the husband's morning-gift or dower. This could involve lands, towns, and revenues. It formed an important part of a queen's endowment and will be dealt with later. The bride also brought a gift or dowry to her husband. Gregory of Tours has described the huge dowry gathered when Rigunth, daughter of Chilperic and Fredegund, went to marry Reccared of Spain. Her father blenched at the sight of so much treasure and had to be reassured by his wife that it had come, not from the royal stock, but from her own hoard. The Franks brought wedding gifts for Rigunth and when presents and dowry were assembled, the gold, silver, and fine clothes filled fifty cartloads. With Rigunth went her escort, families of serfs and highborn attendants who were forced to accompany her. In their distress at forcible exile some hanged themselves, others made their wills, many escaped en route. There were ample opportunities to abscond as Rigunth and her cumbersome baggage train made their slow southward progress. The cities on her route were called on to provide hospitality for the bride and her distinguished escort. They lived off the land, taking grapes and cattle as they passed, leaving desolation in their wake. Gregory's lack of sympathy for Chilperic and his family may have exaggerated the story of suicide and devastation, but Rigunth's retinue was typical of that of other royal brides. When the Merovingian Bertha married King Æthelberht of Kent she brought followers who included her own Christian bishop; when queen Æthelthryth went from East Anglia to Northumbria she took a household in which the future monk Owini was the chief servant. Her foreignness was apt to create difficulties for a new queen. Eanfled brought followers from Kent when she came to marry Oswy of Northumbria, embarrassing the king because the Kentish contingent observed Easter on a different day from the Northumbrians. When Galswinth came to Chilperic's court she was accompanied by maidens from Visigothic Spain. A foreign retinue, like the foreign queen herself, was often suspect in its new home. When Exeter fell to the Vikings in 1003, the *Anglo-Saxon Chronicle* blamed Queen Emma's servant, the Frenchman Hugh. Foreign manners generally excited comment. Ralph Glaber described the arrival of Queen Constance at the court of Robert the Pious in the early eleventh century, noting that her retinue had strange haircuts, lacked beards, and wore indecent shoes. These same shoes so scandalized William of San Benigne that he was moved to foretell that those who wore them were bound for the fires of hell. He presaged the harm that this host of loose-living, fancy-dressing southerners would bring to the decent, honest Franks, who eagerly flocked to the new fashions. The attitudes were recorded later, and are tinged with late eleventh-century moral reform, but the suspicion is genuine.

Wooed and won, laden with gifts, accompanied by her native followers, the bride to be arrived at the king's court. Like the heroine in the Anglo-Saxon poem *Judith*, she was led to the marriage bed, adorned with rings and circlets. It is to be hoped that the king's arrival was not like that of the villain Holofernes, inflamed and stupefied with liquour, but probably like him the king was led by his own men to the bedchamber, where the bride to be lay ready to become the king's wife.

Chapter 3 ⚜ *The King's Wife*

harlemagne succeeded to the throne in 768 at the age of twenty-six. Although at that date he was not married, he already had a concubine, Himiltrud, whose son Pepin was born around 770. Pepin was named after Charlemagne's own father, which suggests that at this date he was considered a full heir in the Carolingian family. Himiltrud was soon cast aside, or eclipsed, when Charlemagne took as a full wife the daughter of Desiderius, king of Lombard Italy. The marriage marked an alliance between the Carolingian house and the Lombards that was favored by Charlemagne's mother, the dowager queen Bertha. By 771 Charlemagne had repudiated the Lombard princess and returned her to her father's house. His actions naturally incurred the wrath of the girl's father and, according to Charlemagne's biographer Einhard, occasioned the only breach between the king and his mother. In his later biography of Charlemagne, Notker the Stammerer claimed that the princess's sterility was the ground of divorce, though Charlemagne gave their marriage little more than a year to achieve success. The marriage and the repudiation in fact mirror the shifts of Charlemagne's early politics, especially his rivalry with his brother Carloman, who shared the Carolingian inheritance.

Charlemagne went on immediately in 771 to marry Hildegard, daughter of a powerful Alemannian family, as Alemannia formed part of his brother's share of the kingdom. The repudiation of his first wife was a repudiation of Bertha's attempts to hold the two brothers together. Charlemagne's new wife Hildegard was too important to him to be a concubine. He took her as a full wife, a status which also legitimized the four sons she bore him. The union lasted twelve years: Hildegard bore nine children before her death in 783 at the age of twenty-five. Her first child was born when she was no more than fourteen and the strain of constant childbearing must have contributed to her early death in April of 783.

In the autumn of the same year Charlemagne remarried, again

taking a full wife in Fastrada, daughter of an East Frankish count. Fastrada's connections were allies for Charlemagne's Saxon campaigns, and the marriage was again fully legitimized. Charlemagne had three surviving sons from his first marriage; the eldest was only eleven. The peril of infant mortality still threatened, so Charlemagne remarried in the hopes of additional insurance through more legitimate heirs. His brief widowerhood, perhaps even the early stages of his marriage with Fastrada, saw the king take another concubine, the unknown mother of his daughter Ruodheid. Einhard was later to blame the troubles of Charlemagne's reign on Fastrada's evil genius; cast in the unenviable role of stepmother she may well have stirred up tensions within the royal family. In her eleven years of marriage Fastrada produced only two daughters, yet she must have hoped for sons and her presence in the royal bed threatened her stepsons with rival half brothers. When Charles's eldest son Pepin rose in rebellion in 792 he blamed the wicked actions of his stepmother; perhaps she taunted him with his mother's concubinage.

Charlemagne did not immediately remarry when Fastrada died in 794. His sons were older now, the fear of losing them in premature death less compelling, and the tensions of step-relationships weighing more heavily. Although the evidence is far from clear, it seems that Charlemagne's next woman, Liutgard, long remained a concubine. He may only have been prompted to legitimize the union by the arrival of the pope at the Carolingian court in 799. Since Liutgard had no children, marriage posed no threat to her stepsons, raised no specter of family disunity. When Liutgard died in A.D. 800 Charlemagne was approaching sixty and took no more full wives to his bed. But his powers were by no means waning. Four concubines occupied his last fourteen years: Madelgard, Gersvind, Regina, and Adellind. He was still fathering children by them in 807 at the age of sixty-five. Although his last two concubines bore him sons, Charlemagne legitimized neither them nor their children with the ceremonies of marriage. In 807 he had three adult sons; moreover two were themselves married, giving him four grandsons. The future of Charlemagne's line seemed assured: his concern as paterfamilias was less now to raise up rival sons than to preserve the concord of his house. Fortune was to ensure that only one of Charlemagne's five legitimate sons outlived him, though his grandsons bore out his calculation of the assured future of his house.

Charlemagne's long marital career was governed by the same principles of political and family need that ruled his choice of bride. Those principles determined the number and timing of marriages, the age at marriage, even the type of union itself, whether full marriage or concubinage. The fundamental needs of family predominated. Charlemagne stands in every way at the center of our period. While the marriage practices he followed did not apply without variation throughout the early Middle Ages, the basic aim remained the same: the security and continuity of the dynasty, achieved by raising up acceptable heirs while at the same time minimizing destructive intrafamily conflict. High rates of infant mortality might require many sons to ensure these ends; varying views on legitimacy might determine the nature of the unions which produced them. But the aim remained the same: continuity of the line. No wife who failed to conceive could ever feel entirely safe.

Marriage and Concubinage

Charlemagne married four wives and took six concubines. The distinction between marriage and concubinage was not entirely simple, nor did it remain unchanged throughout the period. The term *marriage* has been applied to various institutions through history, not all of which have the same legal and social connotations. A bewildering variety of rights can be created by the marriage bond: sexual monopoly for either partner, property rights over the other partner's goods, joint property rights or monopoly on the partner's labor. The usual aim of marriage is to produce heirs; it normally creates rights of property and inheritance for the children of the union. Marriage has even been defined as a sexual union that creates such rights for its children, a definition emphasizing the fact that marriage produces the next generation and reproduces the social order. But marriage can, and in the early Middle Ages did, involve the creation of security for the wife as well as the children, usually by guaranteeing her future through the provision of a dowry. Late Roman law made the dowry a prerequisite of true marriage, dowry here being understood as the property a wife brought to the marriage. Germanic law also required a dowry or nuptial gift if a union were to be a legitimate marriage, in this case signifying the husband's gift to the wife. But for Romans or for Germans society had demanded the protection of the vulnerable partner, the wife, making such protection an indispensable part of that legitimate sexual union which produced inheritance-worthy children. Roman law also stressed the need for free consent of both partners for a lawful marriage.

Marriage as distinct from sex is always a social affair, concerned with the production of future generations, ensuring the survival of society and of its existing property structure, hedged with the support of society's laws. In the early Middle Ages, marriage involved consent and dowry to legitimize the claims of its heirs. The relationship created was stable but not indissoluble. It was usually accompanied by ceremonies aimed at publicizing both the dowry and the consent, drawing attention to the nature of the union being formed. Concubinage, on the other hand, is a sexual relationship, usually of long—even lifelong—duration, but lacking legal protection for the woman and her children, and easily terminated. Concubinage was a private affair between the parties concerned, accompanied by little or nothing in the way of ceremony. Yet in the early Middle Ages the distinction between marriage and concubinage was blurred, partly because of the Church's own attitudes. Concubinage had been legally recognized in the laws of the late Roman Empire. Some protection had been given to the long-term concubine and her children, though the concubine was still distinguished by her total economic dependence; she lacked any of the security which dowry provided for a wife. Early Christian ideas on marriage had chosen to stress consent above dowry as the constituent element of legal marriage. This became a major plank in the Church's platform throughout the Middle Ages. This insistence on consent shifted emphasis away from such demonstrable elements as dowry and publicity. Consent, unlike dowry or public ceremony, was a gray area. The Church condemned concubinage as a loose union, inimical to its own ideas of lifelong monogamy. But how could concubinage be distinguished from clandestine marriage, where consent had been given in secret? The canon lawyers of the eleventh and twelfth centuries were deeply troubled by such ambiguities. Earlier their major effect, in combination with late Roman law, was to narrow the gap between concubine and wife, to aid the easy taking and discarding of concubines, and to justify for kings and others the continuation of practices that they followed for reasons of their own.

The practice of the sixth, seventh, and early eighth centuries suggests that in the crucial area of children's inheritance, concubines and wives were almost indistinguishable. The children of Merovingian and early Carolingian concubines enjoyed rights almost as great as those of the fully legitimate. Thus in the early sixth century Theuderic I, son of Clovis by a concubine, shared his father's inheritance on equal terms with his legitimate half brothers. Theuderic's own son, Theudebert I, succeeded his father, although again apparently the son of a concubine. At the end of the sixth century Theudebert II, Childebert II's son by a concubine, divided his father's kingdom with his half brother Theuderic II, son of a full wife, Faileuba. Ragnetrud, the mother of Dagobert's son Sigibert III, was probably a concubine. In the early eighth century the Carolingian Charles Martel, Pepin's son by a concubine, made good his claims to his father's property: his chief rival was Theudoald, grandson of Pepin's legitimate wife, but himself a concubine's son. Charlemagne's own early practice suggested the survival of similar attitudes. His eldest son, Pepin, born of the concubine Himiltrud, was apparently given hope of inheritance, and Charlemagne later recognized the claims of his illegitimate grandson Bernard. In practice the children of concubines long appear to have enjoyed rights of inheritance, the supposed monopoly of the legitimate.

The situation is actually not so simple, because the language of political polemic has created much ambiguity. *Concubine* was a term often applied to a rival's mother in order to discredit him. Bernard of Italy, that grandson of Charlemagne, was first referred to as "son of a concubine" during the reign of Louis the Pious. Louis had disinherited Bernard in favor of his own son Lothar, and had a vested interest in casting doubt on his birth. Charles Martel's partner Swanhild is called a queen (that is, a full wife) in the Reichenau confraternity book (a book listing those to be remembered in the prayers of the community); in the partisan *Annales mettenses priores*, whose author wrote against the claims of her son Grifo, she is a concubine. With the term bandied about as political abuse, the precise status of individual women becomes difficult to determine. However, the polemical use of concubinage and illegitimacy to discredit claims to the throne in the eighth and ninth centuries suggests that legitimacy mattered, that the claims of a concubine's son were debatable. Otherwise the slur would have been irrelevant. The succession arrangements made by the Carolingians in 806 and 817 excluded the sons of concubines on the grounds of illegitimacy. Charlemagne's own attitude toward the sons of his later concubines adhered to these rules: neither of the two who survived was given any share in the Carolingian kingdom; both were destined to the clerical career that became the normal path of a king's illegitimate sons.

The position of such sons had never been entirely secure even in the sixth century. Germanic laws had recognized the superior rights of legitimate children, though often illegitimate sons were preferred to daughters or remoter heirs. The Church backed such ideas on legitimacy, though its own definition of marriage may have helped the technically illegitimate. Reexamination of the cases where a concubine's son is known to have succeeded shows that in most instances he was the son of his father's first union, often of the concubine taken by a prince before he was of marriageable age. Such concubines were usually of high birth, perhaps for that reason considered more legitimate. Where sons of their fathers' later concubines succeed, there is often no other heir; yet in other cases a possibly illegitimate son like Grifo can push his own claims against those of legitimate half brothers, attracting powerful support to his cause. If clear distinctions did exist, they were muddied by political circumstances: the claim of blood could be strengthened by the support of noble factions prepared to back the sons of concubines for their own ends. As late as 924, on the death of the English king Edward the Elder, Athelstan made good his claims to the throne. He was the son of Ecgwyna, the noble concubine of his father's youth. Edward had designated his younger, legitimate son, Ælfweard, to succeed to the family kingdom of Wessex, but Athelstan had been destined to rule the newly acquired Mercia. Edward had wished to secure inheritance for Athelstan, but preferred his legitimate son for the ancestral lands, governed perhaps by rules of legitimate inheritance. As Ælfweard died only sixteen days after his father, however, Athelstan now had the opportunity to gain Wessex, backed by the nobility of Mercia, where he had been raised. He succeeded over the heads of three legitimate half brothers, at least one of whom was no mere infant. Arguments were certainly raised against him; the German writer Hroswitha of Gandersheim had heard them through his half sister Eadgyth. William of Malmesbury echoed them in the twelfth century, though his story that Edward had fallen in love with a peasant's daughter is a romantic elaboration of accusations that Athelstan's mother, though noble, was a concubine. Athelstan's success arose from a combination of circumstances and support, though it suggests that illegitimate birth was still no absolute disqualification in early tenth-century England.

The late ninth-century Carolingians enjoyed little success in gaining thrones for their illegitimate offspring. Both Lothar II and Charles the Fat tried and failed to legitimize the sons of their concubines; both admitted the difficulty of securing inheritance for the recognizably illegitimate. The Carolingian movement of reform had sharpened the issue, but then politics proved the major determinant. Lothar's attempts to marry Waldrada, the mother of his son Hugh, were blocked by the machinations of his uncles, especially Charles the Bald but also Louis the German; his own brother, Louis II of Italy, was no constant ally. Uncles and brothers could hope at best to gain possession of heirless kingdoms, or at least some territorial concessions: the legacy of the Carolingian family settlement was endless struggle for inheritance. Noble factions used the embarrassments of kings to their own advantage. Charles the Fat, for example, came up against their opposition in his attempts to legitimize Bernhard. Yet Arnulf in the late ninth century became king of East Frankia even though he was illegitimate, and later secured a kingdom for his own concubine's son Zwentibold. In a stronger or less beleaguered position, with sufficient support or a proved military reputation, an illegitimate Carolingian could make his claim stick, though it is significant that Arnulf, like Edward the Elder, felt it prudent to leave the East Frankish throne to Louis, the infant son of his wife Uota, searching elsewhere for kingdoms for his bastards. The marriage practices of kings created doubts and problems ripe for exploitation by enemies.

Moral arguments were a weapon in their armory. The Church's campaigns against royal marital malpractice were always conducted in the sensitive area of succession and legitimacy. Merovingian Frankia, which showed the clearest examples of the rights of the illegitimate, demonstrates how theory and politics combined to erode them. Speaking of the children of his hero, Guntram of Burgundy,

Gregory of Tours made his famous statement of the claims of royal blood per se: the sons of a king have rights to succeed irrespective of the status of their mother. His categorical statement was in fact defensive, called for because such right had been questioned. Bishop Sagittarius of Embrun had denied the claims of Guntram's sons because they were the children of a servant girl. Gregory disliked Sagittarius and relished the opportunity to condemn his ideas as foolish, but Guntram's sharp reaction against the bishop shows how sensitive was the spot Sagittarius had touched. Guntram had already formalized his union with the servant girl Austrechild/Bobilla as a full marriage: Sagittarius's views would be music to Guntram's predatory relatives, for whom legitimacy was a weapon in the struggle for inheritance. Guntram himself used it against Clothar II when he cast doubts on the child's paternity; Brunhild used it in suggesting that her grandson Theudebert II was the son not of Childebert but of a gardener. Such arguments were rarely absolute proscriptions of inheritance, but rather weapons in the battle. They were sharpened by the Church's efforts to establish Christian monogamy.

Marriage practice was the favored battleground for moral reform. Although churchmen did not speak with one voice, when a heroic champion like Columbanus strode on to the scene the tones could be strident. In her attack on Theudebert II, Brunhild had wisely chosen the ground of paternity rather than the fact that his mother was a concubine, as concubinage and the legitimacy of concubines' sons were chinks in her own armor. In about the year 600 Brunhild had been expelled from the court of her grandson Theudebert II and had taken refuge with his half brother Theuderic II in Burgundy. Theuderic never took a wife but kept concubines by whom all his sons were born. This course was allegedly followed at the instigation of his grandmother, who did not wish to see her position at court threatened by a rival queen. Brunhild was undoubtedly concerned for the future of her line, for the claims of her great-grandsons. But in late sixth-century Frankia, concubines' sons had succeeded to the throne; the risks she and Theuderic ran for his sons appeared an acceptable gamble.

She had reckoned, however, without the complicating factor of Columbanus. This Irish monk had arrived in Frankia armed with the rigors of Irish penitential discipline and the errors of Celtic Easter reckoning. He may have felt distaste at Theuderic's sexual practices for some time, but his anger overflowed at the royal court in 609 over a question which raised the specter of succession. On his arrival at court on this occasion Columbanus was met by Brunhild, bringing her great-grandsons with her. The queen asked the abbot to bless them; with that righteous rudeness which is sometimes a mark of great sanctity Columbanus refused. Theuderic should raise his children from an honorable queen, not from whores; he would not bless these children, who should "in no way receive the royal scepter, who were born of concubines." Brunhild ushered the children away, and Columbanus left the courtyard, roaring. From that day, Jonas and Fredegar agree, Brunhild plotted the saint's downfall. To her attempts to woo his retraction, Columbanus responded with threats of excommunication. Overtures of peace gave way to menace. Brunhild and Theuderic mobilized episcopal support and attacked Columbanus on the grounds of the errors of Celtic practice. From the beginning these practices were a major ingredient in the clash, though Columbanus's biographers have been eager to present it as a purely moral issue. In his wide-ranging quarrel with the Burgundian bishops and court, Columbanus had known where to strike. Brunhild's tolerance evaporated when Christian morality threatened her own security and the continuity of her progeny's claims to the throne.

She feared for the future, but also for the advantage her unfriendly grandson Theudebert might take of her discomfiture. The moral pressure of churchmen lay heaviest when there were rivals ready to use the Church's arguments as a hammer with which to beat kings. From the second half of the sixth century the Merovingians took lowborn wives. These marriages occurred at a time when Christian arguments about concubinage and legitimacy were combining with bitter struggles between uncles and nephews over the family property. They regularized existing concubinage or liaisons with the lowborn, which had long been royal practice. A king whose sons were born of these loose unions now felt obliged to marry the mother to protect his heirs. The parallel with the generation of Charlemagne's grandsons and great-grandsons in the ninth century is striking. Other sexual practices changed little. Clovis II in the early seventh century confined himself to one wife, since she bore him sons: his reputation as a libertine shows his appetites otherwise uncurbed. The need to produce heirs whose claims to legitimacy were uncontested forced kings to accommodate ecclesiastical ideas on marriage though not on pleasure. The dialogue between ecclesiastical theory and political situation gradually squeezed out the concubine in favor of the full wife. Yet although disqualified in many cases as a means of begetting sons, concubinage died hard, because it filled other needs in a king's family life.

Even when kings were careful to marry all those women by whom they hoped to raise heirs, concubines or mistresses continued to be kept. Hugh of Arles with his Roman goddesses in the tenth century, Otto the Great with his Slav captive, acted as kings were to continue to do through history. In neither case was there any question of their sons by these unions claiming the kingdom: to this extent the Church's theory had won. In Hugh's case concubines occupied his later years. Charlemagne too had taken concubines in later life, as did his grandson Lothar I. After the death of his wife Ermengard in 853, Lothar took two serving women from the royal manors as mistresses. One of them, Doda, was unfree; the document emancipating her after she bore a son still survives. The last years of Lothar's kingship were passed peacefully with his mistresses before he died as a monk in the abbey of Prum. The concubine of old age is therefore not uncommon. It is possible to label these kings, according to taste, as vigorous or lecherous old men, but not if that means leaving their preferences unexplained. The peace of the family, not to mention a tranquil old age, discouraged kings from full remarriage when they had sons sufficient in number and advanced in age. Lothar's father, Louis the Pious, remarried at forty, producing the classic stepmother and stepsons to disturb the quiet of his declining years. The family wars of Louis's reign resulted directly from his second marriage to Judith and her production of a son to rival his half brothers. Louis may have felt remarriage necessary in 818; his advisers certainly agreed with his decision. Second marriage rather than concubinage with Judith signified not so much a priestridden king, but one whose elder sons were only just of marriageable age and whose younger had barely reached twelve. Not for Louis the sons and grandsons who inspired Charlemagne's confidence in A.D. 800. Securing the future through more heirs outweighed the dangers of remarriage. But Louis miscalculated, and paid a heavy price. His eldest son, Lothar, with two adult sons if no grandchildren in 853, preferred the example of his grandfather Charlemagne.

The concubine of youth was in some dynasties more common than the mistress of old age. Since concubinage did not necessitate the provision of a household for a young prince nor yet of a kingdom, since it did not introduce friction into the royal family by bringing a rival queen into the household, many fathers encouraged their sons to take concubines until age or opportunity provided them with a kingdom. Charlemagne's Himiltrud was probably his concubine before accession in 768; his own mother Bertha long remained Pepin's concubine; Otto the Great had his captive Slavonic noblewoman until his designation as king in 929 brought marriage to Eadgyth. Alfred's eldest son, Edward the Elder, had the concubine Ecgwyna as long as his father lived; Alfred dandled her son Athelstan on his knee. Only after his father's death did Edward take a legitimate wife in Ælfflæd. Merovingian princes ordinarily had concubines until they were fifteen, after which age they were considered able to take up kingship and a wife. In some cases youthful concubinage may be a form of loose marriage, a halfway house, the *Friedelehe* beloved of German historians. Such concubines could, like Bertha, become full wives at a later stage; many Merovingian kings took their first wives in this way. Lothar II had a concubine of youth in Waldrada, and his brother Louis II took Angelberga as a concubine before his father's death. Lothar was later to claim that he had married Waldrada before his father's death, so desperate was he to be rid of his sterile wife Theutberga. Lothar was arguing a case, but his claim may indicate that these early concubines had a specially high status. The Lothar affair proved a crucible for the definition of marriage; it saw the reaffirmation of dowry as a necessary characteristic of marriage. As a result a retrospective dowry document was forged for his sister-in-law, Angelberga. This erstwhile concubine and Louis II wished to leave no doubt over the nature of their union.

Concubines could provide uncomplicated solace to the old, safe indulgence to the young. They filled needs in the family politics of the early Middle Ages and were relinquished only reluctantly, never completely. Some few kings confined themselves to concubines throughout life, preferring the total freedom of action to the relative constraints of marriage. In 746–47 the English monk Boniface and a group of fellow missionaries wrote a letter to Æthelbald, King of Mercia. It had come to their ears that Æthelbald had never taken a lawful wife in matrimony. Had this meant chaste abstinence for the sake of God they would have sung his praise; alas, this was not the case. "Governed by lust," Æthelbald had "stained the fame of his glory" with "the sin of lasciviousness and adultery." Boniface must have felt vindicated when Æthelbald came to the worst of ends, murdered by his own bodyguard at Seckington. Æthelbald left no close member of his family able to make good a claim to the throne. If his marriage practices had any clear aim it may well have been to retain total freedom of choice in the succession, to keep in his own hands the power, even the security of having no obvious heir. Legitimate sons felt assured of inheritance; illegitimate might feel more dependent on their father's wishes, remain more loyal. In theory, to take all concubines and no wives might give a king control over a loyal family. In practice most kings took wives for the political advantages they brought, to ensure the legitimate claims of heirs. No king controlled his succession, which was determined by the alignments of power at his death, and to throw open the question of legitimacy only exacerbated turmoil. Few kings followed the example of Æthelbald; most bowed to legitimate marriage where their prime objective, the peaceful succession of their own line, was involved.

Monogamy, Serial Monogamy, and Polygamy

The Church's onslaught on concubinage formed part of its major aim, the imposition of lifelong monogamy outside the prohibited degrees of kinship. This basic position remained unchanged, although reforming zeal alternated with periods of more muted comment, while some churchmen proved willing to combine theory and practical considerations. Concubinage, repudiation or divorce, finally incest, bore the brunt of attack in turn. Ambiguities and contradictions complicated the Church's stand, but the fundamental truth was always to be defended—one life, one wife. Kings approached marriage from another angle: heirs were high on their list of aims. Monogamy could and sometimes did produce sufficient sons; more often kings were driven to serial monogamy—a succession of wives—or even to polygamy.

Polygamy is uncommon in Eurasian society in spite of its many advantages. Many wives bear more children, are a visible sign (in his ability to keep them) of their husband's wealth and status, and may even contribute to the household economy. Polygamy may appear ideally suited to a society like that of the early Middle Ages to which household and family are central. But a multitude of wives and heirs has its disadvantages in societies where wives and heirs must be endowed with adequate means to maintain their status. Where sources of wealth are finite, polygamy would combine with such endowments to seriously drain family resources. Yet when wealth was plentiful and ideas of joint family property still strong, approximations to polygamy could exist. In Merovingian Frankia the riches provided for the ruling dynasty by booty, and the vestiges of Rome may have fostered polygamous practices.

There are few certain examples of polygamy. Cnut, the early eleventh-century Danish conqueror of England, must qualify. He had two simultaneous wives, Ælfgifu of Northampton and Emma. Neither seems to have been dismissed, though he did allocate them separate spheres of influence: Ælfgifu became regent in Norway for her son Swegn, Emma stayed in England. Emma claimed precedence, no great problem since in polygamy all wives are not necessarily equal. When Emma attacked Ælfgifu's son Harold Harefoot she did not claim that Ælfgifu was not married to Cnut; rather that Cnut was not his father. Many writers noted a tendency to polygamy, or at least to loose marriage, among the Vikings both in England and in Normandy. The comments are late and certainly no foundation for an assumption of large-scale polygamy in these Viking areas. Contemporary Europe could rival them. If Robert the Pious was not a polygamist he must count as a near miss. He repudiated his second wife Bertha around 1005 to marry Constance of Anjou. But Bertha remained at court. In 1008 Robert, who had secured the necessary son from Constance, was considering returning to her, causing Constance to fear Bertha's presence close to the king. Bertha was soon dismissed, for Robert's polygamy remained half-hearted, a broad interpretation of serial monogamy. The clearest example comes from the fringes of Christian Europe, from the pages of Fredegar, who tells of the Frankish merchant Samo. The help Samo gave to the Wends against the Huns led them to make him king. He had twelve Wendish wives, twenty sons, and fifteen daughters, although the tale and the tally may have grown en route to Fredegar's ears.

The Merovingian dynasty remains the most significant and debatable example of royal polygamy. Merovingian kings undoubtedly had a multitude of wives, but it is less certain whether these wives were simultaneous or taken in succession. Merovingian writers distinguish concubines and full wives. Yet since polygamy recognizes differences in the status of various wives, if a king has a wife and a concubine at the same time the arrangement should probably be called polygamy. According to Fredegar, Dagobert I took first a wife named Gomatrud, then repudiated her for Nantechild; after his marriage to Nantechild he took another woman, Ragnetrud, who bore him a son. Yet Nantechild had not been dismissed, since soon after this she herself produced a child, the infant Clovis II. Fredegar was later to remark that Dagobert gave himself up to a life of wantonness, having three queens and a troop of concubines too large to enumerate. Fredegar's moral outrage is leveled at Dagobert because the king had begun to attack the Church and while his abuse implies that Dagobert favored these women simultaneously, i.e., that he was polygamous, he is not being precise.

In the sixth century Charibert I had married Ingoberga before taking her servant Merofled to his bed. Again, Ingoberga seems to have remained at court, for Gregory relates how she tried to poison Charibert's mind against Merofled. Charibert next turned to Theudechild, daughter of a shepherd who tended the royal flocks, and married her. Finally he became enamored of Marcoveifa, Merofled's sister, marrying her even though she was a nun. At this point, Saint Germanus excommunicated king and wife. Plurality of wives might be tolerable; marriage to a nun was not.

Did Charibert's affairs succeed each other, or run concurrently? Only in the case of Ingoberga and Merofled is the evidence for polygamy strong. Charibert's half brother Chilperic repudiated his first wife, Audovera, before marriage to Galswinth. But he had certainly not entirely dismissed Fredegund, who was accused of stirring Chilperic to murder Galswinth. Audovera was a full wife, Fredegund perhaps still a concubine. Gregory of Tours remarked that Chilperic had many wives when he took Galswinth, but again, generalized slander against Gregory's favorite villain is unreliable evidence.

Clothar I presents similar ambiguities. His early marriage to Ingund was ended temporarily when he married his brother's widow

Guntheuca. Ingund returned to his bed in the 530s only to be displaced by her own sister Arnegund. Arnegund in turn was probably dismissed in favor of Radegund; at some stage a concubine, Chunsina, is to be accounted for. Clothar and Dagobert make it clear that supplanted or repudiated wives need not disappear permanently from the royal bed. The exile of a wife who later returns is not quite the same as polygamy, while it is clear that these kings felt it necessary to repudiate and send away full wives. The joint tenures for which there is the most evidence—Ingoberga and Merofled with Charibert I, Nantechild and Ragnetrud with Dagobert—involved a wife and a concubine. Polygamy may mean a man's keeping several wives, only one of whom he favors at any given time; it often involves wives of differing status. Kings like Clothar, Chilperic, Dagobert, and Charibert, who moved backward and forward between their wives, who combined wives and concubines, should count as polygamous. The general obscurity of the period may hide other cases from view.

If doubt must hang over polygamy, serial monogamy is crystal clear. Most kings had several wives. Sometimes they waited decently for the death of one before taking another: Charlemagne remarried after the death of Hildegard, Louis the Pious after Ermengard's, Charles the Simple when he lost Frederun, Otto I after the death of Eadgyth, Henry I of France after Mathilda's. These decencies were not always observed, and many kings repudiated one wife to marry the next. Merovingian Frankia and seventh-century England provide many examples. Ecgfryth, King of Northumbria, separated from Æthelthryth to marry Iurminburg. The excuse was Æthelthryth's vocation to religion and her chastity—she is alleged to have survived two marriages as a virgin. The divorce was required by her sterility.

Repudiation and remarriage were far from barbaric customs confined to the emerging kingdoms of the sixth and seventh centuries. They flourished in all dynasties and kingdoms, green and vigorous as late as the eleventh century. Charlemagne repudiated the daughter of Desiderius to marry Hildegard; Edward the Elder probably dismissed Ælfflæd to marry Eadgifu; Henry the Fowler rid himself of Hatheburg to take Mathilda; Edgar disposed of Wulfthryth to marry Ælfthryth, if not of Æthelflæd to marry Wulfthryth; and Robert the Pious summarily dismissed both Rozala and Bertha. Hugh of Arles,

when he fled from Marozia in Rome, scarcely went through the for-
malities. A tiny minority like Chilperic I and Berengar I made a
thorough job of it by murdering their wives. The majority found legitimate excuses for disposing of unwanted women.

Some kings did not aspire to repudiation, but had it thrust upon
them. Charles the Bald forcibly separated his son Louis the Stammerer from his wife in 875 and chose a second wife, Adelaide, a
woman with suitable connections. Here repudiation ended a son's
rebellion, which marriage had begun. Only three years earlier in
872 Louis II was apparently pressured to repudiate Angelberga and
marry a noblewoman from central Italy. Noble pressure is alleged
in this case, though Louis might have been pleased to exchange a
wife who had borne him no sons. In 958 Archbishop Oda separated
the English king Eadwig from his wife Ælfgifu on grounds of consanguinity: they shared the same great-great-grandfather in King
Æthelwulf. The grounds were technically correct, but many tenth-
century marriages happily survived such degrees of kinship. Divorce
was forced upon Eadwig by the supporters of his brother Edgar.

Divorce was no less political than marriage. While some kings
were forced to dispose of their wives, others were prevented from
doing so. Lothar II was the second son of the emperor Lothar I, becoming king of Lotharingia, the northern portion of the Carolingian
Middle Kingdom. Before the death of his father in 855, Lothar had
had a concubine, the noblewoman Waldrada. Soon after his accession in that year he took a full wife, Theutberga. The marriage was
one of undoubted political convenience, probably undertaken at the
prompting of sections of the Lotharingian nobility. Theutberga was
of the Bosonide clan, sister of Hubert, the head of a family that controlled lands, abbeys, and counties in southern Lotharingia and the
passes into modern Switzerland. The marriage failed to bring the
backing of the powerful Hubert, who even acted against Lothar. By
858 Lothar had begun a process of repudiation, to end a marriage
which had failed in its objective and to defame and attack Hubert.
The grounds of divorce were the alleged incest of Theutberga and
her brother before her marriage, rendering her unfit for the royal
bed. Hubert's known character might almost support such wild al-
legations. Although he was abbot of many monasteries, Pope Benedict III upbraided him, not with his wife and children—many
respectable ninth-century ecclesiastics were married—but with

keeping concubines, installing them in his abbeys, and generally dissipating his ecclesiastical revenues on dogs, falcons, and loose women. The truth of Theutberga and Hubert soon ceased to matter. The brother and sister fled to Lothar's uncle, Charles the Bald. Charles welcomed with open arms these God-given excuses to meddle in his nephew's affairs; he sheltered them both and gave Theutberga a nunnery. Lothar II's divorce was no longer his own private matter. It dragged on from 860 until his death in 869, stirred and fanned by his uncles Charles and Louis the German, often abetted by his brother Louis II of Italy. The rivalries of the Carolingian family focused on it. Territorial concessions and threats of war marked its stages as Lothar moved from defiant remarriage to Waldrada to reconciliation with Theutberga and back again. By 864 the deadly question of inheritance to the Lotharingian kingdom was involved. Whether or not she had ever been incestuous, Theutberga by now appeared definitely sterile, while Waldrada had borne a son, Hugh, who must be legitimized. Repudiation of Theutberga and full marriage with Waldrada had become imperative for Lothar. Prowling relatives began to see an heirless kingdom possibly falling into their hands. The divorce now engrossed Lothar's politics. It was still unresolved when he died in 869, on his way home from the papal court after a final desperate appeal for the end of his marriage.

Christian theory and political reality combined in a trap that caught Lothar and Eadwig, forcing a wife on one, taking her from the other. The trap captured many kings. Henry II was prevented from repudiating the sterile Cunigund in the early eleventh century more by the power of her brothers than by the strength of argument; Edward the Confessor faced the same problem in 1051. Edward had tried to be rid of the family of Godwin and of their daughter, his wife Queen Edith. The king had ecclesiastical backing in the shape of Robert of Jumièges, Archbishop of Canterbury, whose deep enmity with Godwin found him able to urge divorce. Godwin was exiled and Edith sent off to the nunnery at Wherwell, but Edward's triumph was short-lived. The strength that swept Godwin and his sons back to England carried Edith firmly back into the king's bed. Edward had wanted to rid himself of his wife as an adjunct to his attack on her family; furthermore, she had failed to provide sons. Like Lothar II, he found himself with a sterile wife in a situation that precluded her dismissal; Lothar's cousin, Charles the Fat, also failed to repudiate the barren Richardis. The enforced monogamy of these sterile unions proved disastrous for the dynasties involved. It was a major cause of the rapid demise of the Carolingian dynasty in the ninth century, it saw the end of the Saxon line in Henry II, and it finished the Anglo-Saxon monarchy itself when Edward the Confessor died childless. All the marriage practices of kings were designed to avoid this, the worst of all possible fates.

While monogamy was forced on some kings, others apparently embraced it freely: Alfred, Otto II, Guy of Spoleto, Louis d'Outremer and his son Lothar, Louis the German, Ralph of Burgundy, and Hugh Capet were all apparently monogamous. All were survived by their wives, or like Louis the German and Ralph outlived their queens only briefly: none of them thus remarried as widowers. Yet neither did they follow the path of repudiation and remarriage chosen by many kings. Did ecclesiastical pressure have more weight for Alfred than it did for Charlemagne? Or is it rather that these kings embraced the Church's marriage laws because they coincided with self-interest? Where changing alliance or barren unions led other kings to divorce and remarriage, such factors were absent for these kings. In most cases the wife proved fertile and the political value of the marriage remained strong. Tenth-century France saw an unusual series of monogamous kings in Ralph of Burgundy, Louis d'Outremer, Lothar, and Hugh Capet. It was a time of struggle over the kingship itself. Gerberga, wife of Louis; Emma, wife of Ralph; Emma, wife of Lothar; and Adelaide, Hugh Capet's queen, all played a central part during their husband's reigns. Their families proved necessary allies: Gerberga was the daughter of Henry the Fowler, sister of Otto the Great and Bruno; Ralph's Emma was a Capetian, Lothar's Emma the daughter of the empress Adelaide, the virtual mother of Europe. These beleaguered husbands never ceased to value their wives' connections. Gerberga salvaged both husband and son with her brothers' help. All but Emma wife of Ralph bore sons. The chief reasons for repudiation were absent, so these kings could please themselves and the Church with their dutiful monogamy. To discount affection as a ground for successful marriage may appear cynical, and indeed it probably played a part. But given the aims of royal marriage, personal preference counted for little. As far as it is possible to ascertain such facts for the eleventh century, Robert the Pious seems to have preferred Bertha to Constance. But

Bertha had given him no sons; Constance cemented alliance with Anjou. Bertha was repudiated; Constance married. Affection was an irrelevance.

Even in the sixth, seventh, and eighth centuries, when repudiation was easy and often undertaken for political reasons, the need for heirs was an important motive in divorce; later it was to become the overriding reason. Clothar I and Chilperic married and discarded wives with a cynical view to advantage, looking to a widow's claims, a woman's treasure, and her allies. Yet Clothar I returned to the fertile Ingund, discarded the barren Radegund. A century later fecundity was a major criterion to govern the choice of Dagobert. In the early tenth century Henry the Fowler repudiated Hatheburg, who had given him a son; his marriage to the well-connected and fertile Mathilda lasted till death. High levels of infant mortality made a brace of sons essential. Charlemagne and Louis the Pious continued to remarry until a sufficiency of heirs gave them security. Charles the Simple remarried after the death of Frederun, since she had produced four daughters. When a king found his progeny deficient in sex, size, or quality, he took another wife to gain more. Three days after receiving news of the death of his first wife, Charles the Bald took Richildis as his concubine and married her soon after. Haste was essential since the sons of his first marriage were rebellious or dead.

Only a small minority of kings took another wife when their sons were plentiful. Edward the Elder married Eadgifu although he had at least three heirs; he may have preferred the advantage of dynastic security and political advantage to the disadvantages of a second wife. His great-grandson Æthelred II, however, was to taste those disadvantages. Like Louis the Pious he found his later years complicated by the tensions between the sons of his first marriage and his second wife. Emma and her efforts on behalf of her son Edward threatened her stepsons. One of them, Edmund Ironside, rose in rebellion in 1015, dividing English efforts against Viking invasion in defense of his own claims to the throne. Otto the Great showed a wary approach. He remained a widower for six years after the death of his first wife, Eadgyth, in 946. He had a single son, Liudolf, but he was adult, married, and designated heir to the kingdom. Only Adelaide, a widow useful to any pretender to the Italian throne, tempted him into remarriage in 952. His former reluctance had been justi-

fied: Liudolf's rebellions in the 950s were part of a new family align-
ment which ranged his stepmother with his old rival, his uncle
Henry, against him.

Stepmothers were not lightly introduced into the cozy royal
hearth. "To murder your stepson is an old-established tradition,
perfectly right and proper. . . . Wards with rich portions should
have a well-developed sense of self-preservation. Trust none of the
dishes at dinner. Those pies are steaming black with the poison
Mummy put there. Whatever she offers you, make sure another tries
it first."

Juvenal's late Roman *Satire* shows the perennial antagonism of
steprelations. When Gregory of Tours told how the second wife of
King Sigismund of Burgundy instigated the murder of her stepson
Sigeric, he remarked that she acted "in the way stepmothers do."
The widely held sentiment made it natural to impute to Fredegund a
role in the deaths of her stepsons Merovech, Clovis, and Theudebert,
though the claim that she sent Clovis to Berny in the hopes that he
would catch the plague raging there smacks of Machiavelli. As late
as 979 Ælfthryth was conniving at the murder of her stepson Edward to secure the accession of her own son; some sources openly
accused her of the murder and of beating her son Æthelred with a
candlestick for failing to show due appreciation of her actions on his
behalf. It is scarcely surprising if relations with stepmothers were
never easy. Even without sons of their own, their presence held the
threat of half brothers and struck a note of discord. Second marriages were not lightly undertaken; concubines could satisfy lust.
Even in the Merovingian period the family's needs for sons, for security, and for increased inheritance were the major stimuli to take
first or second wives.

Divorce

In the sixth and seventh centuries divorce and remarriage seems to
have been relatively easy. Ecclesiastical opposition existed—Saint
Medard opposed Clothar I's divorce from Radegund—but other
abuses engrossed the Church reformer's attention. Concubinage
may have seemed an easier, more vulnerable target. As in the later

days of the Roman Empire, divorce was common, obtainable on relatively trivial grounds. Merovingian legal formulae in the *Angers Formulary* of 595–96 or Marculf's in the mid-seventh century show divorce by mutual consent because the husband "instead of being affectionate is insupportably arrogant," because "discord reigns between us and communal life has become impossible." The Church's theory was less tolerant, but also less certain, divided over whether repudiation was forbidden in all circumstances or permissible in some. The earliest Anglo-Saxon and Celtic penitentials (books of guidance for priests on sin and penance) were strict, forbidding divorce and remarriage totally, allowing separation, but only where both parties wished to enter the celibate life of religion. Yet in the seventh century Theodore of Tarsus, Archbishop of Canterbury, allowed divorce on grounds of adultery, desire to enter religion, desertion for five years, the reduction of either partner to slavery, or the wife's abduction into captivity. The mid-eighth-century Frankish councils of Verberie and Compiègne spoke with equally divided voices. Verberie allowed divorce only for incest, for the wife's conspiracy against her husband, or if the husband left the country. Remarriage was not permitted. Compiègne allowed all the old arguments of adultery, desertion, impotence, and sterility, and condoned remarriage after repudiation. Strong attempts to enforce indissoluble marriage were made in ninth-century Frankia: at the council of Paris in 829, in the theoretical works of Smaragdus, Jonas of Orleans, Hincmar, and others. Divorce was forbidden, monogamy praised. Even as a remedy for impotence, Hincmar preached exorcism, not divorce. But the councils of the late ninth century saw the battle still fought. The attack continued through the tenth and eleventh centuries, though by now the Church was also showing a renewed interest in incest and its dangers.

The moral campaign mobilized arguments designed to exploit the taboos of sexuality and aimed at the sensitive spots in a warrior society. Its virulence is eloquent testimony to the difficulties of enforcement. Hincmar warned that sexual excess enervated, softened, took away health and sanity, produced physical disability and monstrous births. The moderation of marriage was a source of strength. Boniface, writing to King Æthelbald in the eighth century, warned of the consequences to the English of the foul life of adultery in which they indulged after the pattern of Sodom: from the intercourse with harlots would spring "a degenerate people, ignoble, raging with lust," who would in the end be neither "strong in secular warfare nor stable in faith." Ninth-century reformers abounded with stories of wives forced to connive at their own concubinage; of husbands falsely accusing wives of adultery before murdering them, even taking them to abattoirs to be killed, all to gain freedom for remarriage; of gangs of abductors roaming the country forcing marriage on widows and nuns. The strengthening current of reform in the eleventh century expressed itself in Peter Damian's retrospective ruminations on the incest of Robert the Pious and Bertha: the union had produced a monstrous child with the neck and head of a goose; the king had been considered so tainted that he was shunned by all; only two servants remained with him and they threw on the fire the plates from which he had eaten and the vessels from which he had drunk. By this date divorce and remarriage were widely condemned, yet the abhorrence of incest provided a gap in the laws of monogamy through which a king like Robert the Pious could drive a coach and horses. As long as kings felt the need for repudiation and remarriage, the uncertainties and contradictions in the Church's ideas provided loopholes for exploitation. Attempts at reform provided obstacles, but rarely insurmountable ones. Kings, like others, merely changed the excuses they used.

By the seventh century excuses for divorce were customary, as the Church's preaching was taking effect. Ecgfryth of Northumbria divorced Æthelthryth because she was sterile, his pretexts being her failure to consummate their marriage and her religious vocation. She was repudiated and sent to a family nunnery. The spectacular growth of female monasticism in the seventh century had produced a double benefit. Nunneries were suitable refuges for repudiated wives, and desire to enter them was an acceptable excuse for divorce. Clothar I had placed Radegund in a nunnery in the mid-sixth century, an unusually early example. Even the penitentials allowed divorce in order to take the veil, though they insisted that both partners follow this path. A related excuse was later used to cover the actions of Henry the Fowler in repudiating Hatheburg: she had supposedly taken religious vows prior to marriage. Ecgfryth's arguments included the claim of nonconsummation. Bishop Wilfrid reported that Æthelthryth remained a virgin, but his knowledge is not independent corroboration. He had heard Ecgfryth's own protests that the queen had pestered to be allowed entry to a nunnery, his loud promises to give lands and money to anyone who could persuade her to sleep with him. Wilfrid approved of Æthelthryth, disliked her supplanter, Queen Iurminburg. His praises of Æthelthryth's virginity flow from that general approval of female celibacy that formed part of Christian thought. Ecgfryth's protests echo Clothar's claim that Radegund deserted his bed for the chapel, that his wife might just as well be a nun. The ground was well chosen. Nonconsummation long remained the strongest argument for divorce, accepted by many churchmen. In the twelfth century, stories of Edward the Confessor's chastity were current. By then they were used to back the process for his canonization. Do they perhaps garble an argument used in 1051 against Edith, repudiation for failure to consummate? In the late ninth century Charles the Fat loudly proclaimed that he had never physically known Richardis. His queen was sterile and he long sought to divorce her in order to legitimize his bastard. The allegation could be leveled against any barren wife. Its technical truth can no longer be investigated, but its utility to a king seeking remarriage is undeniable.

Charles the Fat added the accusation of adultery to strengthen his hand. Richardis had indulged in a liaison with Bishop Liutward of Vercelli, Charles's chancellor. Adultery, usually committed with officials of the royal household, was the most common charge leveled against queens. Richardis, Uota wife of Arnulf, Emma wife of Lothar, Judith wife of Louis the Pious, and Angelberga all stood accused. So too did Edward the Confessor's Edith. A late story tells of the adultery of a queen, variously garbled as Edith or Emma, with the bishop of Winchester. The queen cleared herself by walking unharmed over burning plowshares; the king was suitably repentant. The story must apply to Edith and to 1051. William of Malmesbury alleges that the accusation still troubled Edith on her deathbed, where she took an oath as a final proof of chastity. Accusations of adultery were not always part of divorce proceedings. They were leveled against queens by their enemies; even when they occur in process of repudiation they may have special significance. Adultery throws doubt on paternity, it is a weapon of rival claimants to the throne. Such was certainly its use against Emma, Lothar's wife, by her brother-in-law Charles of Lorraine. These accusations form part of the politics of succession and as such will be treated more fully in their place.

The sons of Louis the Pious, when attempting to justify their separation of Judith and Louis, accused the queen of adultery with Bernard. They added a charge of incest, for Louis was Bernard's godfather and relationships created at the baptismal font counted equally with those of blood. Bernard, in effect, had committed adultery with his own mother, or at least his father's wife. When Lothar II was divorcing Theutberga, he too alleged incest. Like nonconsummation, incest had the advantage of prohibition by ecclesiastical law. In these ninth-century cases it is a smear, a slur on the fitness of a woman to be queen. By the tenth century, however, it was a technical loophole in Church law. If a marriage was incestuous it was not valid: partners whom God had never joined together could readily be put asunder. An archbishop of Canterbury could separate Eadwig and Ælfgifu in 958 without qualm. The endless intermarriages of the tenth century produced a rash of technically incestuous unions.

The Church's weapon could be turned against it to a king's own ends. The life and loves of Robert the Pious began with a brief sally into matrimony in 988. At his father's instigation Robert married Suzanne/Rozala, widow of the count of Flanders. The marriage had ended by 989, perhaps even without consummation—Robert refused to hand over her dowry. In late 996 Robert was married for the second time to Bertha, widow of Eudes of Blois, the erstwhile implacable enemy of the Capetians. Robert was merely legitimizing an affair that had begun early in 996 against his father's wishes. Bertha had two underage sons, and Robert hoped for their wardship. Unfortunately Robert had stood godfather to one of these sons. Bertha was already a cousin by blood: their respective grandmothers Gerberga and Hathui were sisters. As the baptismal font added a further relationship, the incestuous nature of their marriage was beyond doubt. In 996 the union caused scarcely a ripple in Capetian France, but provoked a storm of indignation from Pope Gregory V. Gregory called Robert and his compliant bishops to Rome to account for their actions. He anathematized them in 998, and continued with fulminations and excommunications. A decade of such treatment left Robert unmoved, but matters closer to his heart brought belated repentance. By the early 1000s it was becoming clear that Bertha would bear him no son. In the manner of King David before him Robert saw the light, acknowledged his sin, and repudiated Bertha on the grounds of incest. It was a precarious repentance. Once Constance, his new wife, had produced a son he showed signs of relapsing: in 1008 he set out for Rome, with Bertha hastening in his wake, to petition for divorce from Constance and thus remarriage to Bertha. He never made his request, so the papal reaction remains unknown. Constance had been left at Theil near Sens, where, in fear of imminent dismissal, she prayed to Saint Savinien, the first bishop of Sens, who appeared to her in a vision. Robert was duly deflected from his purpose, and the king's love was restored to her.

Robert achieved his own ends in his own time with his adversary's weapon. Contemporary churchmen struck rival postures that served both to help and hinder the king. The pope was his implacable opponent, a standard-bearer of moral reform. Gregory's stand squared nicely with papal politics. The popes were already at odds with the Capetians over the powers, jurisdiction, and appointment of French bishops. Moreover Gregory V was cousin to Otto III, and the Ottonians were in conflict with the Capetians in the Rhineland. By marrying Bertha, daughter of the king of Burgundy, Robert stood to gain advantage here. When Gregory was expelled from the Holy City by the Romans in 997, he prevaricated with Robert; restored to power in the same year, his condemnations rang out once more. Papal politics affected royal marriage now as they did in the later days of Henry VIII. In the ninth century popes Leo IV and Nicholas I had found themselves in conflict with the Carolingians Lothar I and Charles the Bald. Leo and Lothar could not achieve an acceptable demarcation of their respective claims in Italy: Charles and his bishops found Nicholas's pretensions inconvenient. Both popes supported, even harbored, the abductors of daughters of these kings. Judith, daughter of Charles the Bald, fled to Nicholas with her lover, Baldwin of Flanders. She was contracting a third marriage in the face of paternal opposition. The Church did not demand parental consent, though it frowned on its absence, but it did urge chastity on widows and forbade constant remarriage. Nicholas was unabashed. He embraced the couple and their cause, leaving Charles to impotent protest. At other times the interests of the Holy See contrived a wondrous convergence with those of reform. Henry I, the son of Robert the Pious, took great care to keep his marital conduct above reproach. His adversary Pope Leo IX was a reformer, a pope, and a German.

Like Lothar II before him, Robert found the pope in opposition but his own bishops in support. The interests of popes and bishops frequently failed to coincide and most bishops preferred their king and lord to a remote papacy whose ambitions were often a threat. Few marital situations were so clear cut that contradictory positions could not be defended. A handful of ecclesiastical reformers made genuine attempts to find a firm path through the quagmire of marriage law and practice, although few of their efforts remained entirely independent of politics. Hincmar, Archbishop of Rheims, was one such reformer. His position on indissolubility of marriage was as clear as he could make it. He opposed divorce with a reasoning set out in his monumental treatise on the case of Lothar II. This work was not simply a tool forged for Hincmar's master Charles the Bald, who had his own reasons to oppose Lothar's divorce; the archbishop's complex treatise is not the stuff of simple propaganda. But while Hincmar's position may have been taken up innocent of base motivation, the views of this eminent theologian were seized upon by Charles, who gave them currency and prominence in his own campaign against his nephew.

To sort out genuine reform from politically motivated argument is a difficult, perhaps a fruitless task. Archbishop Dunstan spoke the language of reform in tenth-century England, directing it at Eadwig and later at Edgar's third wife, Ælfthryth. His moral arguments were useful to Eadwig's enemies, with whom Dunstan was numbered, and to the opponents of Ælfthryth's son Æthelred, among whom the archbishop stood. The bite of a Hincmar or a Dunstan was rarely turned on their own party. Hincmar was silent when Judith, daughter of Charles the Bald, married her own stepson; his tones were muted when Charles forcibly ended the legal marriage of his son Louis and joined him to a new wife. Reforming churchmen were interested in the marriage affairs of kings for good reason. As Boniface reminded Æthelbald of Mercia, kings were the example their people followed: they should be wary not to lead them into the pit of death.

In 797 the English cleric Alcuin wrote from the court of Charle-

magne to Ealdorman Osbert of Northumbria. He urged the ealdorman to admonish kings Cenwulf and Eardwulf against adultery,
against repudiating wives to take noble concubines. Yet Alcuin lived
at the court of a king who repudiated one wife and kept six concubines. In his voluminous correspondence there is no hint of Alcuin's moral criticism of Charlemagne. Kings who were generous to
churchmen could hope for support and a good press. Only when he
records Dagobert's attacks on the Church does Fredegar drag in the
king's lusts and adultery. Helgaud, a monk in Robert's favored abbey of Fleury, was only momentarily embarrassed by the king's affairs, even turned them to advantage. Critics of Helgaud's *Life* had
drawn attention to his omission of Robert's incest and divorce. Filling the lacuna in his second version, Helgaud likened Robert to King
David, pointing out that sin is human and repentance, however belated, a more than royal virtue. The acceptance of Christianity may
have made divorce more difficult; the lengthy war of attrition took its
toll. But the strength of a king's enemies determined his marital
practice as much as moral dogma. If kings became warier of divorce
it was not simply because the Church's weapons were sharper, but
because they were wielded by more hostile hands.

Infertility and Childbirth

Infertility remained the strongest reason, as opposed to pretext, for
divorce. Failure of heirs was intolerable. But especially by the tenth
century, divorce and remarriage was not always the first resort. In
the sixth and seventh centuries barrenness worried kings, but ter-
rified their queens and wives. With divorce so easy, a wife's very survival depended on the production of sons. Fredegund, Chilperic's
wife, lost three sons in infancy. In her distraction she threw her tax-
lists in the fire, fearing that her oppressions had brought this judgment on her. She accused her stepson Clovis of using magic to secure
the death of her children. When her fourth son Theuderic was born
in 582, Chilperic was so delighted that he opened the prisons and
canceled fines to the treasury. Alas, the child was dead of dysentery
before the age of two, and Fredegund was again certain that her en-

emies were practicing magic arts against her. She superstitiously burnt all her dead child's belongings.

A wife whose sons died feared for her own security; even more so did the barren woman who failed to conceive. She might be repudiated, even murdered. Bilichild, wife of Theudebert II, was exposed to this fate through her sterility. After divorce from Æthelthryth, Ecgfryth took Iurminburg to wife. The queen showed an understandable anxiety about conception. She confiscated Bishop Wilfrid's reliquary, perhaps to act as a fertility charm, and wore it in bed. But the magic turned against the thief: Iurminburg was racked with pain, but no children were born.

The barren wife feared summary dismissal, the woman without sons divorce or an insecure fate. When Balthild was pregnant in 649 she confided to Bishop Eligius that she feared to be carrying a girl. Eligius made her a prophetic gift, a toy suitable for a boy, and Balthild went on to bear a son. The Church was increasingly called in to work the fertility magic sought by Iurminburg. Charles the Bald had a lively appreciation of the practical value of religious intercession and consecration with holy oil. When his young daughter Judith married the elderly Anglo-Saxon king Æthelwulf in 856 and Charles had her consecrated, the accompanying prayers referred to the fruitful earth and requested fertility. Charles's dissatisfaction with the sons of his own marriage to Ermentrud saw him call in the Church's aid on his own account. In 862 he took an unprecedented step, requesting annual prayers and feasting to celebrate his wedding anniversary. This was no modern nostalgia, but a call to God that the aims of that wedding be fulfilled, that more sons be produced. By 866 three infant sons had been lost and a fourth was on the point of death. Charles now had Ermentrud, a woman at least thirty-six years old, consecrated as queen. The step is again novel, undertaken more than twenty years after the wedding. The consecration prayers evoke those great Old Testament figures Abraham, who begot a son at the age of one hundred of his ninety-year-old wife, Sarah, and Isaac, whose prayers to the Lord caused his barren wife to conceive. After his second marriage to Richildis, Charles continued to invoke supernatural aid. Again annual prayers were ordered to commemorate the marriage, and the "fecund virgin" of Notre Dame was called on to provide more sons.

Kings might repudiate their wives, but they could not ignore the problems divorce could entail. By the tenth century royal couples increasingly prayed and persevered. When his wife Theophanu was pregnant with her first child in 975, Otto II made two grants to the abbey of Fulda, for the health of his dear wife and the stability of his kingdom and empire. That stability depended to a large extent on her safe delivery, preferably of a boy. Theophanu produced a girl, and went on to have three more. The mounting anxiety of the royal couple can be sensed as Adelaide followed Sophie, only to be succeeded by Mathilda and yet another girl—four daughters in the four years between 975 and 979, until in 980 the long-awaited son Otto III was born. Between 1045 and 1048 the emperor Henry III and Agnes produced three daughters before the necessary son appeared in 1050.

Fertility shrines profited from this deep anxiety. The cult of Saint Verena at Zurzach was largely a tenth-century phenomenon. Verena was the fertility saint of the Burgundian royal family and the Alemannian dukes; she specialized in the provision of sons. When she chose girls, foresight, not error, guided her hand. Duke Hermann of Alemannia received a daughter Ida in answer to his heartfelt prayers, but she grew up to marry Liudolf, son and heir of Otto the Great. It was to Saint Verena that Conrad of Burgundy and his wife Mathilda came in their distress. Conrad had no children by his legitimate wife, no heir to his kingdom. He suggested to Mathilda that they travel to Zurzach and beg the mercy of the virgin Verena, "that we may have sons." They went, they prayed, they vowed great vows and made great gifts, and then returned home. "On that self-same night the queen went in to the king, conceived and bore a son." Virgin though she was, Saint Verena delivered prompt answers to requests, to the delight of her devotees.

The rates of infant mortality remained so high that the birth of a son offered only temporary security. Fredegund lost four sons in infancy. From all his marriages Hugh of Arles had only one legitimate son. The baby Lothar fell ill, and his parents carried him into the church, where he was given a drink from the cup of Saint Columbanus to cure him. When the infant Robert the Pious, only son of Hugh Capet and Adelaide, sickened, his distraught parents prayed and made a gift of a golden crucifix to Sainte Croix at Orleans for his recovery. Fears of mortality, coupled with the desire for sons, made the lives of many fertile queens one long childbearing. Theophanu produced five children in as many years; Æthelred II's first wife produced ten children between 985 and 1002; Hildegard produced nine children in twelve years; Ermentrud's eleven children make Charles's prayers for fertility an impertinence. Many queens must have died, like Hildegard at twenty-five, exhausted by the dangers of constant childbearing in circumstances often less than ideal. Childbirth was an ordeal. The daughter of the Lombard King Agilulf died in childbirth and she cannot have been alone. The missionary Paulinus claimed that his prayers had secured the safe and relatively painless delivery of Eanfled, the daughter of King Edwin of Northumbria, a fact that prompted the grateful father to have her baptized. Henry the Fowler's wife, Mathilda, built and embellished a nunnery at Nordhausen in thanksgiving for the safe delivery there of Henry and Gerberga: there, with the help of the Virgin Mary, she had twice navigated the perils of childbirth. The author of the *Life of Edward the Confessor* provides a clue to the hazards of birth when extolling the Church as a spiritual mother blessed with numerous progeny, but a mother who did not endure the anguish of a stillborn child, did not bring forth with the pangs of birth after a tedious pregnancy.

Carrying and bearing children required some attention to health and circumstance. Some queens proved cautious where the birth of a royal heir was concerned. Theudelinda gave birth to Adaloald in the palace of Monza. The place was specially chosen, being a site above the plain of Lombardy, a refuge from the intemperate climate of Italy known to Theoderic the Ostrogoth. Gerberga was confined with three of her children by Louis d'Outremer in the safety of Laon's fortifications, while Louis was off on campaign, just as in 778 Charlemagne left the pregnant Hildegard in the royal palace of Chasseneuil in Poitou while he marched toward Spain, so that Louis the Pious and his twin brother were born during their father's absence. Royal manors were favored as safe places of confinement. King Alfred was born at the royal vill at Wantage, Edward the Confessor at Islip in Oxfordshire. But circumstances and especially the life of constant travel which queens shared with their husbands could produce complications. Hildegard produced her second child, a daughter named Adelheid, in a military camp outside the walls of Pavia in 774. The infant was separated from her mother and sent back to Frankia, but died en route through the Rhone valley. The Ottonian Mathilda bore at least two children in the security of Nordhausen, while her granddaughter-in-law Theophanu regularly used nunneries as places of confinement. Yet when Lothar of France led a surprise attack on Otto II at Aix-la-Chapelle, Theophanu and her husband had to flee even though the queen was pregnant, while only a few months after the birth of the much-desired Otto III she and the baby were following Otto II into Italy, making the difficult journey across the Alps. The nunneries where Theophanu bore her children in safety and comfort were located as close as possible to the royal itinerary, from which she was absent for only the briefest period.

Central as they were, pregnancy and childbirth were not allowed to interfere too greatly with the life of a queen. Gerberga, wife of Louis d'Outremer, gave birth twice in 948, but in April 949 she was hastening to Aix on her husband's behalf to make an alliance with her brother. She had twins in 953, but had negotiated with Hugh Capet, her husband's enemy, during the pregnancy. The extent to which constant childbearing reduced the political involvement of queens should not be exaggerated. It is true that we hear little of the political activities of Æthelred the Unready's first and fertile wife, nor of Edward the Elder's Ælfflæd, who bore most of his children. And it is a fact that Paul the Deacon in his epitaph for the fecund Hildegard could say no more than that she was the mother of kings and had pleased Charlemagne. It may be argued that Judith, with only two children, had time on her hands to stir up trouble for the elderly Louis, that Fastrada, with her two daughters, had energy and leisure for scheming. Certainly where constant childbirth may have produced weakness or illness, a wife's political role may have been restricted. But Gerberga and Theophanu combined fertility and activity, while Judith and Fastrada would have caused even more trouble with more children to fight for. Childbirth is a poor answer to the question why some queens are more powerful than others: the reasons lie elsewhere.

Childbearing after the age of about thirty was in any case comparatively rare. Hildegard, we remember, died at twenty-five; the Ottonian queens Mathilda and Theophanu each produced five children before thirty; Judith's children by Louis the Pious belong to the first years of their marriage and her youth; while Louis's older children belong to the first, not the last, twelve years of his marriage to Ermengard. Emma of Normandy's childbearing was extended by her second marriage to Cnut, but she was little over thirty when her last child was born. Queens like Gerberga, still bearing twins in her mid-thirties, were apparently rare. Charles the Bald's hopes of sons from Ermentrud in her late thirties may have needed all the help ecclesiastical magic could bring. The fortunate queen produced her sons and produced them quickly. The birth of Liudolf within a year was the perfect consummation of the marriage celebrations of Otto the Great and Eadgyth.

The war between the Church and lay society over marriage was lengthy. It was neither simply nor primarily a struggle between sexual practice and moral code, but one between Christian ethic and social requirements. The Church rarely fought it as an undivided army. The major theater of operations was the royal family itself, the trendsetter for the lay aristocracy, the apex of society and the especial concern of bishops. There were great battles and long truces, and not all victories were consolidated. It had its petty skirmishes, as when Bishop Medard unsuccessfully opposed the repudiation of Radegund, or Dunstan accused Edgar and Ælfthryth of adultery in their marriage bed. It had its great single combats between armed champions, few more resounding than the clash between Brunhild and Columbanus. Its sustained battles were fought over affairs like those of Lothar II or Robert the Pious, battles that revealed the divisions within the Church's ranks, the readiness of those who might agree on principle to part for political advantage. They were battles that only gradually affected the course of the war. Kings with good records of protecting the Church won silent victories and indulged a sexual and marital life of their own choosing. Sustained attacks were undertaken during the movements of moral and ecclesiastical reform that swept Frankia in the seventh, eighth, and ninth centuries, and the whole of Europe in the tenth and eleventh. Except possibly in the eleventh century progress was painfully slow; the greatest achievement no more than to change the rules of the game so that kings first regularized their unions with more care, then found appropriate excuses for divorce. Each side had its soft underbelly exposed to attack: for the Church, internal doctrinal and political divisions; for the royal family, succession, legitimacy, and the lay enemies ready to profit from discomfiture. At no stage did divorce in case of necessity become impossible, although it might be prevented in individual cases and was increasingly problematic.

In most areas of life abundance brings cheapness, and marriage practices that multiply the numbers of wives and facilitate their replacement do little for the status of wives or women. The desperate insecurity of a woman like Fredegund is eloquent witness to her unprotected position. Monogamy works in favor of women, as wives cease to be prey to the arbitrary caprices of their husbands. Concubines, wives of lower status, gradually disappeared. With some spectacular exceptions monogamy was winning by the eleventh if not the tenth century. The current of thought favored one wife, though a king could still divorce her if need be. Marriage practices recorded a slight shift in favor of the king's wife, but many other factors determined whether she was to enjoy any real power, whether a wife was to be the queen.

Chapter 4 👑 *Mistress of the Household*

etween 830 and 834 the three sons of Louis the Pious's first marriage rebelled against their father in an attempt to control the ordering of the Carolingian succession. The crisis involved local rivalries, noble factions, and provincial separatism, but at its heart lay a struggle for power over the king within the royal household. The major object of the sons' attack was not Louis but his second wife, Judith, and her supporters. It was Judith's dominance at court, the fear that Louis's will was in her hands, the belief that he would receive no one without her approval, that incensed them. Their aim was the separation of their father from his wife, the removal of her faction from court and the substitution of their own control of the king. Judith was accused of adultery and incest with her husband's godson Bernard, the court chamberlain and lynchpin of her party. She was imprisoned in the nunnery of Saint Radegund at Poitiers. Bernard fled, but other members of Judith's court party were taken. Her brothers Conrad and Rudolf were tonsured as monks and sent to Aquitaine to be imprisoned by the second son, Pepin; Bernard's brother was captured, blinded, and incarcerated in Italy under the surveillance of the eldest son, Lothar. Judith had been accused of manipulating, together with Bernard, both the palace and royal counsels, of securing the retention of those men who agreed with her and the expulsion of those who did not.

The crisis saw a series of palace revolutions. When the brothers' victory was overturned and Judith restored to court, she in turn expelled the counsellors who had worked against her, Abbot Wala among them. The revival of revolt in 834 was marked by an immediate move against the queen, who on this occasion was sent to Italy to be held safe by Lothar. Their propaganda may have exaggerated her vices, but Louis's sons had correctly identified Judith as their problem. When the crisis had abated, Judith returned permanently to court to continue her efforts to secure the inheritance of her son Charles by working on Louis. Judith's power had certain formal bases, but its strength lay partly in her personality, in the capacity of this sweet-tongued, pliant, and musically gifted woman to influence an elderly husband and secure the future for her son and herself. She exercised her power almost exclusively within the confines of the palace, with the help of allies from her own family and among the great court officials. The Judith affair demonstrates how central palace politics were to *all* politics at this date. Through personal influence with the king, patronage was secured and, more important, the consuming questions of succession and inheritance could be decided. These questions, which divided the royal family, drew into themselves all other divisions and rivalries. The queen's position at court put her at the heart of politics.

Palace Intrigue

Judith was accused of adultery with Bernard of Septimania as part of an attempt to be rid of both. Adultery was the charge most frequently leveled at the queens of the early Middle Ages. When Charles the Fat repudiated Richardis in 887, he not only alleged that she failed to consummate their marriage, but that she had denied the king her sexual favors only to bestow them on his archchancellor, Bishop Liutward of Vercelli. Richardis meekly retired to the nunnery at Andlau, though not before she had cleared herself through the ordeal of burning plowshares and a solemn declaration of virginity. In the mid-eleventh century, Edith was accused of intimacy with the Bishop of Winchester and was later also said to have walked barefoot over hot plowshares to prove her innocence. Accusations against Emma, wife of the penultimate Carolingian Lothar, continued for a decade. Long before Lothar's death there were rumors of her adultery with a household ecclesiastic, Adalbero of Laon, bruited most persistently by her brother-in-law Charles of Lorraine. The bishop's involvement led to a public debate of the whole affair at the Synod of St. Macre, deliberations unfortunately now lost. After Lothar's death Emma and Adalbero were again attacked, now with force as well as words. The queen was imprisoned by Charles of Lorraine. This climax clarifies the entire affair.

Charles was a claimant to the West Frankish throne of his brother Lothar. Even before Lothar's death he suspected, surely correctly, that Emma was working against him at court. Emma naturally supported the claims of her own son, Louis V; any provision for Charles threatened Louis's interests. Emma's influence on Lothar was exercised within the palace, with the help of her own supporters. Charles's own attack was directed there, taking the form of an accusation that her alliance with Adalbero had gone further than the merely political. Such an accusation served a double purpose for a claimant like Charles. Not only could he hope to discredit Adalbero, the queen's ally, and perhaps secure the repudiation of Emma herself, but also, a charge of adultery would cast doubts on the paternity of Emma's son, his own major rival for the throne.

Defamation of character offered glittering prizes to the successful. It was used, as we shall see, in many disputed successions to discredit a mother and her son. Accusations of adultery usually help identify the queen's supporters as well as her opponents and their aims. During the last illness of Arnulf, in 899, Uota, his legitimate wife, was accused of adultery by a magnate faction which included Adalbero of Augsburg and Hatto, Bishop of Mainz. At one stage their aim seems to have been the exclusion of her son, Louis the Child, from the throne, and the advance of the claims of her illegitimate stepsons. The claims to regency which Uota, and especially her family, might put forward were to be discredited. But in this case the factions shifted and realigned during the course of accusation and ordeal. A group led by Adalbero and Hatto came to feel that a legitimate Carolingian was preferable, doubly so if, like Louis, he was an infant and was under their control. Having accused Uota and checked the power of her kin, they took control of the child themselves and then acquitted the queen.

Even when accusations are made by a king in the course of divorce proceedings, they may still form part of a palace revolution. Charles the Fat accused Richardis because he wished to be rid of a sterile wife. His final charge of adultery came in 887, when Charles was already aware of his own imminent death. After his unsuccessful brain operation, Charles spent the summer of 887 in final, desperate attempts to arrange the succession. His court was the scene of vigorous lobbying by supporters of legitimate and illegitimate Carolingians alike, and his own last hopes may have been for his bastard child, Bernard. Richardis was at court in these months with her close ally Liutward. The cry of adultery now raised against them came as part of a final palace revolution that replaced Liutward by his enemy, Liutbert of Mainz. So closely were queens bound in with palace factions that their removal might be a necessary part of political change.

It was not only great ecclesiastics who debauched the queen and the morals of the court. Judith was accused of adultery with a personable young count; Fredegund of liaison with a mayor of the palace, Landeric; Brunhild of taking the court official Protadius as her lover. The common factor is the position of all these men within the court, the alliances they had forged with the queen. If great ecclesiastics figure frequently it is less because of the strains of celibacy than because of their central place in the courts of the early Middle Ages. It is difficult now to know whether real fires of passion lay behind all the smoke of propaganda; courts have ever provided the opportunity and the leisure for pleasant dalliance and idle flirtation. The certainty is yet further confirmation of the palace as the heart of politics. If a woman's power there was buttressed by that of her family, both might need to be removed. If her support came, as it so often did, from palace officials, adultery was a neat charge to encompass a double ruin.

While the court coinage often bore stories of incest and adultery, it could also be struck with the more sinister devices of malevolence and murder. Sudden deaths that served the purposes of queens could scarcely fail to throw suspicion upon them. It was alleged that when Brunhild wished to advance her own lover, Protadius, she found Bertoald, the mayor of the palace, standing in his way. Bertoald was despatched on a tax-gathering mission to a notoriously dangerous region and accordingly met his death. Fredegund was said to have connived at the death of her own husband, Chilperic, aided by a court official who was her lover and who would soon rise to power. Eadburh, wife of the West Saxon Beorhtric, was accused of poisoning those counsellors who thwarted her.

The story of Gundiperga and Charoald from seventh-century Italy is set in the crosscurrents of court politics. Queen Gundiperga had passed favorable comment on the appearance of a certain Adalulf, a noble at Charoald's court. Sensing an advantage, Adalulf had attempted to seduce her, only to be summarily dismissed with a queenly rebuke—she spat in his eye. To forestall the queen, and in the hope of revenge, Adalulf rushed to Charoald and accused Gundiperga of plotting with Duke Taso to overthrow the king, marry the duke, and together rule in Charoald's stead. The queen was exiled for three years. The story simplifies a complex situation into a series of personal preferences and encounters. But even so, it bears eloquent witness to the atmosphere of intrigue and suspicion that is the inevitable concomitant of personal rule and court politics.

The truth behind the rumor becomes hard to disentangle. Edward the Confessor's queen, Edith, was said to have engineered the murder of the northern English magnate Gospatric at court at Christmas in 1065. The deed was done on behalf of her brother Tostig, Earl of Northumbria, as part of his totally inadequate attempt to deal with mounting opposition to his rule in the north. Tostig was Edith's favorite brother. Yet the very reasons that might have led her to perform the deed were precisely the reasons that made her a prime suspect when the sudden death occurred. The guilt of Constance or her allies in the death of Hugh of Beauvais is clearer. Hugh was an official at the court of Robert the Pious, a supporter there of the interests of the house of Blois and thus of Robert's first wife, Bertha. Circa A.D. 1006 Robert repudiated Bertha and married Constance, a member of the family of Anjou, traditional enemies of the house of Blois. Hugh remained at court, still pressing the cause of Bertha and inevitably incurring the ill feeling of the new queen. Ralph Glaber blames the murder of Hugh in 1008 on Constance herself. A likelier candidate is her kinsman, Fulk of Anjou, who saw Hugh standing in the path of Robert's Angevin friendship. Assassination is a frequent weapon in the personal world of palace politics, where the literal removal of an enemy may appear the only path to success. The domestic nature of this world makes stealth, and especially poison, a normal means. Since Tacitus's Livia, if not before, this secret method of encompassing death has regularly been imputed to queens.

The queen's trusted servants would hope to advance at court to a position where their utility was assured. Brunhild was suspected of ridding herself of Bertoald so that she could advance her own man,

Protadius. Leudast, count of Tours, won the favor of Marcoveifa, wife of Charibert I, growing rich in her service and becoming influential as count of the royal stables. In the mid-eleventh century, Edith secured a bishopric for her own chaplain. But queens did not always find the courtiers who surrounded them congenial. They could find themselves at odds with the powerful officials, even in conflict with them for influence over the king. Ælfthryth, King Edgar's wife, found a sympathetic ally in bishop Æthelwold of Winchester. Her relations with Archbishop Dunstan, another great figure at Edgar's court, were less happy. Their mutual distrust became focused in the dispute over the succession to the throne, in which Dunstan favored Ælfthryth's stepson and not her own son Æthelred. Adelaide found herself in open enmity with Berengar, the chief official at the court of her first husband, King Lothar of Italy. Berengar's power rivaled that of the king, and he may have entertained hopes of the succession even before Lothar's death. Berengar was quick to make himself king when opportunity presented; his first action was to capture his old enemy and rival, Queen Adelaide. She had formed her own alliances at Lothar's court, and her later dramatic escape from Berengar's prison was effected with the help of one of them— Adalhard, Bishop of Reggio.

The queen's power at court depended partly on the centrality of that court to all politics, then on her capacity to influence the king. The nature of personal rule ensures that she who has the king's ear may help direct the course of events. Political change thus comes to involve the replacement of the king's advisers, and central to them, the king's wife. Attempts at the separation of such queens as Judith, Richardis, Edith, or Angelberga signal attempts at such palace revolution, whether engineered by the king or his enemies. In 589 a plot to replace the court faction in Austrasia entailed first a plan to persuade Childebert to drive out his mother Brunhild, repudiate his wife, and marry again; or, failing this, to remove the king himself and replace him by one of his own small children. The alternatives are significant: total control over a pliable infant was in some ways comparable to the power a dominant wife or mother could exercise. Where queens successfully filled the role of most intimate counsellor, formidable possibilities were brought within their reach.

Household Powers

The queen's power within the household rested on formal as well as informal bases. In 882 Archbishop Hincmar of Rheims wrote a tract *On the Governance of the Palace* for the instruction of the young King Carloman. He drew extensively on an earlier account of the palace of Charlemagne, written by Adalhard about A.D. 814. The tract offers a unique picture of the Carolingian royal palace at work; on every page the personal, household nature of ninth-century rule is apparent. Adalhard divided government in two: rule of the kingdom and ordering of the palace, placing both on an equal footing. The organization of the palace was the preserve of the queen and the great officials. Her especial responsibilities were the management and day-to-day running of the household, the maintenance of the royal dignity—covering the whole area of the outward appearance and estate of royalty—and the annual provision of gifts for the highest officials. Throughout the description of palace government, the giving and receiving of gifts appears as the way in which friends were made, obligations created, and the whole system of personal rule cemented.

It was also the affair of the queen and the great officers to isolate the king from the minutiae of administration, to preserve the essential distance and impartiality of royalty. This left them with favor to bestow, solving the problems of lesser officials, and controlling crucial access to the king, the fount of patronage and justice. Here lay the major source of the power of household officials. The queen's special responsibilities placed her to advantage in exercising such power herself. Adalhard's Carolingian palace is the center of a vast melee, as the poor, the old, and debtors, not to mention officials and nobles, sought access to the king. It is a world in its own right, within which the greatest officials seek constantly to bind to themselves factions of lesser fry, giving gifts to the young men and vassals, inviting them to dinner. The tract ends by describing a meeting of the general assembly, nobles of all ranks gathered from all the kingdom to discuss its affairs, in the open air if the weather permitted. Through them all the king himself moves, receiving presents, greeting old friends, deliberating with the important, chatting with those from afar, gathering news from all quarters of the vast Frankish realms.

The tract is in many ways an idealized picture. It has many features that would apply only to a static court such as Charlemagne had in his later years at Aachen. But its ideas are reflected in the theory and practice of ninth-century Frankia. Everywhere the king in his household appears as the center of government; often the queen's role in that household is stressed. For Sedulius, it was the queen who ruled the household and influenced her husband; from her wisdom good flowed to the household and the kingdom. As she ruled household and children, so would the kingdom be ruled; her foolishness would bring problems to both. For Agobard, the queen had the care of the palace, but also held the reins of the kingdom. She was the essential helpmate of the king in both spheres. It was Judith's inability to rule herself that made her unfit for these important tasks. There is an element of special pleading in these attacks on Judith, but there can be little doubt that the Carolingians saw themselves and wished others to see them as a family, a household in which the queen as wife and mother had her roles. However distorted they may be by borrowing from antique authors, the pictures created by the court poets for Charlemagne show the importance that king attached to court, family, and household. Charlemagne is the quintessential family man; his court is a center of education, of friendly intercourse with his nobles, of songs, even of communal bathing, at the heart of his kingship and of its success. The women of that court were important. When Louis the Pious cleansed it and expelled his sisters, he was not merely reforming morals but effecting a palace revolution. The tone of Louis's court changed. According to Thegan, Louis had little love for stories, poetry, and popular songs; Walahfrid Strabo has left a stylized picture of Old Testament solemnity and Byzantine rigidity of etiquette. But still the queen is there, Judith, strong in spirit, sweet in conversation, the beautiful Rachel leading the infant Benjamin by the hand.

The personal nature of rule made the court, where the king and his family lived, a center and symbol of the entire kingdom. In some nineteenth-century African states the parallelism has been exact: in Dahomey the palace mirrored the external organization of the kingdom; in Mossi the palace layout symbolized the kingdom as a whole, its life and death and its extension by conquest. In most of these states, the palace was organized partly or wholly by royal women. The Frankia of Hincmar and especially of Adalhard may have offered especial powers to women in palace and kingdom, but their general importance in household and family is not unique to Charlemagne's kingdom.

At a time when the royal hall was the focus for raiding parties, for companies of warriors and their loot, *Beowulf* describes the functions of Wealtheow, Hrothgar's queen. Her concern is with royal hospitality and generosity. Adorned with gold, she greets the warriors, proffers them their cup; it is she who gives Beowulf gifts and speaks his praises. Hygd, wife of Hygelac, goes through the hall offering mead vessels to the guests, giving gifts and treasures freely; she is not too proud. When Clothar and his followers uttered criticism of Radegund as a queen, they cited her failures in these areas. She left the care of the royal hall to others, came late to meals, and did not preside at the feasts with the nobles. In the tenth century Mathilda's biographer can speak approvingly of the queen's presiding over the royal table and maintaining her dignity. The motif of the queen feeding the poor, as Mathilda did, is only a specific extension of the ideal of hospitality and generosity. Helgaud's Constance was in charge of dispensing patronage from Robert's household, and like Edith in the court of Edward the Confessor, with the maintenance of royal dignity. Whatever the individual variations in the queen's power and control within the court, it remained throughout the period an accepted and important area of queenly activity.

Marriage created whatever rights a queen possessed in the household. When Brunhild supposedly encouraged Theuderic to take concubines rather than a wife, it was because she feared to lose her own dignities and honors in the royal hall to a wife and queen. Marriage created property rights for the wife that formed a basis of a queen's power. On joining her new family, the wife was provided with a dowry from its property. For all wives, these dowries provided security for the wife within her adopted clan. Almost all dynasties provide examples of queenly dowries of varying size and composition. Galswinth was given the towns of Bordeaux, Limoges, Cahors, Lescar, and Cientat as morning-gift when she married Chilperic. Desiderius gave the monastery of San Salvatore in Brescia as dowry to his wife Ansa. It still formed part of the dowry of Italian queens in the ninth century, when Lothar I gave it, together with other lands like Erstein in Alsace, to Queen Ermengard. Angelberga received a dowry from Louis II although the charter formally recording it was not produced until 860, some years after the marriage. Charles the Bald gave Feuquières-en-Amienois to Ermentrud; Charles the Fat dowered Richardis; Charles the Simple granted his first wife, Frederun, both Corbeny and Ponthion, his second wife, Eadgifu, received Tusey on Maas. Robert the Pious gave Montreuil to Rozala as dowry, then took it back when he repudiated her. When Rudolf III of Burgundy married Ermengard in 1011 he gave her the town of Vienne, plus the counties of Viennois and Sermorens, Aix-les-Bains, and Yvonant. Rights in the towns of Winchester and Exeter formed part of the dowry of English queens by 1002, and in the eleventh century they received much of the county of Rutland. Some of the largest dowries are those recorded for the Italian and Ottonian queens and empresses of the tenth century. When Adelaide was betrothed to Lothar in 937 she received a promise of 4,580 *mansi* in Italy plus three abbeys. When she married him in 947, Corano was added, and her marriage to Otto I brought further unspecified lands. When Theophanu married Otto II in 972, her dowry consisted of enormous properties in Italy and in Germany, plus the nunneries of Nivelles, Herford, and Nordhausen. The document recording the gift was written in gold letters on purple parchment.

Dowry lands provided revenue for the queen during her life and especially in widowhood. But queens could enjoy other lands and revenue allocated to them from the royal estate. In 1066 Queen Edith held lands scattered throughout southern England and the Welsh marches, far more extensive than the dowry lands of the Anglo-Saxon royal house. She had a share in some of the miscellaneous revenues that accrued to the king, the annual gifts to the queen mentioned in the Warwickshire and Northamptonshire *Domesday*. Queens held and had opportunities to acquire lands far more extensive than their dowries. At Andelot in 587 the property, revenues, and cities belonging to Brunhild and her daughter-in-law Queen Faileuba were guaranteed, as was their free disposal. The right of disposal, but especially the fact that any lands they may acquire in the future are so protected, suggests that Andelot was concerned with more than dowry lands. Many queens were granted land during their husband's lifetimes, over which they had rights of disposal. A series of such grants have survived for Italian queens from the time of Angelberga onward. Ageltrudis received grants from Guy and from her son Lambert; both Lothar and Otto I added property to Adelaide's already extensive dowry. In tenth and eleventh-century England queens like Eadgifu, Ælfthryth, Emma, and Edith all acquired land in this way. A desire for clear distinctions would suggest three types of property providing revenue for the queen as king's wife: her dowry lands, which in many cases seem to have been inalienable and returned at her death to the royal estates, a share in the revenue of the royal demesne itself to provide for her queenly estate in the household, and properties acquired in a more personal capacity with rights of free disposal.

Unfortunately such neat distinctions may often in practice appear blurred. The concept of an inalienable royal demesne governed by generally accepted rules for the provision of the royal family was neither universal nor unchanging. The royal wills, coupled with the evidence of land grants, suggests that in ninth- and tenth-century England there were certain lands regularly allocated as dowry to queens, regularly returning to the royal estates. In Lombard and early Carolingian Italy certain estates were used in the same way. It is difficult to say whether the provisions of Andelot prove that Merovingian queens could dispose freely of their dowry lands, but early tenth-century Frankish queens like Frederun appear to have done so.

The problems that dowry and rights of alienation could pose are illustrated in the struggles over such lands in the Ottonian house. In the 970s Adelaide waged a long battle with her son Otto II and her daughter-in-law Theophanu over her dowry. In the Italian charters that recorded the dowries of Adelaide and later of Theophanu, these queens were given complete freedom of disposal of the lands involved. Adelaide was claiming such rights of alienation in the 970s. Otto II and Theophanu opposed the permanent loss of such a substantial portion of the royal demesne. They were prepared to guarantee only lifelong enjoyment of lands, which would then revert to the royal estates. The issue was a major factor in the rift between Adelaide and her son—and perhaps especially with Theophanu—that caused her exile from court. When Otto II died and the infant Otto III succeeded, Adelaide tried again to establish total control over her dowry. Again Theophanu, now as regent, stood in her way. The conflict may partly have been one between tenth-century Italian legal provisions, which greatly favored women, and German family practice. It certainly helped sour relations within the Ottonian dynasty.

Dowry could be a bone of contention between mother-in-law and daughter-in-law even when alienation was apparently not in question. Henry the Fowler's widow, Mathilda, was deprived of her dowry by her son Otto I and his wife Eadgyth in 936, and forced back on to the ancestral lands of her own family. Her dowry lands were later returned to her, but a lingering sense of insecurity may have remained. She was especially anxious to gain Otto's backing for her nunnery at Nordhausen. Dowry and other royal lands enabled a queen to live in appropriate state. As such they should ideally have belonged to the family, which would need them to endow future queens, and not to the queen herself. Even in such circumstances they could be a source of friction, but when queens sought to alienate those lands the friction was even greater. In tenth-century England and Ottonian Germany, perhaps also in sixth- and seventh-century Frankia, queens often desired to use their property to endow the burgeoning monastic movements. Difficulties could scarcely fail to ensue.

Some queens controlled the household wealth in a more general fashion. The capitulary from Charlemagne's reign, which deals with the organization of the royal demesne, places king and queen on an equal footing in the running of the royal lands. Orders sent to stewards and other officials are to be obeyed promptly whether they emanate from king or queen. No royal envoys are to take unauthorized lodgings on the royal manors; they must have specific permits from king or queen. In Merovingian Frankia queens controlled all or part of the royal treasure. When Fredegund fled to Paris after the murder of Chilperic she had a great deal of treasure with her, most of it subsequently taken from her and sent to her nephew and enemy Childebert. When Alethius plotted to oust Clothar II, he approached Queen Bertetrude with a plan to marry her and acquire the royal treasure. Brunhild was in Paris with treasure as well as with her children when Sigibert fell in battle. In the seventh century when the final share-out of Dagobert's treasure was made, Nantechild successfully claimed a third.

Merovingian queens may not have controlled all the royal treasure; certainly they did not do so unaided. There is evidence for treasurers, officials attached to Merovingian royal households. Similarly, when Eadburh fled with treasure after the death of her West-Saxon husband, King Beorhtric, it is unclear whether it was her own or part of the royal hoard. Queens could amass their own treasures: Fredegund protested to Chilperic that Rigunth's dowry came from her own store of gold, not from the king's. Queens certainly continue to be associated with treasure. Plectrud, wife of Pepin, Carolingian mayor of the palace, acted like a queen. On Pepin's death she ruled briefly and attempted to control the succession. Her actions included taking possession of Pepin's treasure and using it to buy support. Relinquishing control to her stepson Charles Martel meant giving up to him his father's treasure. When Otto II suffered his disastrous defeat at Cortona in 982, Theophanu was in the nearby town of Rossano, in charge of the royal treasure.

The Merovingian treasury contained gold, silver, precious stones, cash, weapons, and royal documents such as tribute lists. Its possession was always crucial to pretenders to the throne, and we have seen such claimants rush to gain treasure, royal residence, and widow. For them, as for Plectrud, the treasure meant the possibility of buying support. The queen's association with its control gave her similar opportunities during the lifetime of her husband, but especially after his death. In 1035 Cnut's widow, Emma, took care to strengthen herself and her faction by taking control of the royal treasure at Winchester; by this and other means she was able to hold off the claims of Harold Harefoot for two years. As late as 1100, when Henry I was making good his claims to the throne, his first concern was the royal treasure and he hastened to Winchester to claim it.

Sometimes the treasure contained the royal insignia themselves, so that possession gave additional control over the succession of a new king. After the death of Lothar of Italy, Berengar moved immediately to capture the young widow Adelaide. According to Hroswitha, he took not only Adelaide, but the royal treasure: gold, jewels, and the crown. In 877 the dying Charles the Bald left the royal insignia in the hands of Richildis, to strengthen her hand in negotiation over the succession. The emperor Henry II on his death bed left his wife Cunigund in possession of the royal insignia and it was she who brought them to Conrad after he was chosen as king. Charles the Bald and Henry II may be special cases: Charles profoundly disliked his son and heir, Louis the Stammerer, while Henry II was a childless monarch with no obvious successor. These instances cannot be used to argue that the crown and other emblems of royalty were always possessed by the queen, though they underline her concern with the succession to the throne.

Merovingian, probably Carolingian, tenth-century Ottonian, and eleventh-century English queens all controlled treasure. To them as to kings it brought the influence wealth could purchase, and special advantages in deciding the question of succession. The actions of Merovingians and Lombard pretenders suggest that this control of treasure should not be divorced from the queen's role as mistress of the household. She possessed it, and other revenues allocated to her, in order to provide adequately for the royal household, to maintain that splendor and those outward expressions of wealth and status that are understood in the term *dignity*.

Even in her widowhood Mathilda maintained the dignity suited to a queen, and her biographer approved. Edith, wife of Edward the Confessor, was virtuous, prodigal, religious, and took care of the worldly dignity of the king and his household. She ensured that Edward was clad in sumptuous finery, embroidering some of it herself. As mistress of the royal household, the appearance of the monarch, like the provision for his table, was her concern. Though his biographer explains that Edward inwardly rejected the finery, he does not condemn Edith. Her concern for the royal dignity is enumerated with her other virtues. In the hands of an unsympathetic writer this concern can easily become avarice, and in practice the line between the legitimate function of the queen and its perversion may have been fine. Constance saw her function as maintaining the dignity of Robert the Pious, a difficult task given a husband allegedly so simpleminded and prodigal. It was she who was concerned when a silver candlestick was stolen from the royal chapel under the nose of the praying king. In anger she swore to torture the guardians and put out their eyes if they failed to find the thief: Robert helped the robber escape the wrath of the "inconstant Constance." When Robert himself helped a poor man break off the silver from a lance which Constance had given him, the astonished queen hoped in exasperation that he would gain joy and glory from the action. Constance's true concern, that the king should appear kingly before his subjects, is expressed in another of Helgaud's anecdotes. Robert the Pious was seated at table, when a holy beggar at his feet stole a gold ornament from the king's knees. Constance's reproach was that the loss would dishonor him. Helgaud's Robert is a new image of kingship, pious and ascetic; Constance represents older ideas and attitudes toward royal wealth.

The external attributes of royalty openly displayed the king's wealth and position, marking him out as above other men; stripped of them he lost his distinction. The motif of kings and queens in disguise is relatively common. Not dressed in appropriate finery, unattended by crowds of retainers, an Adelaide or an Alfred could pass unrecognized by humble fishermen or peasant women. In a society that relied on outward marks of distinction, the queen's provision for the royal appearance provided for the charisma of royalty itself. Iurminburg engineered the downfall of Wilfrid, because the bishop rivaled the king in the splendor of his dress, the size of his following, and his general estate. Eddius gives vent to his antifeminism, but underlines the proper role of the queen in her concern for such matters.

Edith arrayed Edward in embroidered robes that she had worked herself, and his biographer notes her skill at spinning and embroidery. Industrial society has devalued such traditionally important household tasks as spinning and weaving. These domestic duties have customarily been the sphere of women. At the practical level, they provide the necessities for the family; at the level of the queen and the royal household, they provide for royal finery, for the working of truly royal gifts at a time when the giving and receiving of gifts mattered. Ermengard wife of Lothar I made an embroidery on the life of Saint Peter for which Sedulius Scottus composed inscriptions. Ermentrud wife of Charles the Bald was a skilled needlewoman, while her mother-in-law, Judith, had worked a cloak for Louis the Pious. Among the sumptuous gifts made by Athelstan to Saint Cuthbert in 934 was an embroidered stole worked on the order of, if not by the hand of, Queen Ælfflæd; it is now one of the treasures of Durham Cathedral. Adelaide, wife of Hugh Capet and mother of Robert the Pious, embroidered a chasuble in fine gold, with Christ in majesty on the back and the Lamb of God on the front, together with a gold cloak, two silver ones, and two other chasubles of marvelous workmanship. All were worked by the queen as gifts from the royal family to the royal shrine and mausoleum at St. Denis.

The importance of such domestic tasks can easily be undervalued. In a household of the size and significance of the king's they took on an extra dimension. Distributing hospitality, providing for the royal table, and presiding there in suitable splendor were queenly contributions to the pageant of royalty that had constantly to underpin early monarchy. Edith preferred to sit at Edward's feet, except at the royal table, when she assumed fitting dignity. Constance was rightly disgusted when Robert allowed himself to be robbed at table. The public nature of royal life is a constant surprise. Charlemagne's palace was thronged with suitors; when a ninth-century English king was in residence on his estate, men journeyed there from all around; Robert's royal board was surrounded by a melee of the poor and sick; Queen Mathilda presided at a table thronged by the poor; the sick flocked to the court of Edward the Confessor to be cured. The public image of kingship had to be maintained in what are apparently intimate domestic scenes, at table, at private prayer. Those who came to the king's household must enjoy his royal hospitality. The most regular record of the queen's activity here concerns the poor, though this was far from the sole area of its exercise. The pressure of numbers involved in gifts of food and clothing could produce a need for institutionalization. Clovis allocated an almoner, Genesius, to help Balthild perform these duties. The real household functions of the queen added point to the hagiographical conventions that show Radegund and others performing such menial household tasks as washing dishes, sweeping out corners, fetching wood, and cleaning lavatories.

Royal women not only organized the concrete spectacle of royalty in its domestic context; they were themselves an important part of that spectacle. Queens appeared loaded with gems and finery, displaying their husband's wealth. Iurminburg wore Wilfrid's reliquary as charm and ornament. Mathilda, widow of Henry the Fowler, had a heart internally acceptable to God, but outwardly she wore gems and silk, and even grief and widowhood could not persuade her to discard her finery. In the will of the ex-queen Ælfgifu from tenth-century England, the present queen was bequeathed a valuable necklace and armlet. The best way to display wealth was to wear it. When Radegund entered the religious life she divested herself of queenly ornament—circlets, armlets, and brooches all of gold adorned with gems. She broke up her golden belt; Balthild later gave her own royal girdle to the abbey of St. Laurent. So closely were royal women associated with ornament and finery that their virtues are described in terms of jewelry and their ascetic practices become a travesty of them. Radegund parodied her queenly attire with iron bands around arms and neck; Æthelthryth of Ely saw her neck-tumor as a punishment for the weight of jewelry she had worn there as princess and queen. Descriptions of Charlemagne's court picture the king surrounded by his daughters, clad in precious stones, gold, and purple. At the hunt near Aachen they were all present, his queen, Liutgard, shining with beauty, clothed in precious stuffs and gems. Charlemagne kept all his daughters at home and brought the daughters of his dead son to his court. His family arrangements deterred these women's marriages, but they were also kept as a sign of his wealth: just as the number of wives may indicate a man's wealth in polygamy so Charlemagne demonstrated his by his ability to keep at court a multitude of royal women and deck them out with suitable ostentation. Other kings might need to dispose of their daughters— he did not.

Royal women in general and queens in particular cannot be divorced from ideas of wealth and status. When exchanged in marriage they are the greatest of gifts, their worth to be measured and appreciated. At court they are part of the royal ostentation, concrete symbols of status in a society where wealth and power was measured by its visual expression. As *Hausfrau*, keeper of treasure, maintainer of royal dignity, the queen personifies the household's need for treasure, for its management and its display. And women create wealth, supremely as bearers of children, but also in weaving and embroidering gifts and adornments.

As mother of the family, the queen should stand at the center of family unity. The royal family and its unity were so crucial to early medieval kingdoms that they are regularly idealized in the sources. Charlemagne has been seen in his role as father, served by sons, feted by daughters, kissed by his sister, the queen presiding benevolently over all. Ottonian Germany presented the same ideal. Its histories were family histories in which women were to the fore; they delighted in depicting the royal family in its intimate moments, children and grandchildren gambolling, emotional scenes between mothers and sons. Otto I went out of his way to demonstrate the family unity at Cologne in 965, gathering the Ottonian house together. The scene was graphically described in the oldest life of Mathilda, when "all the royal progeny of either sex gather, brought together by divine mercy and in love at seeing one another . . . and that renowned mother queen Mathilda, rejoicing in the birth of such great children, was received in great honor, by the emperor and then by all the rest. She embraces them in her joy at seeing her grandchildren and especially her son safely returned." The ideal of unity and of the queen's role in creating it was an image whose potency derived in part from the reality of family tension.

We have encountered queens as stepmothers, sources of household discord. As vengeance-takers they could wreak havoc. Where wives and mistresses clashed in rivalry over royal favor, enmity could erupt into tragedy, and a concubine like Fredegund could provoke the murder of a rival wife. The royal household could equally become the focus of the age-old tensions between mothers-in-law and daughters-in-law. Retirement of a queen mother at the time of her son's marriage could obviate problems. Æthelred II did not marry his second wife, Emma, and make her his queen until his mother Ælfthryth had retired to Wherwell, perhaps even died. Emma herself retired to Winchester when her own son Edward married Edith. In the tenth century Eadgifu had already retired to her nunnery in Laon when Louis d'Outremer married Gerberga. Gerberga's own disappearance from court does not coincide with Lothar's legal majority, but with his wedding at the age of twenty-four to Emma in the winter of 965–66. Lothar's marriage was unusually delayed, perhaps at his mother's instigation. Brunhild had broken the betrothal of her son Childebert and the future Lombard queen, Theudelinda. She did not oppose his marriage to Faileuba, a complaisant woman who allowed Brunhild to remain at court and exercise the powers of queen. Brunhild's later rude expulsion from the household of her grandson Theudebert coincided with his marriage and coming of age. Gregory of Tours remarked on the amity of Brunhild and Faileuba; it was sufficiently unusual to provoke comment.

Other mothers-in-law found their daughters-in-law less congenial. Queen Mathilda was estranged from her son Otto I during the lifetime of his first wife, Eadgyth, and did not return to court until after Eadgyth's death in 946. No relationship became more bitter than that between Adelaide and Theophanu. Otto was married to Theophanu before his accession in 973, but it was his mother, Adelaide, who ruled at his court during the first year of his reign. From June 973 to May 974 she was by his side, participating in the great royal progress which inaugurated his rule. Suddenly in August 974 it was Theophanu, not Adelaide, who appeared in Otto's charters. Adelaide was still at court seeking confirmation of her lands in 975, but she was soon in exile, first with her brother Conrad of Burgundy, later on her estates in Italy. Only the dire political events of 982–83 reconciled son and mother and brought Adelaide back, not as his venerable mother, but as august empress. The reconciliation between Adelaide and Theophanu was one of convenience, not affection, and Adelaide was in retirement again when Theophanu became regent for Otto III. The bitterness of these years and the part her daughter-in-law played in them never left Adelaide. In old age, when she reminisced to Odilo, thoughts of the dead Theophanu still rankled. She could not bring herself to use the name of the daughter-in-law; all references in Odilo's biography are to "that Greek woman."

The personal causes of these tensions are now lost: the clashes of personality, the distrust of the in-marrying stranger, the psychological reaction to replacement in a son's affections—these can only be guessed at. Concrete sources of difficulty existed. Adelaide and Theophanu quarreled over dowry and the forty-year-old dowager was galled, like many mothers, to be at the mercy of her daughter-in-law. Most queen mothers whose dowry demands were less extravagant than Adelaide's secured their lands with little trouble, but most were still forced to retire from court. There was room for only one queen in the household; the functions and power of that position could belong to one woman only. When a young king took a wife and queen it was time for his mother to bow out gracefully. It was dignity in the royal hall that Brunhild feared to lose to a new queen.

The handful of queen mothers who survived their sons' marriages unscathed eclipsed their daughters-in-law. Brunhild's partnership with Faileuba was unequal; Eadgifu overshadowed the two wives of her son, the tenth-century English king Edmund; Æthelred II's mother, Ælfthryth, exercised the functions of queen during the first half of his reign, obscuring his first wife completely. Only after Ælfthryth's retirement did Æthelred take a wife whom he made queen. Robert the Pious married twice before the death of his mother in 1006, but it is she who still enjoys the title of queen. Only after her death did Robert take a third wife and make Constance his queen. Precisely because of her powers in the household, the queen's position was unique. When a dowager like Adelaide attempted to hold on to power and found herself faced with a daughter-in-law as determined as herself, the stage was set for a classic drama of family life.

As mother of the family, the queen might be responsible for the upbringing and education of the children of the royal household, including the heirs to the throne. Judith oversaw the education of the young Charles the Bald, for whose future well-being she took such care. Freculf of Orleans dedicated part of a universal history to her for her son's instruction, and a world history since the time of Augustus, which she commissioned from Florus of Lyon, was intended for young Charles's enlightenment. Brunhild took over the education of Childebert herself. Pope Gregory commended her efforts, though perhaps with a little flattery. Praetextatus of Rouen accused the probably unlettered Fredegund of neglecting the education of her son Clothar II, a criticism for which he is alleged to have suffered the death penalty. It was Alfred's mother who encouraged him and his young brothers to learn poetry by heart, offering the book from which they learned it to the most able. Ælfthryth, mother of Æthelred II, was probably responsible for the upbringing of the children of his first marriage. Her eldest grandson, Athelstan, recorded fond memories of her in his will. Although Edith had no children of her own, she had control of the son of Ralf of Mantes, reared at court after his father's death, and the empress Adelaide kept the daughters of Berengar II at her court after their father had lost his kingdom.

Royal children were not invariably reared at court by their mothers. The tenth-century English kings Athelstan and Edgar were brought up by foster mothers, though in each case their natural mothers had died or been removed from court during their infancy. Fostering need not have permanently separated a prince from the queen; Æthelred's eldest son had a foster mother, but retained close links with his grandmother. Athelstan was reared in another royal household, that of his aunt Æthelflæd in Mercia, where he built up links that aided his later bid for the throne. Even if princes were removed to other courts, queens might still have responsibility for the education of the multitude of other young men who were raised in the royal household. Balthild was in charge of the "tender nurturing" of young men at court, as was Eanfled in seventh-century Northumbria. Young men reared in a queen's service would later form useful supporters. When Wilfrid left home as a boy he entered the service of Queen Eanfled, commended to her by those followers of his father who had previously served in her household. Their connections had never been severed. Systems of fostering out and rearing the sons of others were designed to create the personal links and loyalty through which early kingship functioned. Through her control of the household a queen might also reap their benefits.

Control of heirs to the throne, whether of one's own or another kingdom, was a desirable asset. Brunhild wrote pleadingly to the empress and emperor of Byzantium, asking them to free her little grandson Athanagild, who had been captured after the death of his mother and taken to Constantinople. She appealed as a grandmother, woman to woman. But however genuine her affection, possession of a young Visigothic prince, a claimant to the Visigothic throne, would have been as important a card in her own hands as it was in that of the emperor. Heirs to one's own kingdom were doubly important. In an early plot against Brunhild, her son's nurse was a conspirator, offering the crucial access to the royal infant. In later life Brunhild faced Rauching, Ursio, and Berthefried, who aimed to get control of her grandsons to increase the chance of their plots' success.

There is no clearer indication of how crucial the control of heirs to the throne could be, of the general opportunities that the royal household offered, than the story of the mayors of the palace in Merovingian Gaul. These officials shared with queens the upbringing of royal sons and the organization of the royal palace. Condan raised the young Theudebald, Gogo had responsibility for Brunhild's own son, Grimoald reared the son of Dagobert. The role of mayors of the palace so dominated Merovingian politics in the seventh century that by its close their royal charges were mere ciphers, the real struggles being those between their noble guardians. By the mid-eighth century the Carolingian mayors had replaced the royal dynasty itself. Their powers had many roots, but among them control of heirs to the throne and the royal household must rank high. When the succession was still central to political maneuvering, he who had an heir to the throne had a loud voice; when the royal household was central to government, he who controlled it might whisper to effect in the corridors of power. It may be no coincidence that the Merovingian period witnessed great officials and great queens.

When Edith was banished from court in 1051, it was allegedly a greater blow to the officials and courtiers than the fall of Godwin himself. Her eulogist claimed that she was indispensable in royal counsels. Edith was at the heart of a politics that revolved around the person of the king and the court. She had used her position to secure appointments and favors, to gain the gratitude of clients. She had helped the career of her brother Tostig by influencing his appointment as earl of Northumbria, perhaps even murdering his enemy Gospatric. She possessed land and revenue as large as that of any great noble. She appeared as a queen and was careful that Edward strike the correct stance before his subjects. Although childless, she controlled the rearing of potential heirs to the throne and had her own plans for the English succession in 1066. What formal powers her position as queen brought, Edith used to the full. Yet that position was precarious and personal. As the king's most intimate adviser she depended on his caprice; sterility threatened her very survival in 1051. Her power being a corollary of that of her menfolk, a crisis between her father and husband sent her to a nunnery. When the revolt against Tostig in 1065 divided her brothers, and her husband proved powerless, she wept over the frustration of her counsels. Edith was ultimately bound by the limitations of queenship itself.

Chapter 5 👑 *The Queen*

In 999 the life of the dowager empress Adelaide and the tenth century drew to a close together. No twentieth-century journalist would have resisted the chance for a retrospect celebrating the way that she and the women of her family had dominated the history of that century. Her sister-in-law Gerberga had been queen of France and had twice rescued the faltering Carolingian dynasty. Her daughter Emma had married Gerberga's son Lothar and had spent her time trying to shore up the power of her husband and son against their Capetian and other rivals. Her daughter-in-law Theophanu had reigned at the court of Otto II, had been regent for her son Otto III. Adelaide's own daughter Mathilda had become abbess of Quedlinburg and herself exercised regency in Germany during the late 990s. Her mother had been queen of Burgundy and Italy, her mother-in-law the saintly ancestress of the Ottonian house.

A history of Adelaide's own career is a history of the tenth century. Born a Burgundian princess, she became wife and queen of Lothar of Italy in 947. His premature death plunged her into the prisons of Berengar II, whence she fled to the welcoming arms of Otto I. Married to Otto she became queen of Eastern Frankia and of Italy, and in 962 was crowned his empress in Rome. She and Otto promoted the new Cluniac monasticism that swept tenth-century Europe, and she became a close friend of Mayeul and Odilo, two great abbots of that house. The death of Otto precipitated her into a family controversy that saw her exile from the court of Otto II, but not the end of her influence. In 981 her daughter Emma was appealing to her to salvage the fortunes of the Carolingian house, if necessary by assassinating Hugh Capet. In 983 she was at Otto's side, making peace with the Venetians; in 983–84 she was helping decide the fate of the infant Otto III. The death of Theophanu in 991 left Adelaide regent for the child-emperor. Only Otto III's legal majority in 996 ended her political life and left her a few final years of contemplation. At the very end of her life she was still helping pacify the troubles that disturbed Rudolf III's Burgundy. Her influence under husband, son, and grandson is charted in her interventions in charters; grants of land, especially to the Church, were often made at her request or instigation. Although exercised throughout the Ottonian Empire, her role in royal patronage was 'greatest in Italy, and at its height during her regency for her grandson Otto III. Unlike Theophanu, Adelaide never issued charters in her own name, but coins were struck in Italy bearing jointly the names of Otto and Adelaide.

Adelaide personifies queenly power. As with so many other queens, that influence was at its peak after the death of her husband, during her regency for an underage grandson. Unlike many queens, she was also important during the lifetime of her husband, and even under son and grandson exercised considerable power in her own right. Her place at the center of a web of dynastic relationships goes far toward explaining her position. Daughter, sister, and aunt of three consecutive rulers of Burgundy; sister-in-law, mother-in-law, and grandmother of three successive kings of France; wife, mother, and grandmother of three Ottonian emperors; mother or aunt to a host of abbesses and bishops—it sometimes seems that to follow any family line in tenth-century Europe is to come back to Adelaide. Wherever she moved she was received by children, grandchildren, nephews; she found refuge at their courts and they appealed to her when in need. In exile from the court of Otto II, she could retire with dignity to that of her brother Conrad of Burgundy. In direst straits her daughter Emma could request her aid, reminding her mother how well she liked her son-in-law the king of France. Adelaide's power cannot be separated from its familial context, but equally it cannot be confined within the backrooms of female intrigue and influence. Her family relationships made Adelaide the "mother of kingdoms," but her career was acted out on the broadest stage. Her life, and to a lesser extent those of other women of her house, call for explanations of the circumstances that brought them into the limelight.

Queens and War

When she intervened on behalf of her nephew Rudolf in Burgundy, Adelaide was a peacemaker, presiding over a meeting of the king and his vassals, attempting to solve their discord. Yet her daughter Emma did not feel that her mother would shrink from the use of violence if necessary. She wrote to Adelaide in 981, informing her that Hugh Capet was on pilgrimage in Italy and asking her to take what steps were necessary to prevent his return to France. Since Adelaide did not know Hugh, Emma included a detailed description of her enemy, down to the shape of his nose and the tenor of his accent. Emma, like most tenth-century French queens, was no stranger to the exercise of force. She had often accompanied her husband Lothar on campaign and her role was not always passive. After the capture of Verdun it was Emma who was left to defend the town while Lothar returned to Laon. Earlier in the century, her namesake, Queen Emma, wife of King Ralph, had played a determined military part. This granddaughter of the Capetian Robert the Strong was a bulwark of Ralph's beleaguered kingship; according to Ralph Glaber she was instrumental to the negotiations through which Ralph was accepted as king, and gave an earnest of her own forcefulness by immediately securing consecration as queen from Archbishop Seulf of Rheims. During the attempt to restore the deposed Carolingian Charles the Simple in 927, it was Emma who organized the defense of the key royal city of Laon; she led a military offensive from the town, and only the fact that Ralph himself capitulated to Herbert of Vermandois forced her reluctant evacuation. In 931 she took Avallon from Gilbert son of Manasses; in 933 she was leader of the siege of Château Thierry against Herbert, and the castle was surrendered not to Ralph, but to Emma herself. Her death in 935, only a year before her husband, removed one of the strongest props of his rule.

Emma was not the only battling queen, nor need one return to Boadicea for parallels. The next French queen, Gerberga, wife of Louis d'Outremer, conducted semipeaceful negotiations with her husband's enemies, especially during the crises of his captivity. In 948, when Louis was prisoner in Normandy, Gerberga led the defense of Laon. During her regency for her son Lothar, Gerberga accompanied him on campaign and helped direct the sieges of Dijon and other towns. Angelberga had been at the side of Louis II during his campaigns in central and southern Italy, and in 982 Theophanu was not far from her husband when Otto II was defeated at Cortona. Angelberga's daughter Ermengard held Vienne for her husband, King Boso, in 882. When Arnulf attacked Lambert of Spoleto in 896, it was Ageltrudis who masterminded the defense of Rome; after taking the city Arnulf exacted an oath from its citizens that they would not support or give aid to Lambert nor to his mother Ageltrudis. The much-reviled Willa embattled herself on the island of San Giulio after the fall of her husband, Berengar II, in 962. Otto I paid her the compliment of besieging her before he turned against her sons. But the greatest of these warrior queens was Æthelflæd, the virtually independent ruler of Mercia from 911 to 918. She built and defended a line of fortresses in the north Midlands against the Vikings and the Welsh. She captured the towns of Leicester and Derby from the Viking armies that held them. Her military reputation spread across the Irish sea, and before the end of her life she was architect and leader of a great alliance of the kings and rulers of northern Britain, subduer of Welsh princes, Lady of the Vikings of York.

Æthelflæd was, as we shall see, heir to a tradition of Mercian queenship with its origins at the court of Offa. But like these other queens she was also involved in a form of warfare centered on the siege and defense of towns, castles, and fortified places. The earliest and most enigmatic references to the military activity of queens support the same correlation. In 722 Æthelburh, Ine's queen, demolished Taunton, while Merovingian queens were regularly associated with the holding of towns. The direction of the immobile warfare that centered on fortifications may have been considered suitable for women, and may in practice have proved more suited to them. In the early eleventh century the empress Cunigund rarely accompanied Henry II on his mobile and distant campaigns, but she was left in charge of the defense of Saxony, which she ordered from fortified towns like Merseburg. Charlemagne's queens were not with him during his lengthy, mounted campaigns in Saxony, north Spain, or Aquitaine, but Hildegard was by his side during the siege of Pavia.

Queens rarely took part in the military maneuvering of the summer season. When Pepin was moving through Aquitaine on campaign in 767–69, he left Bertha at Bourges after the army assembled at the camp in May of 767. He returned to spend the winter with her there, but when the next campaigning season began she was sent first to Orleans and then to hold the fortification at Chantoceaux. It was there that he returned to meet her after his victories.

The association of women with siege rather than mobile warfare may explain why we hear most of the military activity of queens from the late ninth century onward. Such warfare came to predominate during the successful English resistance to the Vikings and in tenth-century France. Italy, where the warlike actions of queens are often recorded, was always a land of towns and here, as in Merovingian Frankia, military action often consisted of the siege and capture of fortified cities. The shift toward this type of warfare and its continual importance in Italy opened opportunities for queens as military leaders not present in the conditions which obtained in, for example, Charlemagne's Frankia. They permitted a heroic role for women outside the confines of palace intrigue.

Tenth-century French queens found themselves cast in the mold of heroines not simply because of the nature of contemporary warfare but because of the strains of contemporary politics. In this century of great insecurity and rivalry for the French throne, when dynasty replaced dynasty, kings were driven to feel that a wife or mother was the most loyal and trustworthy defender of their interests. A wife, especially one with a powerful family, might be the safest ally. During Ralph of Burgundy's brief usurpation of the Carolingian throne of France, his wife Emma was his most constant supporter, her brother Hugh the Great a powerful aid. In 926 Hugh married the sister of the English king Athelstan. At that date the house of Vermandois was attempting to restore Charles the Simple, calling on Athelstan as Charles's English brother-in-law. Hugh's marriage defended both himself and Ralph. Gerberga stood by Louis d'Outremer and her son Lothar while other allies shifted ceaselessly in and out of the Carolingian camp. She called on her brothers Otto I and Bruno, Archbishop of Cologne, whenever possible; she was ready to negotiate in person with her Capetian enemies and when necessary took up military cudgels herself.

There can be no more loyal ally than the queen whose own survival depends on that of husband or son. When those husbands and sons were insecure queens were permitted, even thrust into, a larger role. Ermengard in the late ninth century had a husband, Boso, and a son, Louis the Blind, whose claims to rule Provence were never uncontested. In ninth-century Italy Ageltrudis was the wife of Guy of Spoleto, the mother of Lambert, neither of whom was allowed peaceful enjoyment of their brief tenure of the Italian throne. In the mid-tenth century Willa's husband, Berengar II, ruled by a title which had neither the legitimacy nor the might to calm the turbulence of Italian politics. Like the tenth-century French queens who inhabited this same shifting, post-Carolingian world, all three found themselves fighting battles and wielding powers we do not often associate with queens.

Queens and the Church

Adelaide was a patron of the Cluniac movement, the friend and ally of its great abbots Mayeul and Odilo. Most queens found Church affairs and ecclesiastical politics a fruitful area of activity; some obtained significant advantage from the supporters they so gained. The cult of the divine was a permissible and even an obligatory arena of female action. Influence in ecclesiastical appointments and royal patronage, alliance with the court bishop—here a queen could use to maximum effect her accepted powers as royal counsellor and mistress of the household. If such activities bulk large in records of the lives of queens, it is not simply because contemporaries approved such female involvement, but because they provided opportunities for female action.

The tribal gods, the dynastic saints, and the royal dead watched over the world of early medieval kings, being tutelary deities for people and ruler. Through properly regulated relations with these powers, kings hoped to ensure success in war, personal fertility, a multitude of followers—all those good things which they understood by "good fortune" and "luck." When a queen married into a dynasty she became involved in these relationships and might be called on to play an important part in maintaining them. The royal dead needed keepers to tend the shrine, so royal women watched over the welfare of kings in death as in life. In seventh-century Northumbria, Queen Eanfled retired in her widowhood to Whitby, where she succeeded her sister-in-law as abbess, watching over the tomb of King Oswy. Mathilda was being more than merely a dutiful wife when she scrupulously observed the anniversaries of her dead husband, Henry the Fowler, and she handed on to her granddaughter and namesake the guardianship of the royal mausoleum at Quedlinburg.

The royal dead were the particular preserve of dowager queens and unmarried daughters; securing the beneficent intercession of the saints was a function of queens at all stages of life. Radegund avidly acquired the relics of saints, including a great prize in part of the True Cross. She wrote to King Sigibert emphasizing that she collected them for the good of the king and the kingdom. When plague raged in Pavia in 950 the relics of saints Sinesius and Teopompus were brought there in the hopes of relief; it was the young queen Adelaide who went out from the city with a great crowd to formally receive them. Magic powers clustered around relics; their capture and movement transferred those powers, weakening and symbolically subjecting those who lost them. At the beginning of the tenth century Æthelflæd and her husband Æthelred of Mercia moved the bones of the Northumbrian royal saint Oswald into Mercia. In 874, after a campaign of subjugation in southern Italy, Angelberga returned north bearing the relics of Saint Germanus from Capua. She placed them in her monastery of St. Sixtus at Piacenza, where the strength of their sanctity might reinforce the fortune of her family.

Where queens appear to follow a religious policy the desire to strengthen their dynasty through contact with the divine is always uppermost. Balthild together with her son Clothar attempted to enforce a rule of life on the greatest monasteries of Merovingian Frankia. This was no arbitrary act of centralization but, as the Rebais charter states, so that the monks would thus be able "the better to pray for the king and peace." Balthild reared Anglo-Saxon slaves and prisoners at court, freed them, placed them in monasteries, and ordered them to pray for herself, her husband, her sons, and peace. Eadgifu, last wife of Edward the Elder and mother of kings Edmund and Eadred was a patron of the tenth-century monastic revival in England. She acted as her sons and grandson did, amassing the support of the saints for her family, furthering a monastic movement whose rule of life later required daily prayers for the well-being of the royal dynasty.

A queen's marriage made her part of a new family and she was expected to adopt and propitiate the gods of her new people. When Brunhild married the Merovingian king Sigibert, she was a Visigoth and thus an Arian. Arianism was a branch of heretical Christianity abhorred by the Merovingian Franks, whose orthodoxy was to them a sign and guarantee of divine favor. Brunhild obligingly changed her faith. She also wholeheartedly adopted the Merovingian dynastic saint Martin, restoring churches in his honor, dedicating new foundations to him, receiving a poem from Fortunatus on the subject of the saint's life. Some years later a marriage alliance was arranged between Brunhild's own daughter, Ingund, and the Arian Visigothic king Hermangild. Ingund was received at the Visigothic court by her grandmother Goiswinth. But Ingund refused to identify with Visigothic ways and become an Arian, stubbornly clinging instead to her Catholicism. Goiswinth fell into a passion. She seized the unfortunate girl by the hair, kicked her until she was covered with blood, stripped her, and attempted forcible conversion by throwing her into the baptismal font. Goiswinth was already in a delicate position at the Visigothic court. King Hermangild was her stepson, relations with him uneasy, a recalcitrant Catholic granddaughter the last thing she needed. Goiswinth's reaction was strong, and Gregory of Tours may have overdrawn it, for he was no Arian sympathizer. But she was merely intemperately demanding what was required of any in-marrying queen. To have one's queen worshipping a different god, or the same god in a different way, was not simply a source of friction but threatened those harmonious relations with the divine that queens should help guarantee. King Oswy of Northumbria followed the practices of the Celtic Christian church, but his queen Eanfled lived according to those of Rome. Their differences were epitomized by the fact that they found themselves observing Easter on different days. For Oswy such disharmony was no triviality. At the synod of Whitby the king decided in favor of the Roman usage. The argument between rival Celtic and Roman saints was won by might; Rome's Peter held the keys of heaven. Oswy wished to choose his saints from the winning side.

Oswy changed his own practices to accord with those of his queen, and the Roman Christian writer Bede approved. Most of our sources are written by men of these same Roman and Christian persuasions, quick to praise those queens and princesses who stubbornly clung to their faith and often converted their husbands. These attitudes are probably not typical; they certainly hide the acute tensions such a recalcitrance must have generated. Clotild, the Catholic wife who allegedly aided the conversion of the pagan Clovis, was rewarded with adulation from Gregory of Tours and with sanctity. Theudelinda, who converted her son if not her husband from Arianism, received accolades from no less a person than Pope Gregory the Great. Bede celebrated Bertha, the Catholic wife of Æthelberht of Kent, the first English king to be converted, and also Æthelberga, their daughter, who was responsible for the conversion of Edwin of Northumbria.

Yet the imperious tone of Pope Boniface writing to Æthelberga that "the unbelieving husband shall be saved by the believing wife" hides a situation probably the opposite, as a rule. Those queens who did succeed in converting their husbands (and Theudelinda should not be counted among them) normally had a long struggle and powerful help. Had Christianity not been able to conjure with the name of Rome, had there been no missionary bishops like Augustine to back them, had the Christian god not proved a victorious god of war, it is doubtful whether many queens would have succeeded in flying in the teeth of convention. The slightest reversal threatened their unnatural victory. Clovis expected good fortune from the Christian god. When his newly baptized sons sickened and died still in their christening robes and his sisters fell ill immediately after conversion, he raged at Clotild over the ill-luck she and her faith had brought upon his house.

Conversion to Christianity opened new areas of action for queens, enlarging the strong tradition of female involvement in mediation with the divine. If women played a part in the original conversion, so did they also in most movements for reform and in the extension of Christianity before the eleventh century. Throughout the period queens figure prominently in royal patronage to the Church. Their interventions in charters—that is, the record of their requests that the king grant land—appear overwhelmingly in those for ecclesiastics. In Italy, the only beneficiaries for whom Lombard and Carolingian queens normally intervened were the royal monasteries like Bobbio and Nonantola. Not a single charter of the late Carolingian king Lothar granting land to the Church before 965–66 fails to record the counsel or order of his mother Gerberga. Tenth-century Ottonian queens, and especially Adelaide, often appear in charters. Yet even Adelaide herself, whose general political importance is indu-

bitable, intervenes most often on behalf of ecclesiastical beneficiaries; the interventions of others, like Eadgyth and Mathilda, are
virtually confined to religious houses or bishops.

The monastic reform movements of the tenth century would have
faltered without the support of English queens like Eadgifu and
Ælfthryth, or Ottonian women like Adelaide. Eadgifu used her key
position at the courts of her sons Edmund and Eadred to influence
them in favor of reformers. She helped advance Dunstan and Æthelwold, driving forces behind the English monastic movement. Her
granddaughter-in-law, Queen Ælfthryth, took over her position at
court and some of her sympathies. Ælfthryth's support went especially to Æthelwold, bishop of Winchester. She used her influence
with the king to settle land disputes in Winchester's favor and co-
operated with Æthelwold in the foundation of her nunnery at Wherwell. The Cluniac revival attracted the favor of a succession of Burgundian queens. Mathilda, wife of Conrad the Pacific, Ageltrudis
and Ermengard, wives of Rudolf III, often intervened to gain grants
of land and privilege to the Church and especially to the abbey of
Cluny. Ermengard made many land grants to churches in the Viennois and especially to Cluny itself. The empress Adelaide in her support for Mayeul and Odilo shared the interests of the women of her
family. As the movement for reform gathered strength in Ottonian
Germany, queens were again involved; Cunigund shared Henry II's
interest, and the decrees of the reforming synod of Dortmund in 1005
were issued in both their names.

The sixth- and seventh-century period of conversion and the peak
of reform and religious revival in the tenth century were times when
royal women enjoyed their greatest power. When Church movements requiring royal patronage and backing stood at the center of
politics, royal women stood with them. Together with kings, queens
must tend to the worship of the Christian god and his saints, now
become their royal deities. Their motivation embraced both piety
and political advantage, and a too-cynical and rationalist view of
their actions must be avoided. Balthild improving the religious life at
St. Denis, Ælfthryth supporting reform at Winchester, Mathilda extending and embellishing Quedlinburg, were ensuring the correct
ordering of the mausolea of royalty. We shall find many queens
founding and endowing religious houses as refuges for their own
old age and death. All sponsored a Christianity that in the early

Middle Ages was committed to prayer for king and kingdom. When changing ideas produced accusations that the worship of God was inadequate or ill-directed, as happened in, for example, the tenth century, neither kings nor queens could afford to ignore the threat to their harmonious relations with the Divine. They were inevitably swept into reform movements so long as it was believed that the affairs of Church and kingdom were linked.

This belief affected bishops and abbots as much as kings. They were not simply churchmen, but key figures in the kingdom and the royal court. Queens moved in the world of court politics, seeking allies through the influence and patronage they could dispense. Those regular accusations of adultery between queens and high ecclesiastics signal less a continuing crisis of debauchery than a continuing alliance between royal women and churchmen. The distortions of court intrigue presented these alliances in salacious terms, while adulatory saints' lives spoke of the pious support of an Eadgifu or an Adelaide for the cause of reform. The reality is more complex. Piety existed, but so too did political friendship: queens found a natural outlet in Church patronage, but they chose the recipients of their largesse wisely. The career of Dunstan suggests less a blanket alliance between queens and reform than the support of individual reformers and particular religious houses.

Dunstan dominates the history of tenth-century Anglo-Saxon politics. First abbot of Glastonbury, then bishop of London, and finally archbishop of Canterbury, his ascent through the hierarchy was far from smooth. Dunstan came to court during the reign of King Athelstan, but resentment generated by his aims and influence had led to his expulsion before that king's death. When King Edmund succeeded to the throne Dunstan returned, but not unopposed; moves against him came close to success. Under Edmund's brother Eadred he successfully demonstrated the capacity for attracting massive royal patronage for his plans that must have been one source of his unpopularity. When Eadred was replaced by his nephew Eadwig, Dunstan's enemies, supporters of the young king, ensured his exile from court and kingdom. Dunstan may already have been involved in attempts to place Eadwig's brother Edgar on the throne. When Edgar became king, the bishop's star rose fast. In 975 he was involved in another disputed succession, supporting Edgar's eldest son Edward against the younger Æthelred II. His final years under

Æthelred were not uniformly happy. In over half a century in and around the royal court Dunstan revealed that combination of moral and ecclesiastical reformer with political figure so typical of the churchmen of the early Middle Ages.

Dunstan's career brought him into contact with at least three queens: Eadgifu, mother of Edmund and Eadred; Ælfgifu, the wife of Eadwig; and Ælfthryth, third wife of Edgar and mother of Æthelred II. Even more than his coreformer, Æthelwold, Dunstan was Eadgifu's close ally. Their friendship was struck early and their fortunes became closely intertwined. Both were very important under Eadred; neither wished to relinquish power on his death when disgruntled nobles supported the new king, Eadwig. They became involved in the succession dispute in the early months of Eadwig's reign, acting against the young king and falling from grace. Both were restored by the accession of Edgar. Each found the other a congenial and useful helpmate. Dunstan's opposition to Eadwig incurred the enmity of Queen Ælfgifu, the young king's wife. She may have represented the rival factions that had triumphed on Eadwig's accession, and when Dunstan and his party forced her separation from the king in 958 it was a clear sign that Eadwig was losing ground. The author of the life of Dunstan holds Ælfgifu responsible for Dunstan's exile; some role here is probable. Later, when the influence of the aging grandmother, Eadgifu, was replaced at Edgar's court by that of Ælfthryth, his enemies at court may have found a new leader in the queen. There was little friendship between Ælfthryth and Dunstan. As a moral reformer he could certainly object to the adulterous nature of the marriage, but the sources of tension between them probably went deeper and wider. When Edgar died in 975 Dunstan opposed the claims of Ælfthryth's son Æthelred. When she and her son were victorious, Dunstan suffered partial eclipse.

Dunstan's queens did not oppose or accept monastic reform as such; Ælfthryth was a close friend of Dunstan's coreformer Æthelwold and a patron of monasticism. They opposed or allied with Dunstan for reasons of politics, personality, or preference now too often obscure. The crosscurrents of wider issues focused in the royal court drew queens towards particular churchmen, led them to seek influence in episcopal appointments in order to win and keep allies. Eadgifu persuaded her sons to advance Dunstan and he stood by her in her own crises. Balthild had Genesius elected to the bishopric of

Lyons in 660; together with Audoenus of Rouen, Chrodobert of Paris, and Eligius of Noyon he was a prop to her regency. Brunhild influenced the elections of Desiderius of Auxerre and Aridius of Lyon; Syagrius of Autun was her ally. Aridius was a leader of the anti-Columbanus bishops of Burgundy, and Brunhild's own monastic foundation at Autun followed the Rule of Caesarius, not Columbanus. Here is an added dimension to the great clash over succession and marriage between Brunhild and Columbanus, an offshoot of Brunhild's ecclesiastical alliances.

Queen Making

Ælfthryth crossed swords with Dunstan, but found a friend in Æthelwold of Winchester. Not only did he support the claims of her son Æthelred, but he gave Ælfthryth the intangible benefits of ideology. It was at Æthelwold's Winchester that the iconography of Mary as Queen of Heaven was elaborated in the late tenth century; it was there that the Rule of Life for the reformed English monasteries was written, a rule that laid great stress on the queen's role in supervising nunneries. It was probably at Winchester under Æthelwold that the idea of Ælfthryth's queenly anointing was conceived.

The anointing of Ælfthryth as queen was a momentous change in England in the 970s, although it was merely the adoption of a practice known on the continent from the late ninth century. Anointing transformed a king's wife into a queen, but it was certainly not the only ritual or ceremony that could do so. Not every king's bedfellow became his queen; those who did seem to have enjoyed particular powers at court. Before the use of anointing ceremonies for queens, full marriage appears to have raised a woman to this dignity, though the evidence is far from clear and earlier rituals of enthronement or crowning may have been involved.

The earliest history of king making, before the practice of royal anointing, is obscure; that of the inauguration of queens is a virtual blank. Writers of the sixth to ninth centuries knew a queen when they saw one, but they rarely clarified what they understood by that term, or how a woman rose to the dignity. At the end of the sixth century Gregory of Tours in Merovingian Frankia consistently dif-

127

ferentiates queens from concubines, suggesting that a queen is distinguished by the nature of her union, that is, by the fact that her marriage is full and legitimate. Fredegar's terminology in the early seventh century confirms the impression. Columbanus tells Theuderic that he should raise up children from an honorable queen, not from harlots. When Dagobert took Nantechild in 628 he "took her in matrimony, raised her as queen," and Fredegar lists the women with whom Dagobert indulged his licentiousness as three queens and many concubines. Brunhild was accused of encouraging Theuderic to have concubines, since a queen would deprive Brunhild of power in the royal hall; full marriage entailed a property settlement and control in the household.

Throughout the eighth and ninth centuries *queen* continues to denote at least legitimate wife. Offa of Mercia made his bedfellow Cynethryth a queen. Offa was anxious to secure the succession to the throne for her son Ecgfryth; he underwrote ecclesiastical legislation that confined the royal succession to the children of a legitimate wife. Whatever else the term *queen* meant when applied to Cynethryth it certainly marked her out as properly married. Politics have sometimes obscured the terminology. An early ninth-century confraternity book produced by Adalhard at Corbie, now preserved in the *Reichenau Confraternity Book*, ostensibly lists as *reginae* only those Carolingian women we can show to have been wives, not concubines. But there are two problems: Swanhild is listed as a queen although the *Annales mettenses* call her a concubine; Ruodheid, Pepin of Italy's woman, originally had the title, but it had been scratched out, and her son Bernard is elsewhere termed "son of a concubine." The sons of both women were involved in disputes over power. Bernard, for example, was deprived of the kingdom of Italy by Louis the Pious and it is only in sources associated with Louis's court that Bernard's mother is called a concubine. But complexity is compounded since Adalhard of Corbie was a supporter of Bernard and a kinsman of his mother; his use of the term *queen* to describe Ruodheid may itself be politically motivated. Yet behind the confusion there is some clarity. Both sides felt that *queen* meant "wife": Louis wished to deny that Ruodheid was legitimately married, Adalhard to stress it.

All the early evidence for ceremonies of queen making point to its association with marriage. The first certain anointing of a queen was that of Judith, daughter of Charles the Bald, in 856. It formed part of her marriage ceremony. In 853 Æthelwulf of Wessex gave his daughter Æthelswith to King Burgred of Mercia; she became Burgred's queen at a marriage ceremony celebrated in royal fashion at Chippenham. When Theudelinda married Agilulf in the late sixth century, the marriage was celebrated publicly before the warriors of the Lombard nation on the field of Sardi near Verona. The title of queen was later used to describe her, though it remains debatable whether this ceremony created it.

Queen certainly denoted "wife," but are the two terms interchangeable or was a queen a wife and more beside? In his *Life of Alfred*, written at the end of the ninth century, Asser stated that the ninth-century West Saxon kings did not have queens; by this he certainly did not mean that they were celibate. A century earlier Æthelbald of Mercia had debauched himself with women whom he never married; did West Saxon kings likewise eschew matrimony? Admittedly Archbishop Fulk of Rheims, writing to King Alfred in 890, remarked on the laxity of English morals, on the prevalence of incest and concubinage. But Asser leaves us no room for doubt. West Saxon kings had wives, but not queens; they allowed their women only the title of king's wife and not that of queen; they did not permit them to sit next to the king on the throne of the kingdom. For Asser and perhaps for others the making of a queen entailed more than marriage and had a significance in terms of politics and power that led the West Saxons to shun it.

Asser suggests that a queen should sit on a throne, and many did. The tenth-century West Frankish texts giving the rituals for the consecration of a queen refer to her sitting at the king's right hand. The *Life of Edward the Confessor* describes how normally, even by law, a throne was prepared on which Edith sat at Edward's side, although she often spurned it, preferring to sit at his feet. Although there is no direct evidence before Asser, enthronement may have formed part of early queen-making ceremonies. Crowns and other royal clothes appear much earlier. Merovingian queens wore regal vestments: Clovis's wife was dressed "in the royal manner," Brunhild was "adorned with royal attire." This could mean simply the rich apparel of royalty, but something more formal is suggested when Fridiburg was espoused to Sigibert II and received from him "royal clothing and a crown." Was Fridiburg crowned and invested as part of the ceremonies that led up to her marriage?

In the late sixth century Theudelinda wore a crown that is still preserved at Monza, though crowns could be worn by royal women who had certainly not received them in formal investitures; the queen and princesses were described as wearing crowns in 799 in a Carolingian court poem. Later Carolingians used coronation in queen making, again often associated with marriage. Thegan describes how the pope anointed Louis the Pious as emperor in 816 and at the same time called Ermengard "Augusta" and placed a golden crown upon her head. The *Annales mettenses priores* note that when Louis took Judith as his second wife she was "crowned as empress and acclaimed Augusta by all." Here the coronations were of empresses; Thegan specifically stated that Ermengard became queen at the time of her marriage to Louis. But at the Lotharingian court in the 860s two queens were crowned, Waldrada in 862 and Theutberga in 865; in Waldrada's case as in that of Judith coronation was part of her marriage. By the tenth century the ritual texts show coronation to have been a customary part of queen making.

From the mid-eighth century kings were often, though not invariably, anointed with holy oil at their inauguration. Anointing symbolized the transmission of strength and magical powers, inner transformations. It came to be used in the medieval church to mark the changes of life: baptism, the making of a Christian; priestly consecration, the creation of sacerdotal powers; and later confirmation, the passage into Christian maturity. To anoint a king was, by analogy, to emphasize that he became a new man with enhanced powers. The practice was adopted more slowly for queens. Although it still denoted enhanced powers and an important change of status, the holy oil made a "new woman" for very specific purposes.

The reign of Charles the Bald (840–77) was as crucial for the anointing of queens as we know it to have been for that of kings. Charles had a lively interest in ecclesiastical magic and its utility to the royal family, and this combined with the presence at his court of Hincmar, a great ritual expert, to produce a series of royal consecrations. In 856 Charles decided to have his twelve-year-old daughter Judith anointed queen as part of her marriage to the aging Anglo-Saxon king Æthelwulf. Charles was worried, as we have seen, at the prospect of his daughter living defenseless in a foreign court. The king's wife in Wessex occupied a lowly position and he hoped to enhance that of Judith. Charles might have remembered the problems that his own mother Judith had experienced as a young wife of an elderly husband with adult sons; Æthelwulf too had sons by his previous marriage and Charles wished to hedge his daughter with security. The anointing was partly a fertility rite; Charles wished to see Judith produce sons, for her own survival might depend on them. With a husband over fifty she might require some spiritual aid in the task. And the claims of those future sons required protection against half brothers, who might plague them as they had once plagued the young Charles himself. What better way than to enhance the status of the mother who bore them? When Charles asked Hincmar to take the unprecedented step of anointing Judith as queen he sought long-term security for his daughter. The holy oil was to render her fertile, and by making her in the literal sense a changed woman, blessed by God, suggest that the male offspring of her fertility would be especially entitled to rule.

Charles's line of thought on the anointing of queens led him to request the anointing of his own wife, Ermentrud, in 866. She was already his queen and had been married to Charles for over twenty years. The sole purpose of her consecration was, as we have seen, to ensure heirs who would be suitable to rule the kingdom. Charles was dissatisfied with his earlier male progeny. Not only did he wish for more and better, but to have new sons whose rights of inheritance would be strong. Once again a ceremony that made of Ermentrud a divinely blessed, new woman suited the king's purposes exactly. These anointings served less to transfer powers to a queen than to underline her function as the producer of heirs to the throne. There is one earlier queen who may have been consecrated: Bertha, wife of the first Carolingian king, Pepin. Her anointing in 751 would have been part of a series of ceremonies that confirmed the transference of royal power to the Carolingians, and covered their usurpation of kingship from the Merovingians. The Franks were no longer to choose kings "from the loins of another." To consecrate the mother of the Carolingian sons, to stress that she too was divinely chosen, would have made excellent sense. These earliest instances of queenly anointing show them to have been devised less for the queen herself than for the throneworthiness of her sons.

It was in West Frankia that the consecration of queens first became standard practice in the tenth century. No English queen can be proved to have been anointed between Judith and Ælfthryth, and in tenth-century Germany only the empresses Adelaide and Theophanu were consecrated. Yet in West Frankia Charles the Simple's first wife, Frederun, had been anointed before 917, Gerberga was consecrated "with holy chrism" immediately after her marriage to Louis d'Outremer in 939, and the actions of Emma in 923 underline the importance attached to the ceremony. Emma's husband, King Ralph, was a usurper in 923, displacing the captive Charles the Simple. Emma went out of her way to secure her own consecration at the hands of the Archbishop of Rheims. When individual kings and dynasties were beleaguered by rivals, when they were attacked and even deposed during their tenure of office, when their sons could not look forward confidently to inheritance, any ritual that set the royal family apart was important.

The anointing of a queen and the special claims that the son of an anointed queen might enjoy mattered in tenth-century Frankia and had a similar significance in eighth- and ninth-century Mercia. Mercian kings from the time of Offa were concerned to stress the throneworthiness of their sons. During the ninth century the situation became critical, as a series of different families disputed the Mercian throne. Few kings were succeeded by members of their own family, let alone their own sons. Faced with a need to guarantee the future, Mercian kings followed a path similar to that of tenth-century French royalty. They may not have anointed their queens, but they raised them to a position of great importance in the kingdom. Offa raised Cynethryth as his queen to buttress the claims of her son Ecgfryth; she appears in many of Offa's charters, and coins were issued in her name to celebrate the anointing of her son—the only coins struck in the name of any early queen outside Italy. Cynethryth was merely the first of a series of ninth-century Mercian queens who stood in the forefront of politics. Once adopted, the tradition acquired a life of its own. In neither Mercia nor West Frankia could kings afford not to emphasize their wives' queenly dignity, for such a failure would have ceded an important argument to their rivals.

Asser's remarks on West Saxon queens, or rather the lack of them, may acquire new meaning. Designating a wife as queen was part of a political strategy of succession; it did not uniquely determine the succession, but it buttressed claims. In 975 supporters of Æthelred II were to argue that he had more right to the throne than his half brother Edward because his mother, and not Edward's, had been consecrated as queen. When rival families aspired to the throne or a second wife needed strength for the claims of her sons, the designation of queens as women uniquely capable of producing royal heirs was one means of action. But it had its disadvantages. It could lower the status of subsequent marriages and of the children issuing from them, and by giving hope of succession to particular sons could sour relations within the royal family to the point of rebellion. Since the queen enjoyed an enhanced position at court, she could more readily acquire a faction in favor of her children and contribute further to tension in the royal dynasty. If the presence of prowling rivals outweighed such disadvantages for Mercians and French, they may have convinced the West Saxons, who suffered from family tension in plenty, that a queen seated beside their king was no pretty sight.

When the West Saxons finally adopted the practice of anointing queens in 973 it was in circumstances that combined the traditions of West Frankia and the glittering example of the Ottonian empresses with a particular English situation. As Edgar's third wife, with an older stepson and a young child of her own, Ælfthryth and her Winchester allies wished to stress the legitimacy of mother and son. Æthelwold of Winchester's *Benedictional*, a beautifully illuminated manuscript, contains one of the earliest representations of Mary crowned as Queen of Heaven. The image was one that also occurred in Ottonian Germany, where the imperial coronations of Otto I and II and their wives contributed to the model for the imperial consecration of Edgar and Ælfthryth in 973. The ritual used for Ælfthryth's consecration was that which had developed in West Frankia. It still bore the marks of its origin and standard use in the marriage ceremony; although Ælfthryth had been married for eight years, she received a ring as a sign of faith. The older coronation practice had been incorporated—the queen was crowned with the crown of eternal glory—but central to all, and associated specifically with the pouring of oil itself, were prayers for fertility and suitable heirs. As the bishop poured the oil on Ælfthryth's head in the presence of the great nobles, he blessed and consecrated her for her share in the royal bed.

By the early eleventh century the consecration of West European queens was standard and no longer reflected contemporary circumstance. The origins of the practice lay in the requirements of fertility and succession, and even before anointing, such ideas must have played a role in the ceremonies that made a queen. Queens enjoyed other powers at court as a result of their position, powers the West Saxons preferred to dispense with. The West Saxons personified their dislike of queens in the character of Eadburh. This early ninth-century queen of Wessex allegedly dominated her husband's court and poisoned his counsellors; the experience of her career was the excuse that Alfred used when he explained to Asser why the West Saxons had no queen. Such individuals played their part in forming traditions of queenship and its powers. Charles the Bald recalled the fate of his mother and had his daughter anointed. Henry I of France remembered his mother, Constance, without affection, and kept his own wives Mathilda and Anne in low profile. Yet Mathilda and Anne were consecrated queens. Anointing may have brought advantages, but they were most clearly marked in those political circumstances that saw the original adoption of consecration. Emma or Gerberga in the tenth century were powerful queens less because of their consecration than because the dynastic insecurity, the nature of contemporary warfare, and their own families created their opportunities. Anointing was a product of their situation rather than a cause of it. A queen received little formal power through consecration, which was designed more for the benefit of the dynasty than of herself. Insofar as it helped her son it could not fail to help her, but it was only one of a series of factors that could make queens influential during their husbands' lifetime.

Italy and Queens

In Italy personality, politics, and tradition combined to allow queens of the ninth and tenth centuries more active roles than in most European countries. Adelaide's power had Italian roots, which fed on the strength of Angelberga and earlier women. Angelberga married the future emperor Louis II about 851; at least she entered his bed, possibly originally as a concubine, at about this date. She was still there at his death in 875, surviving an abortive divorce and the misfortune of producing only two daughters. Her origins lay in the important Supponide clan, and its strength and rivalries dogged her footsteps. When Louis tried to replace her by a new queen in 872, the attempt involved the family of Winigis, who had lost the duchy of Spoleto to the Supponides. Louis had been crowned and anointed before his father's death, so that Angelberga's coronation as empress was delayed until the accession of Pope Nicholas I in 858; from 861 onward she was often referred to as "sharing in the imperial rule" of Louis, though this is no true indication of formal powers. As early as the late 850s Angelberga's influence was clear. She was an advocate of her brother-in-law Lothar II and urged her husband and the pope to support Lothar's divorce. In 860 she was at Louis's side in his campaign in southern Italy. She negotiated with Charles the Bald and Louis the German on behalf of the hapless Lothar. In 871 and 72 she was Louis's regent in northern Italy, in which capacity she convoked and presided over a council of nobles at Ravenna, and arranged to meet her husband's uncles to discuss the Italian succession. After quashing Louis's divorce and remarriage in 872 she remained in southern Italy as regent at Capua, concluded the punitive expedition Louis had begun, and herself led back the southern Italian hostages and relics in 874. No area of Louis's rule escaped her. She consistently supported Bishop John of Ravenna against successive popes, an episode in the long struggle between Rome and Ravenna. When Eleutherius, son of the imperial envoy Anastasius, carried off the daughter of Pope Hadrian II, Angelberga presided at the tribunal that judged him and carefully protected Anastasius himself. Archbishops and bishops sought her aid; Louis the German appealed to her in his attempts to gain the pallium for the bishop of Cologne. She intervened in charters, and coins were struck in the joint names of Louis and Angelberga.

The death of Louis brought no sudden end to her position. It was she who called the Council of Pavia in 875 to decide the succession of the sonless emperor; no claimant to the Italian throne in the 870s ignored the power she represented. Louis the German, Carloman, Charles the Fat, Berengar, and Arnulf all in turn courted Angelberga and confirmed her property. In 877 she was the center of a faction opposing the claims of Charles the Bald, bringing together at her monastery of San Salvatore old supporters like Wigbod of Parma, the archbishop of Milan, and the bishop of Brescia. If she did plan to gain the succession for her own son-in-law Boso of Vienne, she was unsuccessful, but Charles the Fat was wary enough of her power and schemes to exile her to the Swiss nunnery of Zurzach while he established his rights to the imperial crown. As late as 887 Angelberga was still trying to influence the course of the Italian succession, first attempting to persuade the dying Charles the Fat to designate her grandson Louis, then supporting Berengar in his struggle against Guy of Spoleto. Only after 888 does she disappear from the political scene, retiring to the enjoyment of her extensive properties, living in the nunnery she had founded at Piacenza, at last not only "the most glorious and excellent empress" but truly now "the most serene."

Angelberga's power, like that of Adelaide, originated in her family. Its importance determined her choice as bride for Louis and it was still close to her in her final years when she made her will. Twenty prominent years in the Italian court brought her many allies, and the family struggles of the third- and fourth-generation Carolingians provided an arena for her activity. Although she had no sons, a fact which proved her final undoing, she was deeply concerned in the questions of succession. Yet her involvement in the politics of inheritance was not inevitable, even less so her role as regent during Louis's campaigns. Other queens without sons sank into deep obscurity and few exercised powers of regency during their husbands' lifetimes. Angelberga made fruitful use of the dissensions of the Carolingian family and the intricacies of ecclesiastical rivalry, but no ninth-century Carolingian queen north of the Alps was able to exploit these opportunities in the same way. The strength of Angelberga's personality is writ large across her activities. She seized the possibilities and in doing so helped transform the future role of Italian queens. But as an Italian queen she may have been at an initial advantage, enjoying a position that her vigorous character maximized.

From the sixth century onward a series of great queens march across the Italian stage: Amalasuntha, Theudelinda, Gundiperga, Ansa, Angelberga, Ageltrudis, Willa, Adelaide, and Theophanu. The history is not continuous, and most of the Lombard queens between Gundiperga and Ansa were insignificant. However, from the ninth century onward stronger traditions of powerful queens developed and profoundly influenced the position of Adelaide and Theophanu in the late tenth century.

Amalasuntha, Theudelinda, and Gundiperga are usually remembered as dowagers who allegedly transferred royal power to their second husbands. It has been argued that these sixth- and seventh-century queens enjoyed formal powers of regency; that although their sex excluded them from personal rule, they acted as vessels of royal power that they transferred to nonroyal husbands. The individual cases are less clear cut. Amalasuntha was daughter of King Theoderic, the Ostrogoth, and a member of the royal Amal family. Her second husband, who became king after marriage, was Theodahad. But Theodahad was her cousin, himself an Amal by birth, with strong claims that marriage to a royal widow merely strengthened. Amalasuntha, far from being a powerful regent, was in a very weak position once Theodahad had acquired the throne. She was imprisoned and murdered by her new husband soon after the marriage. These Ostrogothic and Lombard queens belong with the sixth-century Frankish royal widows already discussed, married by usurpers for their following, their claims, their treasure, and their expertise. On the death of Hygelac, his widowed queen Hygd had offered Beowulf the kingdom and the treasure, not as a formal regent but in the anxious hope of salvaging her own position. Royal widows were important in the insecure kingships of the sixth and seventh centuries; here is no secure basis for the power of later Italian queens.

Italy was more deeply influenced by Rome and Byzantium than any other part of early Europe. Empresses like Theodora exercised an official part in the Byzantine state: their names appeared on the state seal, they were referred to jointly with the emperor in the preambles to decrees, and received together with their husbands the oaths of officials. Lombard Italy knew and copied Byzantine etiquette. But titles can be empty of power. Similar formal praise was lavished on Visigothic queens, whose political role was virtually nil. Reccared I's wife, for example, was addressed with the Byzantine title "most excellent." Knowledge of Byzantine practice cannot have hindered, but did little to help, Italian queens. Late Roman law laid a firmer basis for Italian women in general.

Early Italy lived under a mixture of Lombard and Italian legal and social custom. Where Lombard law bothers to specify the position of women, it gives a picture of restricted action and severely limited property rights. But surviving Lombard codes say little about widows and married women. Late Roman law guaranteed extensive female property rights. A married woman could hold property distinct from that of her husband and under her own control, her right to that property after the dissolution of marriage was maintained, and a widow's claim to control *all* her dead husband's possessions was defended. This may be the foundation for the undoubted powers of female regents in some of the dukedoms of Lombard Italy. In the late seventh century Theuderada, widow of Romuald of Beneventum, ruled Beneventum in the name of her son Grimoald II, and Scanniperga was regent of that same duchy for her son Liutprand from 751. By the mid-eighth century the Lombard laws of King Liutprand were indicating a distinct improvement in female property rights, enabling legitimate daughters to succeed to land where earlier codes had preferred the claims of male collaterals and bastards.

Such rights to own and dispose of property helped queens like Angelberga acquire great accumulations of land. Louis II made over twelve grants of land to his wife, an almost unprecedented endowment of a queen during the life of her husband. In her will in 877 Angelberga disposed of more than twenty manors to her nunnery of San Sixtus at Piacenza. Ageltrudis received grants from her husband Guy and her son Lambert. These large-scale endowments of Italian queens culminated in the tenth century in the possessions of an empress like Adelaide. The grants made by Hugh and Lothar to Adelaide and her mother, coupled with later acquisitions from Otto I, placed a large proportion of the Italian royal demesne in Adelaide's hands—more than thirty-seven large royal manors, most of which she tried to use to endow San Salvatore in Pavia. It is no surprise that Otto II felt that his mother's support would be a significant prop in the peninsula. Late ninth- and tenth-century Italian noblewomen in general had achieved enviable powers based on rights of property and regency. Bertha of Tuscany, Ermengard of Ivrea, Theodora and Marozia in Rome, ruled as regents after their husbands' deaths, sometimes to the exclusion of their sons. So great had these property rights become that in 1037 Conrad II felt it necessary to restrict them. In his *Edict concerning the Benefices of the Kingdom of Italy* he excluded women and cognates from feudal inheritance. These rights had provided a formal basis for the power and regency of queens like Angelberga.

Italian queens of the late ninth and tenth centuries were hailed in the official documents as "consorts in power"—*consors regni*. Although the title does not indicate formal juridical powers of corule, as once was thought, it is a tribute to these women and especially to the way Angelberga and others transformed the role of queens. The origins of the title were literary and antiquarian, borrowed from biblical and Roman sources to compliment kings and queens. At the Italian court of the Carolingian Lothar I the title was adopted as propaganda for Lothar against Louis the Pious, used to suggest that the king's oldest son was joint ruler with his father. At this date it was only occasionally applied to Lothar's queen, Ermengard. It was the doughty Angelberga who ensured the survival of the title and its application to queens. In the royal documents of the 860s it was used to describe her, and her actions politicized it, filled it with meaning. Applied to Angelberga, it seemed a fitting description of the reality of her power and was permanently adopted by the Italian chancery to describe queens and empresses. It remained a mere title, applied to the greatest and the least of royal women, to an Adelaide or an Anna. It was never a legal term. But its adoption in Italy is one more sign of the tradition of queenship that grew up there.

Adelaide and Theophanu were Ottonian empresses; their power had a German dimension and origin, but they exercised it most fully in Italy. Here their interventions in charters were most regular; here Theophanu as regent used an imperial seal with her own name, dated charters by her own regnal year, issued two imperial documents in her own name and was called by the title *imperator* in one of them. Even before their husbands' deaths, it was in Italy that Adelaide and Theophanu appeared to best advantage. The recognition of female rights in the peninsula enabled them to benefit from the fact that their husbands controlled two kingdoms, Germany and Italy. The Ottonians required regents in one kingdom, and a tradition that accepted female rule granted their queens this regency in Italy. At the beginning of the eleventh century the English queen Emma achieved a prominence under her second husband, Cnut, that she had never enjoyed under Æthelred. Cnut had married her partly because of her knowledge of English politics; she benefited from his control of three kingdoms and from his absences in Scandinavia. Cnut made his first wife Ælfgifu and her young son Swegn his regents in Norway; he may have given similar powers to Emma in England. Tenth-century England, like Italy, gave women wide rights to hold and inherit land. They disposed of land by will and by gift; they defended their landholding in court; they granted land to female kin at the expense of the male and called on other women as legal witnesses and pledges. In such a context queens like Eadgifu and Ælfthryth had developed a tradition of activity that made Emma's role in the eleventh century acceptable in English life.

The presence or absence of such traditions of female power determined the possibilities open to individual queens. Property and regency rights created an Italian situation that Angelberga exploited to the full. Her personal dynamism was soon followed by that of Ageltrudis during the reigns of her husband and son in the 890s, and between them they created a fact of female rule that later helped Adelaide and Theophanu. The deliberate prevention of such prominence for West Saxon queens in the ninth century contributed to the obscurity of their successors. Conversely, a century of Mercian queens culminated in the prominent reign of Æthelflæd at the beginning of the tenth century. Mercian queens were brought to the forefront of politics as a part of the strategies of succession. Throughout the ninth century a number of Mercian queens, now no more than names, stand beside their husbands in the charters, making grants of land jointly with the king. This shadowy power of a Sæthryth or an Æthelswith was the basis for the remarkable career of Æthelflæd, lady of the Mercians.

This daughter of the West Saxon king Alfred was married in the 880s to the virtually independent ruler of Mercia, Æthelred, lord of the Mercians, king in all but name. Together with her husband, Æthelflæd ensured the survival of Mercia against Viking attacks; jointly they made grants to the old churches of Mercia; jointly they moved the relics of Saint Oswald to Gloucester. When Æthelred died in 911, Æthelflæd ruled Mercia in her own right. She organized the building and defense of fortifications such as those at Bridgenorth, Tamworth, Stafford, and Warwick. She sent an avenging army into Wales, which appropriately brought back a Welsh king's wife as hostage. She recaptured the Viking strongholds of Derby and Leicester, and at the height of her power in 918 the people of York bowed to her rule with oaths and with pledges, joining an alliance of the kings and rulers of northern England that she had masterminded. She died on 12 June 918 at Tamworth, "in the eighth year in which she held lawful dominion over the Mercians." After her death her brother, Edward the Elder, King of Wessex, planned to take personal control of Mercia. Some of the Mercians had other plans and raised Æthelflæd's daughter Ælfwyn to rule over them. Edward had to forcibly deprive her of authority three weeks before Christmas in 918. The tradition of Mercian queenship found its fullest expression in these extraordinary examples of women who ruled in their own right.

Queens enjoy exceptional opportunities as royal counsellors, arbiters of royal patronage, the foremost allies of a king at a time of insecurity. But their power should not be divorced from that of other women; societies that favor and permit female rights at all levels offer the greatest opportunities to queens. Angelberga and her successors in Italy were paralleled by a host of duchesses and countesses; Ælfthryth and Emma in England had property rights shared by all their sisters. Adelaide and Theophanu in Germany belong with royal women like Mathilda of Quedlinburg, Sophia, Adelaide, and a host of other aristocratic abbesses. Even where inheritance practices did not apparently favor women, these Ottonian abbesses show how the tendency of women to outlive men in a violent age bring into their hands accumulations of land that cannot fail to guarantee their importance.

A combination of Italian legal and personal traditions, French dynastic insecurity, Ottonian family and Church politics, and a movement of Church reform throughout Europe made the 900s a century of women. For a brief period in the 980s Western Europe was ruled by queen-regents. In England the underage Æthelred II was under his mother's tutelage until 985. Theophanu ruled from 984 as regent in the Ottonian Empire for her young son Otto III. Adelaide, briefly regent in 984, held vast estates and power in Italy throughout the decade. In France her daughter Emma was regent for the young Louis V until 987, while in the neighboring duchy of Lorraine the dowager duchess Beatrice ruled for her minor son. When the wily Hugh Capet wished to treat with Theophanu in 988, he suggested a meeting, not with himself, but with his wife, Adelaide. On the death of Otto II in 983, custody of his infant, Otto III, had been claimed by an uncle, Henry of Bavaria. Henry's revolt escalated beyond a mere demand for regency, and probably entailed a bid for the throne on his own behalf. Adelaide and Theophanu won the struggle for tutelage, and in 985 Henry's revolt was finally ended. Its final resolution was confirmed in that year at a meeting of the female regents of northern Europe, at a *colloquium dominarum*—a veritable Diet of Dowagers. The 980s mark an apogee, but of a significant type of female rule. These were mostly dowagers, not queens. Although women could and did rule beside their husbands, their stature often increased after his death. It was often succession questions that drew queens into the center of court politics; it was as dowager queen mother and regent that a woman might hope for greatest influence.

Chapter 6 👑 *Queen Mother*

Clotild, wife of Clovis, died in 548, a venerable old lady in her seventies. Widowhood had occupied the largest portion of her long life; the death of Clovis in 511 left her thirty-seven years of dowagerhood. Clotild's may not be quite a record. Æthelflæd of Damerham, whom King Edmund married not long before his own death in 946, survived him by at least thirty, possibly more than forty years. Æthelred II's widow, Emma, died in 1052 after packing another lifetime's excitement into the thirty-six years she outlived him. Æthelred's own mother, Ælfthryth, had survived King Edgar by twenty-seven years or so, while his great-grandmother Eadgifu died no earlier than the mid-960s, over forty years after Edward the Elder. The empress Adelaide outlived her first husband by half a century, and her second, Otto I, by twenty-six years. Otto's own mother Mathilda was a dowager for thirty-three years. Brunhild and her archenemy Fredegund carried their feud into widowhood, but whereas Fredegund survived Chilperic I by a mere thirteen years, Brunhild outlived husband, son, and grandsons, not to mention Fredegund herself, to pay a bitter price for her longevity and thirty-eight years of widowhood.

Not all queens outlived their husbands. Charlemagne survived all his legitimate wives and Æthelred II was probably a widower when he married Emma in 1002. The dangers of childbirth made no distinction between queens and commoners, and queens too were prey to the diseases of their times. Ermengard, first wife of Louis the Pious, was probably not much over forty when she predeceased her husband in 818; Louis achieved a ripe age, surviving her by twenty-one years to die at the age of sixty-two. These early Carolingians were long-lived. Louis's own father, Charlemagne, passed seventy, his eldest son Lothar I reached sixty, outliving his wife Ermengard by three years, while Louis the German lived to be seventy and died in the same year as his wife, Emma. But in general a combination of female longevity, the violent deaths of kings, and the practice of re-marriage made the dowager queen a familiar figure.

Many queens reached the age of sixty or even seventy. Clotild, wife of Clovis; Radegund, repudiated queen of Clothar I; Ingoberga, widow of Charibert I—all achieved seventy or more. Mathilda and Adelaide in tenth-century Germany approached this age: Adelaide had turned sixty-eight when she died, and it is possible that Mathilda had reached seventy. Ultrogotha, Brunhild, the tenth-century English queen Eadgifu, and Queen Emma, widow of Cnut and Æthelred II, all topped sixty. Female longevity was a fact of the early Middle Ages as of other periods, though it is still difficult to credit the chronology that would leave Wærburh, widow of Ceolred of Mercia, to die an abbess in 782, 107 years after the death of her own father. Not all women reached a ripe old age; some died young but still had lengthy widowhoods. Theophanu was a widow for eigh-teen years even though she probably died in her forties; Fredegund passed away when only a little over fifty, but still outlived Chilperic by thirteen years. Many kings died young, often in violent circum-stances, to leave young widows and infant sons. Otto II was only twenty-eight when he succumbed to illness in 983 and left Theo-phanu with four children, the eldest of whom was no more than eight. Chilperic's life was cut short by an assassin's dagger. The En-glish king Edgar died when only thirty-two; his brother Eadwig was no more than nineteen at his death in 959, while their father Ed-mund was stabbed to death by a robber at his own court when a mere twenty-six. All three condemned their wives to widowhood. Murder carried off other kings besides Chilperic and Edmund; Brunhild's long years as a dowager were the product of the as-sassination of her husband Sigibert in 575.

Battle, which might be thought of as a major cause of early death for kings, is insignificant when compared to hunting, which claimed many lives. Edmund had narrowly escaped a hunting accident at Cheddar Gorge in his early twenties before he was stabbed in his own household. Aistulf, king of the Lombards, died in a hunting ac-cident in 756. Louis II of Italy was badly gored and rumored dead, while his cousin Charles, son of Charles the Bald, received a blow on the head from a sword during a hunt which resulted in debilita-tion and finally death. Lambert of Spoleto met an early end; he died of the wounds sustained when he fell from his horse in a hunt at

Marengo in 898. A similar fall from his mount while pursuing a wolf ended Louis d'Outremer's life in 954 at the age of thirty-three. Louis's own grandson Louis V ended the Carolingian line in West Frankia when he died in a hunting accident while still in his early twenties, in 987. The crude scenes sculpted on Merovingian sarcophagi depicting fathers and sons involved in the chase are a graphic reminder of the perils of the hunt. This noble sport engrossed so large a proportion of kings' lives that the number of accidents it produced should come as no surprise. Like other causes of early death, violent or peaceful, it left an undue preponderance of widows: the life of the medieval noble male was that of a widow maker. When Louis d'Outremer married Gerberga she was probably the older partner, yet as a result of his premature demise she outlived him by twelve years, to die when she herself was little more than fifty. Louis's grandson Louis V had been forced into a marriage with a widow several years older than himself, a marriage which soon ended, yet his repudiated wife outlived by twenty-odd years the young man cut off in his prime.

The marriage practices of kings also tilted the scales in favor of widows. Louis the Pious reached a good age at sixty-two; his second wife Judith died probably before she was forty. But Judith outlived her husband by three years, since he had married her when he was already forty-one and she still a girl. Judith's granddaughter and namesake long survived her husband, Æthelwulf, no surprise since their marriage took place when he was fifty and she twelve. Otto I did not die young—if he had not reached sixty he was approaching that age. Adelaide survived him partly because she was his second wife, married at twenty-one to a man of forty. Adelaide was more comparable in age to Otto's own son by his first marriage, Liudolf, though the accidents of mortality dictated that she long outlive both. Charles the Simple took Eadgifu as a second wife when he was about forty and she no more than eighteen; both lived to be fifty or so, but the disparity of their ages left Eadgifu twenty years and more of widowhood. Edward the Elder married *his* Eadgifu when he was at least forty; she was his third wife, perhaps no more than twenty herself. Forty years of widowhood was the result.

Faced with a flood of widows and given its own doctrines on sex and marriage, the Church favored a life of prayerful celibacy as the correct condition for the female bereaved. For the royal widow this generally meant entry into a nunnery, where many ended their days in peaceful retreat. Most noble widows faced a choice, not always their own, between the life of religion and remarriage, but relatively few queens took the second option. The most difficult course was an active secular life without a man. Women at all levels of society found this path fraught with dangers and problems, and few queens tried to retain power in their own right. But a man need not be a husband; he might preferably be a son. Widows could continue to be influential and active outside religion as mothers rather than wives. This was not only a possible method of survival, but a route to even greater power; many queens reach the height of their careers not as wives of royal husbands but as mothers and regents for young royal sons.

When Sigibert I was assassinated in 575 Brunhild had been married to him for a mere nine years, by no means years of powerlessness and inactivity. Her enemy Ursio supposedly taunted Brunhild in 581 that though she had governed in her husband's day, he and his supporters would now control her young son. In fact Brunhild's greatest days were still to dawn. After a brief flirtation and marriage with her nephew Merovech, she linked her fate with that of her five-year-old son Childebert. During the years before Childebert's majority in 585 she shared power with Gogo, her son's indispensable noble protector. Later stories of enmity between Gogo and Brunhild and accusations that she murdered him are wildly inaccurate, though they may preserve something of the inevitable tensions between these two would-be regents. Paradoxically, and in distinction to the experience of most dowager queens, Brunhild's position became stronger with her son's coming of age. The minority of an infant king brought danger and advantage in equal measure to his mother; if she could retain influence over an adult son, both could act with greater freedom and independence from noble tutelage. With Childebert beside her, of age but still susceptible to her influence, Brunhild entered into an almost equal partnership in power, pursuing her old feud against Fredegund, controlling Church appointments, protecting and fostering those allies on whom both she and Childebert depended. Her son's marriage to Faileuba disturbed his mother's role but little. Brunhild eclipsed the new queen, and it was she who profited from the death of Childebert in 596, at the youthful age of twenty-six.

Childebert left two sons, the half brothers Theudebert, son of a concubine and now aged ten, and Theuderic, Faileuba's child and a mere nine years of age. Their grandmother became regent for both. Theudebert's majority in A.D. 600 ended her influence in Austrasia; the young king came under the sway of noble factions hostile to his grandmother, and his own gesture of independence may have been marriage to Bilichild, Brunhild's former slave. The enmity between Brunhild and her granddaughter-in-law expressed itself in a long and bitter war of poisonous taunts and countertaunts. Brunhild was expelled from Theudebert's court. The story of the pathetic old lady wandering the roads of Frankia unrecognized is a legendary elaboration, but Brunhild certainly found herself forced to take refuge in Burgundy, with her other grandson, Theuderic. Her actions there show that she had lost none of her taste for queenly power and its continued exercise. It was allegedly at her suggestion that Theuderic eschewed marriage and took only concubines.

Brunhild may have doubted her capacity to eclipse another Faileuba, and she must have feared that Theuderic's queen might prove a second, aggressive Bilichild. Age made her even less inclined to risk a fall from power. She took care to secure control of her great-grandsons: the heirs to the throne were her only hope for the future. It is possible that she played a part in the war between her grandsons, legitimizing if not stirring up Theuderic's actions against his half brother with stories of Theudebert's illegitimate birth, begotten by a gardener, not a king. Theuderic's death in 613 of dysentery at the age of twenty-seven exposed Brunhild once more to the harshness of Merovingian politics. Her last attempt to rule through her great-grandson Sigibert, then aged eleven, foundered. The noble support essential to securing any succession was not forthcoming: Austrasian separatism brought in Clothar II, son of her age-old enemy Fredegund, against her. Her great-grandsons were captured and all but one murdered. Brunhild at the end of her long life found herself without husband, son, or grandson to protect her, left friendless to pay the bill for the power game they had all pursued in partnership with her.

Brunhild inherited the prizes and the problems of widowhood. She extended her political career some thirty-eight years after the death of her husband, exercising the quasi-regal powers of queen mother and regent during the minorities of her grandsons. A series of premature deaths were a key to opportunities but also to difficulties. Only her ability to marshal noble backing secured and maintained her regencies; when that backing failed, when the sands of noble faction shifted beneath her, Brunhild stood in danger of destruction. An adult king was a safer partner, but only as long as he proved friendly and amenable: Childebert hearkened to his mother's voice, Theudebert threw his grandmother out. Brunhild's survival depended on male descendants and on her utility to them. If kings were insecure, queens and queen mothers who lacked the formal protection of kingship were more so.

Brunhild's was not a unique career. Eadgifu married Edward the Elder, King of the English, early in the tenth century. Their marriage was probably little more than six years old when Edward died in 924, leaving Eadgifu with two infant sons: Edmund, two or three years old, and Eadred, even younger. Eadgifu had been Edward's third wife, and at least three half brothers stood between her own sons and the succession. Edward's death precipitated a struggle that first divided the kingdom between two of those half brothers, then brought it together in the hands of the older of them, the thirty-year-old king Athelstan. What part, if any, Eadgifu and her sons played in these events we shall never know. But before Athelstan's death in 939, Eadgifu had maneuvered herself into a better position. If she did not actually secure the succession for her own son Edmund, she had certainly already made a powerful friend in the future archbishop, Dunstan. The accession of Edmund brought her a power that she had never had under her stepson Athelstan, and one that she never enjoyed under her husband Edward. Edmund was adult at his accession, and married twice during his brief reign, which ended at his death at the age of about twenty-six, in 946. Eadgifu eclipsed Edmund's wives as successfully as Brunhild had dominated Faileuba.

When Edmund died, his young sons, Eadwig, aged five, and Edgar, aged three, were passed over in favor of their uncle Eadred. Eadgifu cannot have been sorry to see the accession of her younger son, and may have played a part in bringing it about. Certainly Eadgifu's position remained dominant under Eadred: she advanced and backed her own allies, including Dunstan himself, and no wife was brought to court to rival the queen mother. But Eadred himself died after a protracted illness in his early thirties, and Eadgifu found herself in real peril. Her elder grandson, Eadwig, already of age, declared his independence and secured his position by an immediate marriage to a young woman of royal descent. As the young king looked for the support of nobles disappointed in the politics of previous reigns, Eadgifu and her allies like Dunstan were pushed aside; they were part of the factions now fallen from power as a new king effected a palace revolution. If she had not already done so, Eadgifu now began to back the claims of her younger grandson, the thirteen-year-old Edgar. Hostility between Eadwig and his grandmother mounted to flashpoint: Eadgifu fell from power, deprived of all her lands, her ally Dunstan exiled. Edgar retained sufficient support to turn a struggle for the throne into a division of the kingdom in which he gained Mercia and Northumbria. When Eadwig met a sudden death in 959 before his twentieth year, Edgar secured the whole kingdom, and his grandmother was rewarded by the restoration of her lands. But Eadgifu was not crucial to Edgar. He had other supporters, and when he married an ambitious wife in 965, Eadgifu sank into obscurity. It must be said that his sympathy and gratitude at least allowed her to die in dignity and peace.

The careers of Brunhild and Eadgifu are separated by three and a half centuries, but they touch at point after point, except that happily Eadgifu does not share Brunhild's tragic end. Early deaths provided opportunities for influence over sons and grandsons. Influence was secured by the deployment of allies enlisted during careers in the royal household. Both minorities and majorities threatened both women, and sudden death brought rapid reversals of fortune. Yet these accidents also combined in both cases with an obvious ability to take the tide at its flow, and brought both women long if checkered careers.

Here was the apotheosis of queenly power. To judge from the evidence of the charters, Eadgifu was constantly with her two sons when they were kings and she ranked high among their closest counsellors. Brunhild and Childebert worked together in the same way. Yet it was as regent for her underage grandsons that Brunhild's actions, within the limits of the possible and desirable, were freest. When Otto II died in 983 at the tender age of twenty-eight he left his Greek widow, Theophanu, still young and vigorous and the infant Otto III not quite three years old. Otto III's claims to the throne had already been acknowledged in 982, when his father's opponents had secured his crowning at Verona during Otto II's lifetime. The potential rival was his cousin, Duke Henry of Bavaria. Henry made a bid for regency and control of the young Otto, which many interpreted as an attempt to gain the throne for himself. The years 983 to 984 saw a struggle for regency and tutelage of the child-king. The struggle was won by the women of the royal family, by Adelaide his grandmother and Theophanu his mother, with the aid of their own followers and erstwhile counsellors of Otto II. By the summer of 984 Otto III had been committed to the control of his grandmother and mother, soon to that of Theophanu alone, whose maternal rights were recognized as greater. The women of the Ottonian house always played a substantial role, but Theophanu now entered into a regency which cast her earlier days of glory under Otto II into shadow. She became the invariable counsellor of her infant son, thus in reality the controller of his empire. She was formally associated with him in all his documents and actions; foreign rulers negotiated with her; the Capetian claimants to the West Frankish throne lobbied for her support. In Italy she issued charters in her own name; in one she was even styled "Emperor." Theophanu's power was the peak of dowager achievement, regency in the fullest sense of the word.

Theophanu's was a formal regency; Italian and Merovingian history provide other instances of female regents with clear and open powers. Nantechild, widow of Dagobert, was regent for her minor son, Clovis II, from 639 until her death in 642. She subscribed to her son's charters and called royal councils, like the one at Orleans, where she arranged the appointment of Flaochad as mayor of the palace. Balthild, Clovis II's own queen, ruled as regent for Clothar III from 657 until she was forcibly removed in 664–65; she played a central part in the ecclesiastical politics of these years. Himnechild was not mother but mother-in-law of Childeric II, who had married her daughter, his own cousin Bilichild. The marriage was part of an alliance between kingdoms, and those who supported that alliance also supported the regency of Himnechild for her son-in-law. The formal position of queen-regents in Merovingian Frankia was reflected in the eighth century in the career of Plectrud, the widow of the Carolingian mayor of the palace Pepin. Plectrud took over his powers as mayor of the palace on behalf of her young grandsons, and together with those children "ruled under her wise direction both the king and all other things." Formal regency has already been seen in ninth-century Italy, where Ageltrudis, for example, called councils and gave judgments in the name of her son Lambert between 894 and 898. Theophanu and Adelaide were heirs to these traditions in tenth-century Italy.

We may be searching for too great a constitutional precision in distinguishing such regency from the engrossing roles played by queen mothers such as Eadgifu, though it is difficult to find her exercising any of the formal powers of a Theophanu, easier to define her position as one of dominant influence. Gerberga played such a role in the first years of Lothar's reign; Lothar moved nowhere and did little without his mother at his side. This was the part Lothar's own queen Emma must have hoped to play under her son Louis V, though she was to be bitterly disappointed. Ælfthryth dominated the early years of Æthelred II's reign, and Emma stood at the side of Harthacnut during his brief rule from 1040 to 1042. Such a position hung on the precariousness of a king and the utility of his mother; the greater her faction and the more his dependence on it, the larger the influence of a queen mother over her son could be. Formal regency itself was no guaranteed place; queen-regents could be ousted if the balance at court was upset against them. Queen mothers played for high stakes. Their game had to be calculated in advance and the play was not over once a son was on the throne. The effort was repaid manifold if success were achieved, and a glittering dowagerhood assured.

The rule of primogeniture—that is, the automatic succession of the eldest son to the throne—is not universal; other methods for deciding who is throneworthy and for choosing among the often numerous acceptable candidates have been more common. Primogeniture itself can leave room for argument, especially if the direct male line dies out. Alternative succession practices that produce a larger number of legitimate candidates regularly lead to dispute, even to armed struggle for the throne. Long before a king's death, the question of who will succeed him becomes a burning issue. Factions develop and rival candidates act as foci, around which the discontented and the mutually antagonistic form clusters, some satisfied with the status quo and some seeking change. Succession politics become a center into which other issues are drawn and the resulting struggles over the throne inevitably involve the queen. The choice of a successor determines the fate of her sons. If potential candidates extend to a wide circle of male relatives, a wife will normally fight for the claims of her own sons. If the succession is confined to the sons of the king, but his marriage practices have ensured that those sons were born of different mothers, a woman will attempt to advance her own son over her stepsons, in spite of age or precedence. Even if the throne may pass only to the king's sons and no stepsons are involved, a mother may sometimes espouse the cause of one favorite child, not always the eldest.

Succession politics become a sphere of activity for queens both during and after their husbands' lifetimes. The queen's power at court could win allies for her son; her own family might prove an important advantage. A mother seeking to secure the throne for her son had an eye to her own future, for if the son were a minor and female regency acceptable, she might hope to rule for him. Even if he were of full age, there was possible influence to be wielded at his court, though only as long as the mother proved useful or until a wife supplanted her in the functions of a queen at court. As long as the succession to the throne remained open to question, queens and queen mothers could participate in the struggle and earn the gratitude or dependence of a son. A royal wife without sons, one defeated in her efforts or cast aside by an ungrateful child, often cut a miserable figure. Few maintained an active political career in dowagerhood without a sympathetic son on the throne, though some struggled hard to do so. For a minority of queens second marriage was a possibility; for the exceptional there might be an independent role.

Succession Practices and Regency

In few European dynasties before the eleventh century were the rules of succession fixed and clear cut so that the choice fell automatically on one candidate, either the eldest son or another. The idea that royal blood in male veins carried claims to the throne died hard, and opened throneworthiness to a wide group. Not only could all sons of a king be considered eligible, but often also his brothers, themselves sons of a former king, if not more remote relatives. If filial succession from father to son was common, fraternal succession from brother to brother was not unknown. If the kingdom were divided among claimants, dispute might be staved off, but often the division merely focused the argument on the size of the portions and the legitimacy of the claimants. If a kingdom was considered indivisible, passing to only one heir, the rivalry could be intense.

The claims of all a king's sons to share in his inheritance remained strong throughout the period, from sixth-century Merovingian Frankia even until eleventh-century Capetian France. By the ninth century if not before, the eldest son of a Frankish king was considered to have special claims, but this did not mean automatic primogeniture. The eldest son of a Carolingian king might exercise a quasi-paternal authority over his younger brothers, but those brothers were still allotted kingdoms of their own. The Merovingian and Carolingian divisions of the kingdom did little to assuage argument. The eldest sons of Louis the Pious opposed the provision for their younger half brother, Charles the Bald, and fought incessantly over the details of division. Nor did they accept that any temporary division extinguished their respective claims to the whole family property. Louis the German could present himself as a legitimate alternative to his brother Charles the Bald in West Frankia, and both of these brothers claimed the inheritance of their nephews in the 860s and 870s. For the earlier Merovingians the claims of a brother could be argued against those of a son, and the proverbially wicked uncle might murder or disinherit his nephews. By the tenth and eleventh centuries there was a growing tradition in France, England, and Germany of passing on the kingdom undivided. The Ottonian Henry the Fowler imposed indivisibility in 929, but at the cost of bitter family feeling and smouldering resentment in the cadet line. Robert the Pious designated his own single heir, but not without the active opposition of his wife and younger sons. In England the powerful claims of all sons, strongly backed by rival noble factions and local separatist feeling, forced temporary divisions of the kingdom as late as the 1030s. In none of these kingdoms was the succession dead as a family and political issue by the eleventh century.

For a queen to play a part in the consequent dispute she required the ability to muster support; for the maximizing of her opportunity she needed the acceptance of filial succession, even if the son were a minor, and of female regency. Minorities were dangerous, even

intolerable, at a date when kings ruled in more than name and especially if the need for military leadership was pressing. They encouraged factions fighting for control of the young king, since others
could claim to speak and rule in his name. Because a king's brothers
possessed the requisite quality of royal blood, there might be powerful arguments for preferring the choice of such an adult ruler. Ninth-
century Wessex, faced with ferocious attack from the Vikings, saw
the succession of four brothers, the sons of Æthelwulf, and the tradition remained strong in England until the eleventh century. Only
Æthelred II came to the English throne while still under age, not
after winning in a succession contest but after his mother engineered
the murder of his half brother. Æthelred's own father and uncle had
been passed over in favor of their adult uncle in the mid-tenth century. In Merovingian Frankia minors succeeded when they could secure sufficient backing, but on other occasions their inheritance was
successfully challenged by adult uncles with the might to enforce
their case. Since the claims of brothers remained strong, minorities
were established only with struggle, and much depended on the infant king's mother and her support.

So real was the threat posed to a child ruler by male relatives, especially uncles, that the women of his family and inevitably his
mother emerged as his natural guardians, even regents. When the
Merovingian Chlodomer died in the early sixth century, his mother,
Clotild, emerged to protect and defend the rights of her young
grandsons, but she was unable to prevent the murder of the two
elder boys at the hands of their uncles. In Ottonian Germany in
the tenth century, Otto I's son Liudolf was an object of hatred to his
uncle, Henry of Bavaria; Henry had been deprived of his succession
rights in favor of his brother Otto I and his heirs. Henry's son and
namesake, Henry the Wrangler, claimed regency for the infant Otto
III, Otto I's grandson, in 983. Many suspected his motives. Gerbert
of Aurillac grieved that the lamb had been given to the wolf and others accused Henry of conniving at joint rule, even of planning to
usurp the throne. Those who supported the claims of Otto III turned
for regents to the women of the Ottonian family, first to his grandmother, Adelaide, and his mother, Theophanu, and finally to Theophanu alone. There were undoubtedly strong feelings against
placing such power in female hands. There were those who echoed
Henry's arguments that the young king's guardian should be a male

relative; Thietmar in the early eleventh century felt obliged to compliment Theophanu by stating that she filled her regent's role "like a man." At the end of the Merovingian period, an age rich in female regents, the hostile *Annales mettenses* argued against Plectrud in 714 that "she presumed to hold the reins of power with a child and with womanly counsel." The arguments that would give regency to male relatives later in the Middle Ages were already there. But the tensions between uncles and nephews with rival claims to the throne made such relatives an unlikely and dangerous choice in the earlier period. The women of a young king's family and especially his mother posed no threat; their own survival was bound up with his.

Yet no queen mother could handle the problems of regency without support. Most Merovingian regencies put a large share of power into the hands of a noble leader at the queen's side, and some were joint affairs. Until the majority of Childebert II, Brunhild shared her role with Gogo, and it was only when her son came of age that she felt strong enough, with an adult ruler beside her, to dismiss his noble tutors and take over control. When Dagobert fell ill in 638–39, his queen, Nantechild, was appointed regent for Clovis, but jointly with Aega, mayor of the palace. It was the Austrasian nobility that created and supported the regency of queen Himnechild for her son-in-law Childeric II. The weaknesses of a minority made noble support essential, and in some kingdoms noble rather than female regency was the norm. In Lombard Italy, Wacho's young son Waltari was left in the regency of Audoin; Audoin succeeded Waltari as king, probably after murdering the young man. Cunipert's son Liutpert was left in the regency of Ansprand, who defended him against attacks, but in the end took the throne for himself. The threats to these young Lombard kings were formidable, and if a strong noble regent was arguably necessary, it was itself a threat, especially when the dynasty was insecure. In Merovingian Frankia, female regency was replaced or rather eclipsed by the control of kings, whether minors or adult, by the mayors of the palace. Merovingian politics had come to focus on the rivalries of a few great families in whose struggles possession of the king was but a tool.

Female regency emerged as a protection against the tensions within the royal family itself. It is associated with minorities and thus normally with dynasties strongly enough established and secure enough from external pressures to tolerate the accession of infants and to prefer them over adult uncles. It always requires noble backing, and if the general position of women is low and the dynasty insecure, as was the case in Lombard Italy, noble regency may replace it. Once established, the strength of tradition may assure its survival. In the late seventh century the loss of Merovingian dynastic prestige and power could have resulted in simple noble regency, but female regents survive, if only as figureheads, perhaps because they became themselves tools of their noble families and backers. Had the Carolingian dynasty thrown up a series of minor kings during its early and strong phase, female regency might have reappeared. Tenth-century Ottonian Germany suffered the family strains resulting from recently imposed indivisibility. It was influenced by Italian traditions of female rule, and the power opened up for noblewomen generally by the expansion of female monasticism. Queen-regents emerged again at their most impressive.

Choice of Candidate, Support, and Propaganda

A queen with only one son faced no problem of choice; he was the natural candidate. Brunhild in the sixth century; Judith with her infant, Charles the Bald, in the ninth; Ælfthryth, whom death robbed of her oldest boy, and Theophanu with her solitary son, Otto, could turn their attentions singlemindedly to the future of this male offspring, Judith and Ælfthryth with violent results. But kings and their wives sought the security of a numerous male progeny, thus presenting some queens with an embarrassment of choice, especially if the principle of indivisibility precluded a kingdom for each son. Her choice had to be governed not simply by personal preference and the son's amenability to a mother's wishes, but by the support which her candidate would command. The latter consideration normally drew a mother to her eldest, whose claims were strongest; his greater age lessened the prospect of an undesirable minority. But led by considerations of preference and other factors, some queens chose a younger son. Mathilda, wife of Henry the Fowler, is supposed to have preferred the claims of her second son, Henry, to those of her eldest son, Otto. Her argument was allegedly that Otto was not born "in the royal hall"; that is, his birth antedated his father's accession to the kingship. Faced with a choice between her grand-sons, the English Eadgifu in 956 seems to have leaned toward the younger child, Edgar. Constance, the wife of Robert the Pious, ad-vanced the claims of her younger son, Robert, and opposed the des-ignation and consecration of her older son, Henry, in 1027. The queen's displeasure at the choice of her eldest was well known. Wil-liam of Aquitaine wrote to Fulbert of Chartres announcing his in-tention of absenting himself from the ceremony, since he did not wish to pronounce "for the king or for the queen." Fulbert himself claimed that he dared not attend Henry's consecration, fearing "the wickedness of his mother. When she promises evil she is to be be-lieved, all her actions are witness to the fact." Constance forcibly un-derscored her opposition by riding off on horseback from the event. The consecration was ill-attended, as had been the earlier designa-tion of Henry's older brother, Hugh, in 1017.

Brunhild had found herself supporting a younger grandson against an older in A.D. 600, because the elder had reached the age of majority, married, and cast his grandmother and her counsels aside. Eadgifu's preference for Edgar was born of a realization that the older Eadwig and his new wife presented a threat to her position at court. These queens found the choice forced upon them by a cal-culation of self-interest. Preference for a younger son might always have involved some assessment of the likelihood of future influence; an older son who had reached majority or was nearing it might prove more independent, less reliant on his mother's support, more inclined to replace his mother with a new queen of his own. Few historians have believed Constance's contention that she supported Robert because he had the stronger will and greater energy. Ma-thilda may have preferred the teen-aged boy Henry to the adult Otto, already married with a son of his own.

In a few cases, a younger son had the better chance of success. When Cnut died in 1035 his widow Emma had three potential can-didates: her two older sons by the English king Æthelred II, Edward and Alfred, who had spent nearly twenty years in exile; or her younger son by Cnut, Harthacnut, at that time ruling in Denmark. Emma chose the youngest. She had identified herself with the Dan-ish dynasty through her second marriage to Cnut, and in backing Harthacnut she may have calculated that little sympathy would be

forthcoming from Edward and Alfred, since she had earlier by-
passed them in marrying their father's conqueror. Also Harthacnut
was younger, thus arguably more amenable. But a third reason for
Emma's choice may have been the likely support Harthacnut would
receive from the Anglo-Danish aristocracy who had risen to power
under Cnut. It was among them that she numbered her key ally, Earl
Godwin of Wessex. Godwin and others like him saw a more secure
future in the continuance of the Danish dynasty under Harthacnut
than in the restoration of a son of the English Æthelred. When Edward and Alfred turned up in England in 1036, there was little support for either brother. Emma now had too many candidates, the
most acceptable of them far away in Denmark. Godwin switched his
support to the fourth contender, Emma's stepson, Harold Harefoot,
and the murder of her son Alfred has been laid at Godwin's door.
Emma's cause was lost and she was dispatched into exile. The as-
tuteness, deliberation, and alacrity with which she had acted in
1035 was neutralized by an embarrassment of sons and the absence
of the best contender. Emma's original choice of her youngest son
still looked correct, though events had outflanked her.

Preference and calculation were only two elements in the equa-
tion; as mothers of *all* their sons, queens were the natural champions of ideas of equal claims and of family unity. On the death of
Clovis in 511 his widow Clotild was a major architect of the novel
decision to divide the kingdom, giving all her sons a share; she was
later to appear as guardian of this decision when she emerged from
retirement to defend the rights of her grandsons, children of the
dead Chlodomer. Bertha, the mother of Charlemagne and widow of
Pepin, worked from 768 to 771 to preserve harmony between her
sons and acceptance of the division of the kingdom made between
them. Indivisibility posed an additional strain on family harmony
and posed a particular problem for a queen mother. In 929 Henry
the Fowler had decided to restrict claims to the newly acquired
kingship to his eldest son Otto. According to traditions of noble, let
alone royal, inheritance, his wife Mathilda might well have felt that
her younger son Henry was being unjustly excluded. In the mid-
tenth century Eadgifu was closely identified with both her sons.
Again indivisibility was becoming English practice, but Eadgifu's
influence may have lain behind the decision that the kingdom

should pass from brother to brother, ensuring that both her sons shared in the kingship.

Constance is alleged to have disliked her son Henry and advanced Robert's claims in 1027, and earlier to have worked maliciously against her eldest son, Hugh, who was designated as king by his father in 1017. Her enemies made the affair one entirely of preference, later interpreted as Constance's desire to dominate a younger son and foment trouble in the royal family. But Robert the Pious's decision to designate one son as heir bred the tensions. Hugh had mounted endless rebellions against his father, who gave him assurance of kingship and then parsimoniously refused to provide sufficiently for him to live up to his expected status. Robert's younger sons always felt resentful of their exclusion from the inheritance. In sum, Robert's determined practice of designating a single heir to his kingdom was an answer to the impoverishment of eleventh-century French kingship, but one that brought its own problems. Designation created a certainty of succession which fostered impatient rebellion, especially if adequate substance was withheld, and produced conflict with younger sons. Constance was not alone in opposing the events of 1017 and 1027. She may not only have been defending the claims of all her sons but also attempting to avoid the dangers of the course her husband had chosen. A passionate temperament and a desire for domination may have complicated her motivation and her primary aim may have been personal survival, but the stance which she took was still eminently defensible in the early eleventh century.

Human motives are a complex web to unravel, never more so than when caught up in the dynamics of events. Mathilda's original pressure on behalf of the young Henry may have expressed a mother's preference for her younger son that she could justify as a defense of the claims of all her children; it may have started as little more than arguments in Henry's favor. But for Henry and his supporters, first pressing his claims and then in open rebellion against his older brother, Mathilda's position could be interpreted as outright support, her arguments becoming part of his propaganda and justification. For her eldest son Otto, any favor toward his brother only diminished his own chances; he could not but resent his own mother for displaying it. When Otto's resentment was combined with a wife and thus a rival queen, it could have engendered a hostility driving Mathilda even further in her stand on Henry's behalf. By the time of her husband's death, Mathilda was supporting Henry and Otto was acting to deprive his mother of her land and power. "Choose your candidate well" is a gross oversimplification of the way mothers reacted to the varying claims of their sons and to their own need to survive.

If the choice of candidate was not always straightforward, the objective was clear: secure your son's accession by gathering your supporters, by defaming rivals, perhaps even eliminating them, by strengthening the legitimacy of your own claims, and by a readiness to fight if necessary.

Family connections could be crucial to success. Louis the Stammerer, who ruled briefly after the death of his father, Charles the Bald, in 877, had married twice. By his first wife, Ansgard, he had two sons, Louis and Carloman; by the second wife, Adelaide, a third boy, the future Charles the Simple. Ansgard had been cast aside at Charles the Bald's command, so that both women were there to press the claims of their sons on Louis's death in 879. Ansgard won, thanks largely to the backing of her powerful family. Adelaide and the infant Charles fled to the protection of Adelaide's kin, who were to successfully back Charles's claims to the throne in the 890s. In 975 Edgar's widow, Ælfthryth, could call on her relative Ælfhere, Ealdorman of Mercia, and probably on her brother Ordulf, a substantial lord of southwest England, to support her son Æthelred II against his half brother. In 984 the empress Adelaide was helped in her fight with Henry the Wrangler for control of Otto III by her brother King Conrad of Burgundy. The natural alliances of kin were often reinforced by self-interest. To marry off one of your womenfolk to royalty brought advantages; to keep her at court as mother of the next king and to have a grateful nephew or grandson on the throne maximized them. Yet families can be fickle. Gerberga, widow of Louis d'Outremer, was the sister of Otto the Great and of Bruno, Archbishop of Cologne. When Louis died in 954 Gerberga faced the problem of assuring the accession of her thirteen-year-old son, Lothar; her sisterly pleas fell on deaf ears. Gerberga was forced to turn to an erstwhile enemy and potential rival, who happened also to be her brother-in-law, Hugh the Great. Hugh responded to her request for advice and armistice, and his support allowed the consecration of Lothar not two months after his father's death. Hugh shared with Gerberga tutelage and regency of the young king, and her influence over Lothar might have been much diminished had Hugh not died in 956. Gerberga was later to receive aid from her brothers, but their active support had been lacking in her crucial need.

For an ex-slave like Balthild or a foreign princess like Brunhild, family could not constitute their major allies. Like Plectrud, the widow of Pepin, they could hope to use their possession of the royal treasure to purchase support. But the successful retention of that treasure itself depended on other backing, and without such backing they could not hope to use it to effect. Brunhild looked to noble support; her rival Fredegund found succor rather unexpectedly in the shape of her brother-in-law, King Guntram. Emma seized the treasure at Winchester in 1035, but Godwin was the crux of her success; when Godwin switched sides her fall was swift. Queens turned in their need to the allies they had won at court. In 975 Ælfthryth could add to her own family the support of bishop Æthelwold of Winchester, though the ranging against her of the archbishop of Canterbury and the ealdorman of East Anglia defeated her attempts. Theophanu and Adelaide were helped in 983–84 by many nobles, including such key ecclesiastical courtiers as archbishops Willigis and Hildibald. In 956 Eadgifu was ranged with her old ally Dunstan in favor of Edgar, while the regency of the empress Agnes in 1056 was underpinned by a whole bench of bishops and abbots: Hugh of Cluny, Liutpold of Mainz, Anno of Cologne, Gunther of Bamberg, Conrad of Speier, and Burkhardt of Halberstadt. The major supporters of Balthild and her young son in 657 were the queen's ecclesiastical allies, Audoenus of Rouen and Chrodobert of Paris. The alliances between queens and ecclesiastics bore fruit in such circumstances; it is no surprise that the rival contenders so often defamed them with accusations of adultery.

The struggles surrounding succession were often accompanied by propaganda wars. Desire to discredit an opponent or legitimize a claim was expressed in vicious and wounding words. Theudelinda ruled early seventh-century Lombard Italy beside her son Adaloald, who was opposed and attacked on the ground of unfitness for rule—

it was claimed that he was insane. At their most elaborate, the accusations against him told how the Byzantine emperor had sent him a bath salve, and when the young king anointed himself with it after his bath, he became enslaved in madness to the emperor's wishes and plotted to kill his great nobles. A useful tale for those who would discredit Byzantine connections and support the rival Arioald. Early in his reign, Louis the Pious and his wife Ermengard deprived their nephew Bernard of Italy of throne and life, giving his kingdom to their own son Lothar. A so-called *Vision of a Poor Woman* was soon circulating, claiming to be an account of a visit to the afterlife. The poor woman in question there found Ermengard suffering the torments of hell, crushed by millstones for her part in Bernard's downfall. At the gates of heaven, the Book of the Blessed was opened for her. Bernard's name shone brightly in it, Ermengard's had been erased, and the gold letters of Louis's own title to heaven were fading to the point of illegibility.

Queens regularly feature in the propaganda of succession. They are vilified in the interests of discrediting their sons, or themselves actually produced arguments against their rivals. In eleventh-century England both Emma and Edith commissioned works concerned with the succession. The *Encomium Emmae* was written to justify Emma's actions in the 1030s and to bolster the claims of Harthacnut; the *Life of Edward the Confessor* lauded Edith and the house of Godwin with more than a glance at the approaching death of the childless Edward. In 887 the last legitimate Carolingian emperor, Charles the Fat, was nearing death. Potential claimants included illegitimate offspring of his own and of his brothers, but also the grandson of his cousin, the child of Ermengard and Boso, Louis the Blind.

It was around this date that Ermengard's court circle produced another vision of the underworld, the *Vision of Charles the Fat*, which combined criticism of the civil wars with an unsubtle plug for the claims of Louis the Blind. One Sunday evening after service, Charles was taken in a vision into the afterlife. He passed first through the fires of hell, where he found his own father, Louis the German, plunged in a vat of boiling water and surrounded by those bishops and nobles who had urged war on the Carolingian family. In paradise, by contrast, he found the emperors Lothar and Louis II, great-grandfather and grandfather of Louis the Blind, seated on splendid thrones. They admonished Charles to mend his ways, to leave his empire to the young Louis, who was, like the little children, called by Christ himself—an ingenious attempt to make a virtue out of the liability of Louis's tender age. Like much other propaganda the *Vision* failed in its purpose. Right followed might and Charles's illegitimate nephew Arnulf succeeded.

Many queens followed Ermengard in attempting to bolster the claims of their menfolk; many struck at the sensitive area of birth and legitimacy in their attack on opponents. Brunhild claimed to doubt the paternity of her eldest grandson, Theudebert, and Emma and her supporters in 1035 cast doubts on whether Cnut had sired Harold Harefoot. Some versions of the Harold story involve affairs with clerics, and children smuggled into the queen's bed in warming pans. In all these tales the message was that of the *Anglo-Saxon Chronicle*: "Harold said that he was the son of Cnut and Ælfgifu of Northampton, but there was no truth in it." The argument was used against queens as well as by them. Fredegund's brother-in-law Guntram feigned disbelief that Clothar II was really his brother's son; Fredegund was sufficiently worried to settle the question with an oath sworn by three bishops and three hundred noblemen. Questions of paternity complicate many of the accusations of adultery leveled at queens. The Church's views on marriage opened a range of attack based on the legitimacy of mother and son, and from the sixth century onward rivals were discounting the sons of concubines as unworthy for the throne. As late as 924 the ignoble birth of Athelstan, son of a concubine, was leveled against him by his more legitimate half brothers. Refinements of the argument took account of whether a son was born "in the purple." Henry of Bavaria's supporters pointed out that he was conceived after his father came to the throne, while his elder brother Otto was born not to a king but to a mere duke. In 975 Æthelred's party conceded his half brother Edward's legitimacy, but pointed out that he was born before his father was consecrated king. The development of queenly consecration has already been seen to link with dynastic insecurity and the need to back a claim to the throne with every strength.

A wife who wished her son to succeed was well advised to take the precautions of legitimate marriage and formal designation as queen; some sought a promise of succession for their offspring. When Emma became Æthelred's second wife she allegedly secured a promise that her sons and not those of his first marriage would succeed. An oath was sworn by the nobles to her son Edward while he was still in the womb. When she became the second wife of Cnut in 1017, she extracted a similar promise regarding any sons she had by him. In both cases Emma was a second wife, attempting to gain designation for her sons over older half brothers. Emma's tactics were not unique. Judith's efforts in favor of Charles the Bald were bent on persuading Louis the Pious to allocate the child a kingdom. The issue here was a share in a divided inheritance, but involved the similar principle of deciding the succession *pre mortem*. During the tenth and eleventh centuries, the practice of designation in France, Germany, and increasingly in England was producing a shift toward primogeniture. It was not a practice supported by all queens, as the cases of Mathilda and Constance have shown. But designation was sought by Emma, Judith, and possibly by Edgar's wife Ælfthryth because each as a second wife faced the rivalry of stepsons. Stepmothers sought to oust their stepsons in favor of natural children. The eighth-century Lombard laws of King Liutprand gave fathers testamentary power to choose a favorite son for inheritance. But if that favorite son was the child of a second or third marriage, he might not be preferred before his mother's death, "lest any should say it was done at her instigation." Designation of adult sons without rivals, on the other hand, threatened to raise a rival queen at court and deprived the queen mother of the opportunity to gain influence by aiding her son's claims. Designation and primogeniture eventually helped remove the succession from its central position in politics and thus deprived queens of a major sphere of activity. With hindsight, Mathilda and Constance were right to oppose it.

Arguments about legitimacy and designation rallied support and fanned dispute, but they were rarely decisive. Stronger action was often necessary—a faction struggle or a succession war. Brunhild was ready to fight in 613 to get her great-grandson on the throne; Charles Martel's widow Swanhild fought at the side of her son Grifo, and when his half brothers Carloman and Pepin won, she shared Grifo's fate of imprisonment; Eadgifu, widow of Charles the Simple, rallied her English half brother, King Athelstan, to send a force to France in favor of her son Louis d'Outremer. Many disputes ended in aggression or violence. On the death of King Edgar in 975 rival factions supporting his two sons delayed the consecration of a new king for some time. Emma and her party continued to struggle for two years after the death of Cnut in 1035, a testimony to their strength and her determination.

The final act of such a saga might be the elimination of the rival candidate himself. In 975 Ælfthryth and her supporters failed to win the crown; but Ælfthryth did not give in. King Edward the Martyr, her stepson, was murdered while on a visit to his half brother and stepmother at Corfe Castle, and Ælfthryth's complicity seems certain. Merovingian queens were often loath to leave resolution of their problems so late. If Fredegund played a part in the murder of her stepsons, she accomplished the removal of these potential rivals long before her husband's death. Marcatrude, wife of Guntram of Burgundy, was accused of poisoning her stepson Gundobad, son of Guntram's concubine Veneranda. Suspicion of such murders inevitably falls on stepmothers, but this can be no ground for excusing them all. The bitterest succession disputes occurred when rival claimants were sons of different mothers; a second wife had powerful motives for undermining or even removing her stepsons.

Describing the situation produced by the second marriage of Otto I to Adelaide and the birth of their first son, Widukind remarked on the plight of Liudolf, Otto's son by his first wife. Liudolf complained that his uncle, Henry of Bavaria, now openly despised him. Feelings between heir and dispossessed uncle could never have been cordial, but Henry had struck up an alliance with Liudolf's new stepmother and sharpened the bitterness. The uncle could now turn open contempt on his nephew, stated Widukind, because Henry knew that Liudolf was deprived of maternal aid. Thus crucial did a mother's help appear to a mid-tenth-century German. No one was better placed than she to swing a father's favor toward his son; in no one else would a prince find so dedicated an architect and consolidator of his support. He would never feel the need for that relationship so strongly as when it was replaced by the envy and scheming of a stepmother. When Chilperic I's sons rebelled one after another, Chilperic and his second wife Fredegund had their natural mother, Audovera, put to death. The assumption that Audovera was aiding them was as natural as Fredegund's resentment.

Fate of Royal Widows

In the tenth century Æthelflæd of Damerham outlived her husband, King Edmund, by almost fifty years. Her brief marriage had been barren and with no son to plan and scheme for, her powerful family availed her little; Æthelflæd's widowhood was one of obscurity. Husbands felt impelled to look to the safety of their sonless widows. On his deathbed Edward the Confessor commended Edith to the protection of her brother Harold, while in 875 the dying Louis II had sought guardians for Angelberga in the pope, Bishop Wigbod of Parma, Everard and Berengar of Fruili, and her own kinsman Suppo II. A woman's future was ordinarily bound up with that of her male offspring. When announcing the death of her third son to Fredegund, the messenger added, "You can expect no better fate yourself now that you have lost the hope through which you were to have reigned." Small wonder that queens sought to keep what control they could over their infant sons! Brunhild took care for the rearing of her grandchildren and great-grandchildren. Deprived of her husband, captured by his enemies in 945, Gerberga would not relinquish her eldest son, the hope not only of the dynasty but of herself. Long years of separation loosened the bonds between mothers and sons. The accession of the adult Edward the Confessor in 1042 brought no comfort to his mother, Emma; no filial gratitude warmed his heart toward the woman who had abandoned him in his early teens, and one of his earliest actions was to dispossess Emma of her royal treasures.

Queen mothers were unwise to expect devoted loyalty from their children. When Henry the Fowler died in 936 his widow Mathilda was attacked by her son Otto I; he and his wife Eadgyth had little cause to feel gratitude to the mother who had backed his younger brother. Yet some sources indict that selfsame younger brother Henry for being party to the actions against his mother, both sons accusing her of building up treasure and consuming the royal revenue. Judith, widow of Louis the Pious, may have died in need in 843, robbed of her property by the son for whom she had fought so long. Supernumerary queens eating up royal resources were unwelcome at court, especially when their political utility was ended and their place taken by a new wife. Years of effort could be brought to naught by the rapid shift of political events.

In 986 Emma, recent widow of the West Frankish King Lothar, wrote to her mother, the empress Adelaide, bemoaning the passing of the days when she had flourished and reigned, the bitterness of the day that had deprived her of a husband and left her in misery. But Emma still had hope, in the person of her son Louis V. This last Carolingian king was threatened on all sides, by his own uncle Charles of Lorraine and by the noble families of northern France, especially that of Hugh Capet. Emma implored her mother's aid, for herself and for her son Louis. Only months later, Emma wrote to Adelaide again, now in desperate straits. Louis had abandoned her; the hope she had laid on him was gone; her own son had become her enemy. She was deserted by her dearest friends and her enemies attacked her honor. In the first months of Louis V's reign, Emma had retained the importance she had enjoyed at Lothar's court, helping her son to rule, receiving jointly with him the oaths of loyalty of his nobles. But the 980s were a period of political instability and intrigue; the last Carolingian king sought support where he could get it in a treacherous world. Louis was wooed first by partisans of Hugh Capet himself, deserting his mother and her ally, Bishop Adalbero of Laon. He was soon flirting with Charles of Lorraine, his uncle and chief rival and his mother's lifelong enemy. Emma's bitterness was complete when Louis joined his uncle in the chorus of accusations imputing adultery to his mother and Adalbero. To salvage her own safety, Emma now fled with the bishop to the protection of Hugh Capet. There were signs in 987 that Louis was shifting his ground again before his premature death left the way open for a Capetian succession.

In 1031 the death of Robert the Pious precipitated Constance into an even worse predicament. The designated heir was her son Henry, already twenty-three or -four and with little love for the mother who had opposed his consecration. Loath to relinquish power, or, as accurately, anxious to protect herself, Constance took possession of certain towns in northern France and formed an alliance with her husband's erstwhile enemy, Eudes, Count of Troyes. Henry was forced to flee to Normandy, where he was joined by his brother Robert, allegedly Constance's favorite but now seeing his best hopes in advancement from his brother, and by Fulk of Anjou, enemy of Count Eudes. Their alliance triumphed; Constance lost ground and took refuge at Poissy, a residence she had always favored for the excellence of local fishing. Attacked by Henry, she fled from Poissy by boat, but her resistance was vain and she finally capitulated. Her tearful reconciliation with Henry was rapidly followed by her death in 1034. The Capetian Henry I faced resistance and rebellion not only from his mother but from his brothers Robert and Eudes during the 1030s. Eudes's struggle continued long after his mother's death during a freebooting career as a landless adventurer. Henry was relieved of the embarrassment when Eudes was suddenly struck down after a sacrilegious banquet in the church of St. Saviour, an orgy illuminated by the light of the Paschal Candle. Robert and Eudes faced the fate of the younger sons in a system of primogeniture. Constance's position was the perennial plight of a royal widow, complicated in her case by the tense family relationships created by the adoption of primogeniture and perhaps fueled by her own commanding personality.

The determined stand that Constance made may be a tribute to her character, or a fruit of the tortuous politics of West Frankia. Constance could recruit allies for her desperate gamble from the ranks of those anxious to undermine king and enemy. Many widowed queens shared her reluctance to bow out quietly, if not her readiness to fight to the end. The pious lives of the seventh-century Balthild and the tenth-century Mathilda obscure the fact that both queens were forced into religious retirement by sons or noble factions. Clotild, widow of Clovis, was ready to emerge from retirement to guard her grandsons and rule beside them; only after they were dead or disposed of did she retreat to Tours to live the life of a handmaid of God, chaste and virtuous, to nights of prayer and days of almsgiving and religious endowment. Judith, daughter of Charles the Bald, twice discarded her widow's weeds to marry again. After the death of her elderly husband, King Æthelwulf, in 858, she married his son, her own stepson Æthelbald, a match perhaps not entirely of her own choosing. After Æthelbald's death she was kept at Senlis under the watchful eyes of her father and the bishop. Once again she demonstrated her reluctance to accept widowhood, this time whole-heartedly embracing elopement with Baldwin, Count of Flanders. Twice widowed before the age of twenty, Judith was not yet ready for the sober pleasures of dowagerhood.

It was not only the young and impetuous who sought a new life in widowhood. Late in 951 Eadgifu, the English widow of Charles the

Simple, fled from the abbey of Notre Dame de Laon, escorted by the vassals of the lord of Vermandois. They brought the dowager queen, by now well turned forty, to Herbert of Vermandois, son of the erstwhile captor of her husband and the implacable enemy of her son. Eadgifu and Herbert were married. How far she connived at this series of events we cannot know, though her son, Louis d'Outremer, expressed his anger against her by confiscating her royal lands. Louis's marriage had already relegated his mother from all influence at court. Eadgifu should probably be numbered with those many dowager queens, from Brunhild in the sixth century to the English Emma in the eleventh, who struggled by every means against the obscurity of widowhood. Their actions have drawn down the obloquy of historians from their own day to this. There is no female equivalent of the male virtue of tenacity to describe these women who refused to accept their fate and retire gracefully.

A minority of widows followed the path of Judith and Eadgifu and married a second time. Remarriage of royal widows was, as we have seen, relatively common in Merovingian Frankia and Lombard Italy as part of attempts to claim the throne. The practice long survived the sixth century and became common again in the tenth, where a royal widow like Bertha of Burgundy or Adelaide was married for the claims and wardship she brought with her. Not all such marriages, however, stem from an initiative on the part of the widow. Theudechild, widow of Charibert I, is said by Gregory of Tours to have offered herself to her brother-in-law, King Guntram, who took her treasure and then confined her to a nunnery. Such a statement could so easily have been biased by Guntram's self-justification, cast in an antifeminist mold, and there is no way of testing its truth.

I have just mentioned Judith's second marriage in 858, to her stepson. Such an alliance was by no means unique. In seventh-century Kent, Eadbald had contracted a similarly incestuous marriage with his stepmother, the widow of his father, Æthelberht. Procopius tells a story of an earlier Germanic king, Radger, of the Warni, who married his stepmother at his own father's express instructions. These marriages with stepmothers have sometimes been claimed as evidence for the survival of matriliny, but wherever the circumstances are fully understood they belie such an interpretation. They are specialized forms of the normal pattern of marriage

169

with a royal widow. Æthelbald married Judith because like his father he wanted this prestigious marriage alliance with the Carolingian dynasty; because her unique status as a consecrated queen made her an ideal mother for his sons, just as it had made her a dangerous stepmother for himself; and because he had at least one adult brother who felt his claims to the West Saxon throne the equal of Æthelbald's. Æthelbald was another insecure royal claimant, marrying a royal widow for the advantages she brought him. Remarriage brought its own problems for a royal widow. Where a widow and mother married a usurper and helped legitimize his position, the legacy of bitterness in the family of her first marriage was great. In the classical Greek tragedy, *The Oresteia*, Clytemnestra, widow of Agamemnon, married Aegisthus, Agamemnon's cousin and murderer, who became king. Her own son Orestes avenged Agamemnon's death by murdering his mother. The classic situation was echoed in eleventh-century England in the feelings of Edward the Confessor toward his mother, Emma, who had deserted her loyalty to her first family for marriage with her first husband's conqueror.

In 1060 Anne of Russia, widow of Henry I of France, married Raoul of Valois. The marriage took place soon after Henry's death. Raoul repudiated his own wife on a charge of adultery in order to marry the dowager queen. The affair caused a great scandal, which possibly led to Raoul's excommunication. Raoul of Valois had been an ally of Henry I, a frequent attendant at court after the king's marriage to Anne, and a close friend of the queen. A Capetian queen, even a dowager, was a useful chess piece, and of Raoul's motives, if not his political wisdom, there can be little doubt. Anne's position was more complex. Before his death Henry I had appointed Baldwin of Flanders as regent for his nine-year-old son Philip. Anne could count on no automatic regency and any hopes she still entertained in this direction would require support. Moreover she shared the peculiarly desperate plight of a royal widow far removed from the aid of her own family, from the support they might give her son or the refuge they could provide for herself. Anne of Russia found herself, like Judith in ninth-century England and Eadgifu in tenth-century West Frankia, a widow and a foreigner. Preference could have been only a secondary factor in the remarriage of all three women; like kings themselves royal widows remarried for advantage. Unlike kings, royal widows could rarely choose their fate. Some attracted a second husband, others struggled on more hopelessly.

Widows without children, especially without sons, could hope for little importance after their husbands' deaths. A few aspired to, or were offered by their spouses, a role as king maker. Charles the Bald on his deathbed committed the royal regalia to his widow Richildis, extending her political role by a few brief months. She and her supporters ravaged their way toward a meeting with her stepson Louis the Stammerer, but in the end there was no question of her not investing Louis with the sword and scepter, the royal robes and the crown. The emperor Henry II left his childless widow, Cunigund, in control of the imperial insignia. She exercised a brief regency after his death, chiefly arising from the dispute over the childless emperor's succession, but once the choice had fallen upon Conrad, her time was at an end. Like Richildis she handed over insignia and power to the new ruler. Ermengard, the barren consort of Rudolf III of Burgundy, played a central role during the last years of her husband's reign. The question of succession was her legitimate concern. Her role at court meant that she was courted by the Salian emperor Henry III, and her opposition helped deal the death blow to the hopes that Eudes of Blois had entertained in Burgundy. But again her part was brief; the succession once settled, she had no son to influence and her political life was at an end. Edward the Confessor's childless wife Edith entertained hopes of determining the English succession in 1066; it is difficult to interpret the *Life of Edward*, which she commissioned, outside the context of succession politics. The Norman conquest of England and its aftermath curtailed any ambitions she may have had, though it must be doubted what future would have been hers had her brother Harold retained the throne.

Two queens, Angelberga and Æthelflæd, survived sonlessness at the center of the stage. The death of Louis II in 875 left Angelberga with two daughters. Even before this date she had been deeply involved in the question of succession, negotiating with her Carolingian brothers-in-law, uncles, and nephews during the family maneuvering that preceded Louis's death. Louis's decease left her as formal regent; she it was who called the nobles of northern Italy to a council at Pavia to decide on the succession to the throne. At Pavia and later, Angelberga had influence of her own, exercised directly and through the supporters and clients attracted during her promi-nent career. That influence was not used to favor any one candidacy consistently, but to continue the game of Carolingian family politics to the advantage of herself and her offspring. Her support for the cause of Louis the German was more expedient than policy, though the success of the unsympathetic Charles the Bald in gaining the Italian crown was particularly unwelcome to her. Angelberga had plans, if not for the accession of her son-in-law Boso, at least for the eventual claims of her legitimate grandson Louis the Blind. Her cousin-in-law Charles the Fat considered Angelberga and her plans a real threat to his own aims in Italy. He took her prisoner during his advance into the peninsula in 880, only releasing her in 882 when his own position on the imperial throne appeared assured. An-gelberga's efforts were still not at an end. In the summer of 887 she and her eldest daughter, Ermengard, took advantage of Charles the Fat's advancing illness to press the claims of Louis the Blind to suc-ceed him. Ermengard went in person to Charles's court; Angelberga sent her doctor. Their efforts were in vain. Political realities brought the illegitimate Arnulf to the throne in Germany and opened the Ital-ian succession to further dispute. Still Angelberga sought to wield her influence to determine the outcome. She supported Berengar of Friuli, an old ally and one of those to whom Louis II had entrusted his doughty widow in 875. Her stance did nothing to endear her to the victor, Berengar's opponent, Guy of Spoleto. After 888 we hear little of Angelberga in Italian life.

Like so many queens, Angelberga found herself a widow while still young and vigorous; she can have been little over forty in 875. The role she had played as queen had brought her powerful friends and political expertise, and perhaps a reluctance to accept obscu-rity. All the advantages that she could have offered to the son she never bore were sought by other claimants to the Italian throne. One after another, uncle and cousins sought her favor in their Italian ven-tures; without a son of her own, her part was still cast within the politics of succession. Her wealth and power as an Italian queen and widow combined with a long period of acute uncertainty con-cerning the throne of Italy to provide Angelberga with an extraordi-nary career as dowager. Her politics may appear thwarted by the multiplicity of Carolingian claimants and their early deaths, but these same circumstances created a situation that she could use to advantage. With no son to take the crown, however, her position was limited and her attempts to play king maker fraught with danger. The crises of 875–88 not only provided her opportunities but exposed her to the doubledealing of popes and relatives—the common coinage of a widow's politics, but inflated for one without a candidate of her own. Angelberga found that her extended political role opened her property to constant attack, her person to imprisonment. Her dowager career is not only a tribute to one of the most powerful medieval queens but a witness to the limitations on even the greatest women, especially when bereft of sons.

In the early tenth century in England the Mercian queen Æthelflæd survived such limitations. She outlived her husband Æthelred to rule Mercia alone, to oversee its defense, to lead an alliance of the northern British against the Vikings and to leave such a reputation that some of her followers took the unprecedented step of choosing her only daughter to rule after her death. Æthelflæd's unique position built on that of earlier Mercian queens, but may have owed something in its initial stages to her family connections. The support of her brother Edward, King of Wessex, might have protected her from any internal challenge. His own potential designs on the throne of Mercia were deferred until Æthelflæd's death. The military exploits of Æthelflæd, her husband, and the local loyalties of the Mercian nobility would have made her forcible removal at a time of external Viking threat unwise. Edward contented himself with sending his eldest son to be brought up at Æthelflæd's court, an adoptive heir to assuage Mercian separatism. Only after his sister's death did Edward move to take over her kingdom and oust his niece Ælfwyn from her brief queenship. Few widows found themselves in Æthelflæd's exceptional circumstances.

Succession politics provided the widest opportunities for women. Anticipation of succession struggles and attempts by queens and their allies to influence them *pre mortem* overshadowed the previous reign. The rights of princes were strongly argued, but such rights were enjoyed by numerous candidates and were infinitely debatable. Automatic transitions of power were rare; many successions were decided amid maneuverings and battles in which queens could play a part determined by their individual influence and standing. The struggle served to enhance the importance of a mother to her son, to confirm any nebulous hold she might have over him. As queen mother, regent, even king maker, a queen might play a role in the politics of succession. Once that succession was clearly regulated, these roles were reduced. Forced to anticipate all possibilities, early queens had attracted allies and influence that helped ensure that no chance was missed.

Widows and orphans were easy prey; lacking the protection offered most effectively by the family group, they were often the victims of medieval society, the perennial objects of the protection of kings and princes. Royal widows partook to some extent in this general vulnerability. In the face of the power enjoyed by some queens, it is easy to be seduced into forgetting their problems. The queen's position, power, and status derived almost entirely from husband and marriage. Deprived of these the range of options was limited. The obvious course was to fight on behalf of a son, though success in the enterprise brought no guarantee of continuing security. Even more uncertain was the path of personal power, the hazardous attempt to use a lifetime's alliances to carve out a political career. Two paths remained: return to the securities of husband and family through remarriage, or retirement.

Chapter 7 🝔 *Retirement and Death*

I n the sixth century Venantius Fortunatus addressed a wistful little poem to the widowed queen Ultrogotha on the theme of her garden. His treatment of the subject has a lyrical nostalgia, an impression of genteel retirement borrowed from classical models. The sorrow of the widowed queen contemplating her flowers and arbors is plaintively evoked. Their beauty is a reminder of her departed husband, Childebert, who had loved to walk there, delighted in receiving the blooms plucked by his wife's own hand, enjoying the shade of the trees, the scent of the roses. But King Childebert was dead, and all such delights withered.

The reality of widowhood for Ultrogotha had been the harshness of exile for herself and her daughters at the hands of her brother-in-law Clothar I. Ultrogotha was sonless; not for her a dowagerhood of political influence. If the pleasures of her garden were truly the consolation of her widowhood, and not merely a poet's echo of the classical past, Ultrogotha may have counted herself fortunate. Murder at the king's command brutally cut short the retirement of Audovera, Chilperic I's repudiated wife, and that same king's widow, Fredegund, saw her enemies triumph and herself exiled after her husband's death. It was one of those enemies, Praetextatus, Bishop of Rouen, who taunted Fredegund with her fate. Even in exile, he would always remain a bishop, but she would not always be queen, and once she lost the security of husband and son she lost all.

Four centuries later the widowed Emma, abandoned by her son, wrote plaintively to her mother Adelaide, telling of her imprisonment without honor or dignity, of the endless insults inflicted upon her. Well might Emma say of herself, "I am that Emma, once queen of the Franks, who commanded such armies, now without even domestic companions to accompany me." Deprived of husband and son, far from her own family, Emma personifies the tragedy and danger of the abandoned wife or royal widow. Without husband or son a queen was open to the harshest treatment; retirement to a nunnery appeared to most as the best of ends.

A few widows, and some repudiated wives, returned to their native home and family, their best protection outside the safety of marriage. Emma moaned, "My enemies glory that I have neither brother, relative nor friend to help me." Her own mother, Adelaide, was more fortunate. When exiled from the court of her son Otto II, Adelaide could take dignified refuge with her brother, King Conrad of Burgundy. Emma's grandmother Bertha had twice been buffeted in the storms of widowhood. Hugh of Arles had married her after the death of her first husband, Rudolf II, but when Hugh's passion cooled into indifference and dislike, Bertha was repudiated. She too returned to Burgundy, where her son was king, to live in retirement in the nunnery at Peterlingen and to enjoy her landed possessions. When Suzanne/Rozala was divorced by Robert the Pious, she too sought a home with the son of her first marriage, Baldwin IV, Count of Flanders. Charles the Bald's widow, Richildis, lost all power at the Carolingian court with the accession of her stepson, Louis the Stammerer; she returned to live on her family lands in Lorraine. Gerberga, widow of Louis d'Outremer, was also to retire to Lorraine after her son's marriage, not returning to the home of her family but to the dower lands of her first marriage. Superfluous dowagers were unwelcome at court, but self-preservation rather than dignified withdrawal motivated many royal widows.

Widowhood in a hostile land could prove a dangerous state. A queen like Osthryth of Mercia could be murdered as an act of vengeance even before the death of her husband; a widow was doubly exposed. When murder and revenge took their toll in the families united by marriage in the tale of Finn, the wife Hildeburh was carried back to Denmark by her family to protect her from an ugly fate. Foreign princesses, whose original marriages had been designed to cement uneasy peace, were especially vulnerable. After the death of Edwin of Northumbria, his widow, Æthelberga, felt it expedient to return immediately to her own family in Kent, to take refuge with her brother, King Eadbald. The turmoil of Northumbrian politics, the counterclaims of other princes, put both Æthelberga and her son in jeopardy as long as she remained. Eadbald gave his sister the nunnery at Lyminge to serve the needs of retirement. Cuthberga, sister of King Ine of Wessex, became the wife of Alcfrith of Northumbria. On Alcfrith's death she left the north to become a nun, first at Barking and later at Wimborne in her native Wessex.

Anna, king of the East Angles, married two of his daughters to foreign kings: Æthelthryth became the wife of Ecgfryth of Northumbria, Sexberga was married to Earconberht of Kent. Æthelthryth was divorced by her husband, who placed her in a Northumbrian nunnery belonging to his own family. Æthelthryth preferred the security of her native East Anglia, and returned south to become abbess of Ely. After Earconberht's death, Sexberga first retired to a nunnery in Kent, her own foundation at Sheppey. But when her own daughter Eormenhild sought the safety of her native Kent after the death of her Mercian husband, King Wulfhere, Sexberga gave up Sheppey to Eormenhild, who might now find safety near the bosom of her family. Sexberga herself then returned to East Anglia, to succeed her sister Æthelthryth as abbess of Ely.

Sexberga's leisurely moves suggest none of the urgency of imminent danger, but the precipitous flight of Eadburh from ninthcentury Wessex on the death of King Beorhtric points to a closer threat. The supplanting dynasty of Ecgberht could have found no place for Beorhtric's widow. Eadburh could not return to her native Mercia where her father Offa and brother Ecgfryth were long dead; she fled rather to the continent, to the court of Charlemagne. There she was offered refuge and a nunnery. The generosity and protection becoming in kings obliged Charlemagne to help her, just as it later obliged his grandson Charles the Bald to take in the repudiated Theutberga. But Charles the Bald welcomed the chance to use a divorced wife to embarrass his nephew Lothar II, and Charlemagne might have seen in Eadburh some future pretext for interference in Wessex. Charlemagne had had an object lesson in the utility of widows when his sister-in-law fled to the court of the Lombard king Desiderius. Charlemagne had invaded Italy to prevent Desiderius's using his brother's widow and sons against him. As late as the eleventh century the exiled queen Emma found refuge in Flanders when her stepson Harold Harefoot drove her from England. She was only one of a string of English political exiles to whom the count of Flanders opened welcoming arms.

Charlemagne and Charles the Bald offered exiled royal widows nunneries as places of refuge, and most dowagers returning to their own families received comparable treatment. Once female monasticism was established on a regular pattern during the sixth and seventh centuries, nunneries provided ideal retreats for the unmarried, widowed, or divorced, and many noble and royal families founded houses as provision for their womenfolk. During the sixth century, on the verge of this great flowering of the religious life for women, some widows or repudiated wives retired to enjoy the revenues and security of towns. Audovera lived in Rouen after her repudiation; Fredegund, her supplanter in Chilperic's affections, followed her there after the king's death. Chilperic used Rouen as a refuge and prison for queens: when he captured Brunhild he briefly imprisoned her there. Yet retirement into a town did not preclude a religious dowagerhood. Clovis's widow, Clotild, lived at Tours in her widowhood, but in a small nunnery she had founded there. The empress Adelaide retired to Pavia in the late 970s and became closely associated with the monastery of San Salvatore, just as Queen Emma's final retirement to Winchester in 1045 reinforced her links with the great religious institutions of the city. Emma may have joined one of the foundations, Adelaide certainly did not.

Most queens retired, willingly or not, into nunneries. Many houses were founded by kings' wives, often on their dower lands, with a view to peace and security in old age. Radegund founded Poitiers, though only after her repudiation; Brunhild founded a house at Autun while planning a retirement more tranquil than the brutal reality; Balthild founded or refounded Chelles; Sexberga founded Sheppey, and her repudiated sister, Æthelthryth, built Ely, not in the kingdom she had ruled but in her family refuge. Ansa, wife of the Lombard Desiderius, was founder of San Salvatore in Brescia, which continued to be an important holding of Italian queens, though Angelberga endowed her own house of San Sixtus at Piacenza for retirement. Henry the Fowler and Mathilda founded Quedlinburg, and Mathilda used her dower lands to endow Pohlde and Nordhausen, the latter allegedly being her favored dowager retreat, although she went to Quedlinburg to die. The empress Adelaide founded a monastery at Selz as a place to await death, and Edgar's widow, Ælfthryth, retired to die in her foundation at Wherwell. Adelaide, wife of Hugh Capet, founded two nunneries, one at Frambourg in Senlis and the other at Argenteuil in the Parisis.

Some foundations became associated with several women of the royal dynasty and were regularly used to endow or provide for queens. Edward the Confessor's wife, Edith, made great improvements at Wilton, where she had been educated and hoped to retire. In the tenth century Wilton had been the place of exile for Edgar's repudiated wife, Wulfthryth, and her daughter Edith, and earlier for Edward the Elder's divorced wife, Ælfflæd, and her daughters. Wherwell was founded by Ælfthryth; her granddaughter was its abbess and Edith was sent there in 1051 when Edward tried to divorce her. San Salvatore Brescia was held by Ansa and later by Judith, wife of Louis the Pious, by Ermengard, wife of Lothar I, and by Angelberga, Louis II's empress: all probably received it as part of their dowry. Nordhausen, founded by the Ottonian Mathilda on dower land, was later given as dowry to her granddaughter-in-law Theophanu, who also received Mathilda's family nunnery at Herford. Chelles may have counted Balthild as its greatest queen, but in the mid-eighth century Charles Martel's widow Swanhild was imprisoned there by her stepsons, and a hundred years later Charles the Bald gave it to his first wife, Ermentrud. Zurzach was given to Richardis by Charles the Fat, who later immured Angelberga there, so that Pope John wrote to Richardis to beg her release.

Queens founded nunneries on their dower lands as places of retirement, also receiving nunneries as part of their dowries for the same purposes. Sometimes they took the precaution of founding houses in the lands from which they had come, on their own inheritance. Ermengard, wife of Lothar I, not only held Brescia and founded Agna, but built a nunnery on her ancestral land at Erstein in Alsace. Richardis added to Zurzach a foundation at Andlau on her own inheritance, and it was to Andlau that she retired when Charles the Fat divorced her. Royally connected nunneries were refuges for widowed sisters and mothers, for repudiated wives; a vocation to the religious life was a convenient excuse for divorce. Nunneries were sometimes used for royal confinements and often for the education of female children. They were held jointly by mothers and daughters and passed on in inheritance. Queens like Louis the German's wife, Emma, whose interventions in charters are virtually unknown, appear in those making grants to houses for women. The association between queens and nunneries was close, regular, and multifaceted.

Not all royal widows who retired to nunneries took the veil. Gregory of Tours carefully distinguished the life of Clotild at Tours as "devoted to God"; she was not "consecrated to God" as a nun, as Radegund was. Balthild does not seem to have become a nun at Chelles, but to have lived there humbly with the congregation in obedience to the abbess, whereas those retired seventh-century English queens Æthelthryth and Sexberga became nuns and abbesses of their own respective establishments. Repudiated wives and dangerous women were often forced to take the veil; as an argument for divorce, it was the female equivalent of tonsuring rival claimants to the throne. In tenth-century England Edgar's repudiated wife, Wulfthryth, became a nun at Wilton, Richardis became an abbess after her divorce, and Louis the Pious's sons were anxious to force Judith to take the veil. Conversely, the prevalence of lay abbacies by the ninth century and before may have helped queens and widows to live in nunneries without taking vows. The ninth-century *Vision* of the monk Wetto deplored the effects that such widows had on the religious life, the laxity that their presence fostered. When Charles the Bald gave his nephew's spurned wife, Theutberga, a nunnery she did not become a nun; such a step would have thwarted his purposes of using her to embarrass Lothar. Angelberga did not become an abbess in her retirement, but continued to intervene in Italian life from Piacenza. Adelaide's first exile was spent at Pavia, not in a nunnery, but perhaps associated with the monastery of San Salvatore, to whose abbot Odilo later dedicated his life of the empress. Her last years were spent traveling from abbey to abbey, more in the manner of a tenth-century king taking ecclesiastical hospitality, and she died as planned in the monastery of Selz in Alsace. It would be wrong to simply assume that retirement into a nunnery entailed the taking of vows; many queens kept themselves ready and able to emerge if necessary.

Some dowagers appear to have accepted the religious life with reluctance. Charles the Simple's widow, Eadgifu, fled from St. Mary Laon with the sons of her husband's former enemy Herbert of Vermandois, and the consternation of her son Louis d'Outremer suggests her complicity in the escape. In the sixth century Guntram of Burgundy placed Theudechild, widow of his brother Charibert I, in a nunnery at Arles. She tried to escape with the help of a Goth, but when the abbess discovered her incipient flight she was mercilessly beaten and locked in her cell. Such evidence must be balanced against the undoubted prestige and importance of the life of an abbess, especially during the heyday of female monasticism in the seventh century and belatedly in Ottonian Germany in the tenth and early eleventh centuries. Radegund's position at Poitiers did not isolate her from the political life of Merovingian Frankia, while her saintly reputation can only have enhanced her prestige as a holy woman. The life of an abbess could have its own power and attractions, especially in the double monasteries of the seventh century or the rich dynastic foundations of the Ottonians. In a seventh-century nunnery like Jouarre or Ely the abbess controlled a small, self-contained world. She provided for the poor, for strangers, widows, and orphans, and might be the hostess of kings and synods. The noble virtues of generosity and hospitality were hers to exercise. She managed an organization that was a center of conversion, education, and practical charity. She ruled a large and mixed congregation, and when the priests under her control were summoned to her presence, they stopped at a distance, knelt, and asked her blessing in a low voice. The life of consecrated celibacy was an ideal of total self-effacement in the Church fathers, but in the social realities of the early Middle Ages it could be a great career for women. Here, ironically, a dowager queen might at last be able to act in her own right—not as the daughter, wife, or mother of a man. The abbess was a close seventh-century equivalent of the career woman.

The role of nunneries as centers of learning is becoming a commonplace of early medieval history. Chelles, for example, under Charlemagne's sister, Gisela, was one of the centers of the revival of learning known as the Carolingian Renaissance. Quedlinburg, Gandersheim, and Nordhausen excelled their tenth-century German male counterparts. They were the centers where the historical traditions of the Ottonian dynasty were fostered and developed, a fact that goes some way to explain why the first Ottonian dynastic saint was a woman, Queen Mathilda, and not a man. The extent of dowager queens' participation in this learning is more questionable. Their personal endowments, their association with the nunnery, their very presence, was certainly a stimulus to the sort of historical writing described. Gisela was reputed to have taken a personal interest in scholarly questions. In the court poems her contribution to the Carolingian family gatherings and homecomings took the form of theological queries as much as expressions of affection. Radegund at Poitiers appreciated and patronized the late antique culture of

Fortunatus, and was herself a poet. Some dowagers may have used the opportunities of retirement to acquire new skills; Widukind suggests that Mathilda only learned to read and write during her monastic retreat after her husband's death. But the detailed activities of dowagers in nunneries are as obscure to us as their public activities as queens.

Prayers for the royal dead, whether said personally or by proxy, were an important function of royal widows; Mathilda's biographers insisted approvingly on this aspect of her religious life. How ascetic and pious these widows were is debatable. The details of Radegund's religious practice as recounted by Fortunatus should not be too lightly dismissed, since Æthelthryth of Ely was described in similar, if less extreme, terms, wearing only woollen garments, taking hot baths only at great feasts and then only after washing everyone else, seldom eating more than once a day. Yet seventh-century Coldingham shocked Cuthbert by the laxity of its practices, and the charges brought by her niece Clotild show Radegund's Poitiers to have been equipped with bathrooms, including private ones, and the nuns played dice, a pastime not expressly forbidden in their rule. In tenth-century Germany it was probably the smaller, daughter nunneries which maintained the strict and arduous way of life, while the mother houses like Quedlinburg and Gandersheim pursued an aristocratic mode of life, their abbesses being involved political figures. Like the laymen who founded monasteries in the tenth century, royal and noble abbesses may have seen the value of vicarious asceticism.

The lives of Mathilda suggest that this particular dowager lived well in her religious retirement. She fed the poor, and her miracles, like throwing bread from the hilltop at Quedlinburg that landed unscathed, show a similar royal largesse. Until the time of her death Mathilda continued to travel between her abbeys and estates, accompanied by her noble servants, consuming her revenues, maintaining a royal dignity. Her withdrawal from political life was at best partial. She still appeared occasionally at court, was visited by her family, and attended those great reunions designed to demonstrate the unity of the Ottonian house. Even Radegund was far from withdrawing entirely; she kept up a lively interest in the affairs of the kingdom. Neither the empress Adelaide nor Angelberga lived in true religious seclusion. Offa's widow Cynethryth took the veil and became abbess of Cookham in Berkshire after the death of her husband and son in the 790s. In 798 she was ably defending possession of the monastery against the claims of the archbishop of Canterbury, coming to an agreement with him to exchange lands in Kent for the disputed foundation at Cookham. A queen in retirement may often appear a powerless figure, but it is doubtful whether she ever forgot her dignity.

Odilo gave prominence to the final year of Adelaide's life; ten of the twenty-two chapters in his biography are devoted to these last months and to her death. He was a personal witness of many of the events he described and there is no fuller account of the passing of a great queen. Adelaide was already tired and ill as she spent these months traveling from shrine to shrine, making final efforts to bring peace to the kingdom of her nephew Rudolf. When she arrived at Peterlingen, the abbey she had richly endowed and the last refuge of her own mother, Bertha, the journey had so exhausted her that the crowds of poor, who flocked to meet her everywhere, had to be given alms by a servant. From there she traveled to St. Maurice-en-Valais, where a thousand martyrs were buried. Her prayers at the shrine were punctuated by sighs and tears, and to the attendant Odilo the face of the aged empress surpassed human features, taking on a prophetic quality. As she rose to leave the church a messenger arrived to announce the death in Rome of an old friend, Bishop Franko of Worms. Adelaide foretold how many would die like him in Italy, even her own grandson Otto III, and prostrating herself again, she prayed that she might not live to see that tragic day.

From St. Maurice she traveled to Geneva, to the church of the martyr Victor, and on to Lausanne to worship at the Cathedral of Notre Dame. Her nephews, Rudolf III of Burgundy, Burchard, Bishop of Lyon, Hugh, Bishop of Geneva, and Henry of Lausanne gathered there for a family reunion with their elderly aunt. At Lausanne she talked politics with Rudolf and his princes, but still continued her last acts of piety and generosity to the holy places. A messenger arrived asking alms for the restoration of St. Martin's at Tours, recently damaged by fire. Adelaide obliged, sending a message with her gifts: "Accept these little gifts given by Adelaide, handmaid of the servants of God, for her own part a sinner, by the gift of God empress." It was as she was leaving the church at Lausanne that she encountered an old friend, a monk whom she had known for many years. Both were in tears, and though the empress could not speak her eyes conveyed the feelings of an elderly woman approaching death. "Remember me in your meditations, you will not see me again with your mortal eyes."

After visiting the shrines of the saints and taking a last farewell of the home of her distant youth, Adelaide at last journeyed on to Selz, where she had ordered her tomb to be prepared. When she arrived there, the anniversary of the death of her son Otto II was approaching. As always, the arrival of the empress had brought a great concourse of the poor to receive her alms; they were arranged in lines and Adelaide insisted on distributing alms to them herself, even though it was beyond her failing strength. The commemorative mass for her dead son was said and during the following night Adelaide was taken with a fever. A slight rallying allowed her to call for the last rites, and her bed was surrounded by clergy singing the penitential psalms. Thus she died peacefully in her bed on 16 December 999, only a few months after her youngest daughter Mathilda, Abbess of Quedlinburg. At the age of sixty-eight she had outlived two husbands and all her children.

The moving details of Adelaide's last year are almost unique in the literature describing the lives of early queens. The failure of most queens to attract biographers has denied us even stylized accounts of their passing. Yet such was the nature of tenth-century Ottonian historiography that Adelaide's mother-in-law, Mathilda, received treatment in some ways comparable. Like Adelaide, Mathilda continued the itinerant life of the medieval monarch almost to the end; she was still traveling around her estates until December 967, only three months before her death. Like Adelaide, Mathilda's final journey was to the place she had chosen for her death and burial. Mathilda's choice had fallen on Quedlinburg, where she was to lie next to her husband, Henry the Fowler, in the great family nunnery they had founded. The queen assured the abbess of Nordhausen that her personal preference would have been to rest at Nordhausen, the house she had founded and around which clustered memories of the births of her children. But Quedlinburg's importance to the Ottonian dynasty overcame preference, and on 22 December 967 Mathilda left Nordhausen in time to reach Quedlinburg for the celebration of the Christmas feast.

Her final illness was already upon her, and her arrival brought a great multitude to take leave of the ailing queen. She divided up the remains of her property among the attendant churchmen, leaving herself only the minimum garments necessary for burial. As a result she had nothing left to give her grandson, Archbishop William of Mainz, when he arrived for a tearful interview at her bedside. Even at the last her generosity rose to the occasion: as William left, Mathilda sent after him her last possessions, the burial clothes she had reserved for herself. Her gift of prophecy had not left her and she foresaw that he would die before her; her provision for his final needs echoed the popular saying that parents too often supplied the shrouds as well as the nuptial gowns of their children. Mathilda was not, however, to be buried without all honor, since her daughter, Queen Gerberga, sent a timely gift of a golden pall to cover her parents' tomb. Mathilda's last interviews were with the abbess of Nordhausen and with her own thirteen-year-old granddaughter and namesake Mathilda, Abbess of Quedlinburg. To this young Mathilda she handed on the duty of guardianship of the Ottonian family dead; she gave the girl a book inscribed with the names of the dead for whom she herself had prayed, and commended to her the souls of herself and Henry.

As her end drew near, priests and nuns gathered round her bed to hear her confession. Mass was celebrated and the Eucharist brought to her. Then all stood singing the psalms. Mathilda approached death with her eyes open and her hands raised. About the ninth hour of the day she ordered ashes to be brought, placed them on her head with her own hand, made the sign of the cross, and died. As far as could be ascertained her death occurred at the very hour of the day at which she had habitually tended the poor in Lent. The body was washed and taken to church. It was there that Gerberga's messengers found it when they arrived with the gold pall. Mathilda's last great misery had been the news of the death of her grandson, William of Mainz, on March 2, only days before her own. Mathilda died on 14 March 968, having put all her affairs in divine order, full of days, an example of good works to her posterity, a woman worthy to have seen her children's children even to the fourth generation.

The deaths, like the lives of Mathilda and Adelaide, were public affairs. When Balthild had died quietly and suddenly in her cell at Chelles, the abbess and congregation had been distraught. They did not know even the hour of her death; they had wanted to see the miraculous light, the vision of angels. Death was a solemn and important moment, the death of the great a public spectacle. The attendant signs were to be seen and remembered, the last words caught and committed to memory. Death was a time of prophecy, and the smallest words and actions were not to be missed, especially by those who might later become guardians of a cult. Retrospect might add signs and portents. Thietmar described how the death of Theophanu in 990 was preceded by an eclipse of the sun late in 989; though Thietmar offered rational explanations he noted that many later took it as a presage of the later event.

The deaths of Mathilda and Adelaide, even though publicly enacted, have an air of the dignity of age, of an end attended by the full spiritual preparations. Other royal deaths were more sudden and less edifying. Like so many other northerners, Gunnhild, daughter of Cnut and wife of Emperor Henry III, succumbed to the heat and plague of an Italian summer, dying in 1038 after only two years of marriage. The high temperature of Italy that caused her death made rapid burial advisable. Herman, Duke of Alemannia, died during this same visit to Italy in 1038 and was interred immediately at Trent. But Gunnhild, as a queen, should lie in her husband's kingdom; her body was treated with aromatic substances and carried back in the train of Henry III and his mother for burial at Limburg.

Austrechild/Bobilla, wife of Guntram of Burgundy, had also died of the plague in A.D. 580 at the age of about thirty-two. Guntram subsequently executed the doctors who had attended his wife. Gregory of Tours, who considered Austrechild an evil woman, claimed that the executions were carried out on her posthumous order; she wished the doctors to accompany her in death so that others might be mourned at her funeral. But in fact, Austrechild accused her doctors of murdering her and Guntram acted on her accusations. She had been an object of dislike and intrigue at Guntram's court, being the erstwhile servant of Guntram's former queen, Marcatrud, whose brothers vilified her, calling into question the legitimacy of her children. The bereaved are often inclined to question the competence of doctors; Guntram may have had especial reason to doubt their professional integrity.

Whether or not she received help on her journey out of this world, Austrechild died in her bed, ostensibly of natural causes. In an age which saw the sudden death of many kings, victims of violence or accident, most queens died peacefully. Some probably perished from childbirth and its attendant dangers, the female equivalent of hunting as a cause of early mortality. Others died of illnesses now unidentifiable. Ermengard, wife of Louis the Pious, died in October 818, "worn out by prolonged loss of blood." Like Adelaide's fever, the symptoms are usually too general to pin down to specific diseases, for early medieval writers found the events of death more interesting than its causes. Surprisingly few queens died a violent death; only seven are recorded and five of these are Merovingian. Chilperic I, an excessively bloodthirsty man, murdered two of his wives. By his command, Audovera was put to death at Rouen several years after her repudiation; she was suspected of complicity in the rebellions of her sons. His second wife, Galswinth, the Visigothic princess, was garrotted by one of Chilperic's servants as she lay in bed. Chilperic wished to marry Fredegund and the crime may have been one of passion, though he could have taken Fredegund to his bed without murdering Galswinth. The gratuitous act seems another testimony to the violence of the man. Brunhild's eldest grandson, Theudebert II, murdered his lowborn wife, Bilichild. The full circumstances are unclear, but again the action appears arbitrary in an age when repudiation was easy. Perhaps Bilichild's servile origins, with no family to support and protect her, made her an easy target. Her namesake Bilichild, daughter of Sigibert III and wife of Childeric II, was done to death together with her husband in the forest of Livry. The pregnant girl and her husband both fell victim to the late seventh-century struggles for the throne.

The most infamous death of a queen, arguably one of the most brutal in the period, was the judicial murder of Brunhild at the orders of her nephew Clothar in 613. After his successful elimination of her grandsons Clothar had his aunt brought before him. With a wild disregard for the truth he accused her of the death of a host of kings. Although the details of her death vary, the old woman was apparently tortured for three days, led through the ranks of Clothar's army on a camel, and finally tied by the hair, one arm, and one leg to the tail of an unbroken horse to be cut to shreds by its hooves. What remained of her body was burned and the ashes later interred at the nunnery she founded at Autun. Whatever her guilt, Brunhild's death is a horrific commentary on a violent age. It was the final act in the long vendetta between herself and Fredegund that had begun with the murder of Brunhild's sister, Galswinth. Clothar, Fredegund's son, exacted the final revenge. Vengeance seems also to account for the murder of Osthryth, daughter of the Northumbrian Oswy and wife of Æthelred of Mercia; her Northumbrian sister had been involved in the death by treachery of the Mercian king Peada. Had fewer foreign wives returned home as widows and divorcees in the seventh century, the toll of murdered queens might have been higher. The only other murdered queen was Bertilla, wife of Berengar I, accused, mysteriously, of the crimes of Circe and put to death around the year 911. Just how and why Bertilla had turned the minds of men after the fashion of the ancient enchantress is not specified. Her death is an unexplained episode in the political turmoil of post-Carolingian Italy.

In her last months, Mathilda's thoughts turned frequently to the welfare of her foundation at Nordhausen, or at least the biographies of the queen written at that house stress her concern. The nuns may have hoped that Mathilda would die there, leaving them the fortunate legatees of her royal body. The biographies were a poor second best compared to her mortal remains. Possession of the bodies of the royal dead mattered; they could become important centers of profitable cults. When the emperor Louis II died in 875, the archbishop of Milan and an army of his clergy turned up to claim the body, which they felt was rightfully theirs. Again, Gunnhild's body was brought back from Italy in spite of the insanitary conditions. Such bodies as these had virtues not lightly to be foregone. When Gunnhild's father-in-law, Conrad II, died in 1039 his internal organs were buried immediately, but the rest of his body was carried through the monasteries of Germany, resting at Mainz, Worms, and Cologne, before burial at Speyer. Mathilda and Adelaide thoughtfully brought their own bodies to the place of burial before death, and Quedlinburg and Selz were able to use them to develop their cults. Chelles and Poitiers had profited from the possession of Balthild and Radegund, while in tenth-century England the claims of Ælfgifu, wife of King Edmund, to sanctity were fostered at her burial place at Shaftesbury.

In Baudonivia's *Life of Radegund* far more attention was paid to details of Radegund's burial than to her death. Before death Radegund had fallen foul of her local bishop, so that when the time came for her burial he was not available. The whole congregation stood around her bier, mourning and singing psalms, but the bishop was still traveling around his diocese. After three days' delay it was felt that burial must take place, with Gregory of Tours himself officiating. Radegund was to be buried with due honor in the basilica of St. Mary, and her body was carried in procession, preceded by candlebearers, below the wall of the nunnery. Since the sisters were forbidden to leave the precincts of the house, they stood on the top of the wall singing psalms and awaiting her passing. Gregory performed the rituals of burial, but perhaps fearing some unseemly jurisdictional dispute he left the coffin uncovered until the bishop of the diocese should arrive. The rites had already been disturbed by an unedifying occurrence, which only the power of the saint turned to good effect. Should the candles borne before the body be thrown into the grave or taken back for use? The squabble was cut short by the saintly dead queen, who caused a candle to leap into the air and fall at her own feet in the coffin. Further argument was superfluous.

Mathilda was buried with great honor at Quedlinburg in the basilica of St. Servatius next to the sepulcher of King Henry; there she had decreed she would rest and await the day of judgment. Such a burial of a queen with her husband or in a dynastic shrine was the norm. When Clotild, widow of Clovis, died at Tours, her body was taken to Paris for burial with her husband in the Church of St. Peter, which she had built there. Hildegard, the second wife of Charlemagne, was buried in the Carolingian family Church of St. Arnulf in Metz. Ermentrud, first wife of Charles the Bald, was interred in St. Denis; Gerberga, widow of Louis d'Outremer, at St. Remi, Rheims. In tenth-century Germany, Eadgyth, first wife of Otto I, was buried at Magdeburg; Otto was later entombed there beside her. In England, the dowager Emma was buried in the Old Minster with Cnut, and when Edith died in 1075 the Normans felt it most fitting that she should be taken to Westminster to lie beside Edward the Confessor. The repudiated wife of Eadwig died probably during the reign of her husband's supplanter, his brother Edgar. Her burial with the royal dead in the Old Minster, Winchester, suggests a gesture of reconciliation with her family.

Not all queens were buried with their husbands, though many

were interred in the religious foundations of the royal family. Ælf-gifu, first wife of the English king Edmund, was buried with her mother at Shaftesbury, the house of nuns that King Alfred had founded for his daughter. Theophanu was lain to rest in the monastery of St. Pantaleone, founded by her husband's uncle, Archbishop Bruno of Cologne. Ælfflæd, wife of Edward the Elder, was buried at Wilton. This was not only a royally connected nunnery, but the house where she and her daughters had lived. Many queens, especially repudiated ones, were buried in the religious houses they had founded or to which they retired. Thus the divorced Radegund lay at Poitiers; the ex-regent Balthild at Chelles, the home of her political exile; the ex-wife and widow, Æthelthryth and Sexberga, at Ely. A repudiated wife like Suzanne/Rozala returned home to Flanders and was buried with her first husband in the monastery at Ghent. Another remarried royal widow came to rest with her new family: Eadgifu, widow of Charles the Simple, lay at Soissons, the abbey she received in dower when she fled to marry her second husband, Herbert of Vermandois. Most queens were interred in royal mausolea or in the religious houses of their retirement, which houses in turn were rarely unconnected with royal cults. The bodies of the repudiated, and of some widows with long and checkered careers, might wander farther afield. The empress Adelaide's choice of Selz was eccentric, as it was neither an Ottonian dynastic house nor was she abbess there. In this as in other ways Adelaide appears as a woman with a life and mind of her own.

Some queens predeceased their husbands. Hildegard, Ermengard, Emma wife of Ralph, and Ermentrud all died as queens or king's wives, still actively filling their roles of wife and mother, mistress in the household, or queen. The majority, whether because of repudiation or widowhood, faced many years as dowagers. For some this meant a struggle over the succession, perhaps even a regency for an underage son. Sooner or later for most it meant retirement, usually into a nunnery, a fate not without its compensations. For many the end when it came was a royal way of death and burial, for some a quick affair, for a minority a violent exit. Even in retirement few forgot their position as royal wife, queen, and dowager, the position which had set them and their actions apart from other women.

 *Epilogue*

In most societies women have roles and responsibilities within the family and the household. They are wives and mothers, and enjoy varying degrees of involvement in providing for their families, bringing up their children, maintaining the emotional if not also economic well-being of the family. Depending on the economic organization and inheritance patterns of society, they may own and inherit land and property, use and bequeath it, or find themselves deprived of it and reduced to total dependence on their men. Economic and social conditions, tempered by prevailing ideologies, determine the extent of their involvement outside the home. Royal women live in these same worlds, and to some extent their opportunities and spheres of action are those of all women. However, their position in the royal family adds a political dimension to all their roles and may magnify some of them into important functions. Thus woman's concern for the spiritual well-being of the family may become ritual functions protecting dynasty and, by extension, kingdom; her organization of the household and especially its womenfolk may lead to control of aspects of the palace and its politics. Sympathetic identification and the exclusion of women from direct rivalry in the roles of men may create strong bonds between royal women and their sons or brothers the kings, and allow queens to become regents or chief counsellors in situations where kings have reason to fear other men. In Dahomey fear of the king's own bodyguard even produced a troop of Amazons, the boldest and toughest of the famous elephant-huntresses, who guarded the king's person.

Royal wives in the early Middle Ages were found exercising most of these roles: as concubine or as wife, though often through serial monogamy; as mother of the king's sons; as mistress of his household; as queen, with or without an active political role; as intimate royal counsellor; as daughter of a great family, property holder in her own right, and ecclesiastical politician; as queen mother scheming and gaining succession and even regency for her son; as widow, abbess and keeper of the royal shrines. Some of these roles remain those of the queen as long as personal monarchy persists and the monarch exercises power. A series of queens before the end of the eleventh century was able to make the most of them. The land and possessions these women acquired through inheritance and marriage was a foundation of their power. Transformations of Frankish and Lombard law in the sixth and seventh century allowed women to inherit, first confining them to newly acquired land, then allowing them a share in the family inheritance itself. Women benefited from the great land acquisitions of the settlement period, which provided wealth adequate to endow both male and female children. Female capacity to inherit and control property continued in Carolingian Frankia, and was especially important in tenth-century Germany and England, where women disposed of considerable landed possessions, partly because of their longevity as residual heirs, partly because of the recognition of their rights of inheritance and disposal. The situation was most favorable in tenth-century Italy, where women inherited land in their own right but also, when widowed, exercised substantial powers over a husband's property as well as controlling the land that they themselves brought into marriage. These property and inheritance patterns favored all noblewomen, and queens excelled in those kingdoms and periods where the position of women in general was favorable. But queens may have additional advantages that can enlarge the opportunities open to all women, even allowing royal women a role when most others of their sex are excluded from power.

The position of intimate royal counsellor was always open to queens: palace politics and intrigue were always a sphere for their activities. The roles this creates thus depend on the nature of palace politics. In the early Middle Ages palace politics focused almost all great issues, partly because at the center of family politics lay the question of the succession to the throne. As long as the succession remained a questionable and debatable issue, as long as it was not a foregone conclusion, it was a burning question, dominating not only the years after a king's death, but also the maneuvering and intriguing which long preceded that event. These intrigues were centered within the royal family itself and opened up a series of important roles for royal women during the lifetimes of their husbands

and after. A second great issue throughout this period was that of
the Church. All the early movements, first for preliminary conversion, then for Christianization, reform, and organization, were
played out in an alliance between churchmen and king. The palace
was the center of Church politics; the wealth, education, and ideologies of churchmen made Church politics significant.

The obvious role queens could play in palace intrigues was aided
by the landed wealth they could personally dispose of in favor of the
Church. They were often aided by forms of religious life which favored women; in seventh-century England and Frankia and again in
tenth-century Germany, movements of monasticism and Christianization were dominated by nunneries. The role of great abbesses,
itself linked to female property holding and family needs, helped
enhance the practical and theoretical position of noblewomen.
Again, where all noblewomen were advanced, queens profited,
both in the practical roles open to them—especially in retirement—
and in the ideological gains from the acceptance of female power.
Queens can excel in the politics of influence and patronage; their
opportunities are much rarer on the battlefield. Yet even here they
were not totally excluded. In the period of chronic insecurity of the
last Carolingians and the first Capetians, kings, like their vassals,
came to rely heavily on their own families, appointing close relatives
to key bishoprics, marrying to gain territory and wardships. Wives,
often the most loyal and reliable members of families, were entrusted with negotiations, even with defense.

But relatives, especially male relatives, were only loyal up to a
point. Mothers and sisters were more reliable, and with succession
disputes opening up rifts and creating tensions within families,
women often appeared as the natural regents for underage sons, the
best allies even in adulthood. Where large territories, long campaigns, and possession of several kingdoms strained personal rule,
women could sometimes become regents, usually where the ideology and the general position of women created favorable circumstances and traditions.

Historical development being continuous, all finishing points are
arbitrary. To end the history of queens in the mid-eleventh century is
just such an arbitrary decision. But it has some justification in a series of developments occurring between the tenth and twelfth centuries that helped to remove or change the conditions within which

earlier queens had achieved their power. A series of interrelated changes in the succession and treatment of the royal inheritance had profound effects. There was a shift away from division of the kingdoms toward the passing on of a unified inheritance in France, Germany, and England. Partition had been a possibility when the crown was sufficiently wealthy (at least vis-à-vis the great nobility), when there were sufficient separate kingdoms to endow sons and when the great nobility were prepared to accept an underking. The first moves to pass on unified kingdoms and not divide them among all sons intensified the struggles over the succession, and certainly contributed to the bitter conflicts of tenth- and eleventh-century England in which queens played a great part. But the attempts were accompanied by moves toward designation. As the lay nobility were soon to do, kings sought to confine the succession to the eldest son, to establish automatic primogeniture, to underpin it with pre-mortem designation and consecration and to virtually exclude younger sons. By the twelfth century these succession practices were becoming entrenched. They were aided by accidents like the ability of the Capetians to produce adult male heirs, and retarded by the extinction of royal families, as happened in tenth and eleventh century Germany. They long remained practices backed by a growing weight of tradition rather than rules and did not solve dynastic problems overnight. But they helped eclipse succession dispute, and with it the whole sphere of succession politics and the queen's role in them.

Later in the Middle Ages, even when a minor succeeded to the throne, female regency was rare. This may partly be explained by a growing involvement of the nobility in government, their increasing reliance on crown patronage, and hence their reluctance to give up control of such an important power. But this is a very partial answer, since it is highly doubtful whether the great nobility were ever unconcerned in the question of regency in the earlier period. The right of the royal family to exercise regency over its own seems always to have been recognized, and the triumph of the idea of primogeniture removed the most important obstacle to allowing a young king's uncles to be regents for him. This, plus the accidental lack of need for regencies in many dynasties in the late eleventh and twelfth centuries, helped to kill the tradition of female regency. The powers of tradition, the argument, This is what we have always done, had formerly aided female regency. The breach of that tradition, coupled with the lack of later circumstances that would demand a female regent, helped to end it.

There were other changes afoot which were inimical to the idea of female rule and power. From the tenth century onward in West Frankia, and gathering ground in the eleventh century throughout Western Europe, the rights of women to inherit and dispose of property were curtailed as part of general attempts to preserve family property. In the late eleventh century and early twelfth century a set of ideas, which themselves originated in tenth-century Cluniac movements, won a temporary triumph. The Gregorian movement of moral reform, which favored marriage and opposed sex, contained a strong current of antifeminism. It was not universally successful, but it marks a nadir in ideas of what women could and should be, setting ideals of womanhood which were both impractical and passive. After the great period of female monasticism in Ottonian Germany, women found themselves playing less and less of a role in the religious movements of the later Middle Ages. They were increasingly the outcasts, the second-class citizens of the religious life. When Æthelthryth's double monastery at Ely, over which she had presided as abbess in the seventh century, was refounded in the tenth, it became a house for men. This and not Ottonian Germany was the shape of things to come. Queens and other women controlled less property, had less power to patronize and influence churchmen. Insofar as the position of queens is linked to that of all women, these changes in inheritance, property holding, ideology and career opportunity affected them.

It has been suggested that the eleventh and especially the twelfth century saw a shift away from household politics toward greater bureaucratization in Western Europe. It has been argued that that shift removed some of the queen's powers in control of revenue and influence, even distancing her from the king himself through the development of a formal court of her own. There may be some truth here, though like all generalizations it carries dangers of oversimplification. However far administration may go along the road of bureaucracy, politics remains an area for personal influence. Those queens who had enjoyed certain quasi-administrative powers in the royal household certainly lost them. But influence over the king remained the center of medieval politics, because government was essentially personal rule.

Some aspects of household politics had changed, probably to the queen's detriment. Removal of the succession question made such politics less and less those of the family, where the queen had an obvious role, and more and more those of the kingdom, where she did not. Great ecclesiastical movements with wide ramifications were increasingly removed from the royal court; questions of fundamental Christianization and organization in which king and churchmen worked in close and necessary alliance ceased to be central. The courts of the Merovingians, the Carolingians, the English, and the Ottonian kings had been centers of educational and especially religious ferment. These movements and their patronage were now more diffused and their origins as often radical as royal. The easy alliance between king and churchmen was itself shaken during the late eleventh and twelfth centuries. For all these reasons, opportunities for queens were reduced.

But when, in later centuries, conditions similar to those of the early Middle Ages were re-created for a while, queens could play similar roles, becoming latter-day Adelaides and Brunhilds. The Angevin Empire of the late twelfth century was a far-flung grouping of kingdoms and duchies. One of its important elements, the duchy of Aquitaine, was the personal inheritance and contribution of Henry II's queen, Eleanor. The royal couple produced four sons, three of whom were adult before their father's death. Several kingdoms and duchies, providing arguments for division and provision of inheritance for all sons, in combination with a large family and the power of a woman who had personal control of part of the inheritance, produced conflicts of family and succession within which Eleanor was able to dominate. Even later, in fifteenth-century England, succession questions again opened a female role. Control of the king was the original issue in the mid-fifteenth century. Royal insanity, the regency, and the hopes of succession this gave to a disgruntled cousin, Richard of York, when followed by the birth of a son to the king, transformed this desire for control in the 1450s into a struggle for the succession. It was Henry VI's wife, Margaret of Anjou, the mother of his infant son, who emerged as the political and military leader of the Lancastrian party, a queen mother in the most traditional of roles, defending the rights of her son against a "wicked uncle."

In the juridical sense of formal powers and duties, there was rarely any question of queenship in the Middle Ages. The position of queen was whatever these women could make of it, determined by the framework of roles contemporary practice and theory allowed them. In the early Middle Ages that framework was wide, and many great women were able to use it to the full.

🜲 Bibliographical Notes

Chapter 1

The debate on the origins of Theophanu has most recently found expression in M. Uhlirz, "Studien über Theophano, I" and A. Hofmeister, "Studien zu Theophanu." The latter discusses other aspects of Theophanu's life, and his conclusions on her origin, children, age at death, and so on have generally been followed here, though the order of her children has been further clarified by O. Perst, "Zur Reihenfolge der Kinder Ottos II und der Theophano." I have adopted Perst's conclusions.

K. Werner, "Die Nachkommen Karls des Großen bis um Jahr 1000" traces the descendants of Charlemagne, and the numbers of male and female descendants are taken from his work. Werner has also reconstructed the facts on Queen Adelaide, wife of Louis the Stammerer, in ibid., Exkurs 2, pp. 429–41. The elusive Osyth is tracked by C. Höhler, "St. Osyth and Aylesbury."

The purpose of the *Encomium Emmae* is discussed by S. Körner, *The Battle of Hastings, England and Europe, 1035–66*, and its authorship, content, and intention by A. Campbell in his introduction to the edition of the *Encomium*; the purpose of the *Life of Edward* is treated by F. Barlow both in his introduction to the edition of that work, and in his *Edward the Confessor*, appendix A. E. Delaruelle, "Sainte Radegonde, son type de sainteté et la chrétienté de son temps" and L. Condanne, "Baudonivia, moniale de Sainte-Croix et biographe de S. Radegunde" discuss the two lives of Radegund, and Delaruelle is especially illuminating on the contrasts between the two. The lives written about Mathilda are considered by M. Lintzel, "Die Mathildenviten und das Wahrheitsproblem in der Überlieferung der Ottonenzeit," a discussion that deals especially with the problem of interpretation and use of such lives. The sources and intentions of Odilo's *Epitaph of Adelaide* are dealt with in the introduction to Paulhart's edition. The lives of all these Merovingian and

Ottonian women, together with the sources on Carolingian women and the classical, biblical, and Christian views of women are well reviewed by M-L. Portmann, *Die Darstellung der Frau in der Geschichtsschreibung des früheren Mittelalters*. J. Verdon, "Les Sources de l'histoire de la femme en occident aux Xe-XIIIe siècles," is less concerned with the image his sources present of women than is Portmann, but provides a good guide to the type of material in which women can be studied in this later period. K. Leyser, *Rule and Conflict*, especially pp. 63–73, discusses Ottonian women and nunneries.

The views of women that the early Christian West inherited from the Old Testament may be studied in further detail in P. Bird, "Images of Women in the Old Testament" and B. P. Prusak, "Woman: Seductive Siren and Source of Sin?" The Church fathers are discussed by R. R. Ruether, "Misogynism and Virginal Feminism in the Fathers of the Church," and the further development of their ideas in the Middle Ages by E. C. McLaughlin, "Equality of Souls, Inequality of Sexes: Woman in Medieval Theology." R. Fossier, "La Femme dans les sociétés occidentales," reminds us that the position of women was not uniformly low in the societies of the Middle Ages and stresses their economic importance within the household, a point also developed by J. A. McNamara and S. Wemple in "The Power of Women through the Family in Medieval Europe." J. T. Schulenberg, "Sexism and the Celestial Gynaeceum from 500 to 1200," however, shows how women were differently viewed by ecclesiastical thinkers at different stages of conversion and reform, and stresses the changes of the images of women, often to their detriment, towards the end of the period. M. Warner, *Alone of All Her Sex: The Myth and Cult of the Virgin Mary*, is a stimulating consideration of the changing views of Mary and their impact on the image of all women. She deals with Maria Regina, as does, in the specific context of the tenth century, R. Deshman, "*Christus rex et magi reges*: Kingship and Christology in Ottonian and Anglo-Saxon Art." The weakness of scientific knowledge, on which many misconceptions about women were based, is treated by V. Bullough, "Medieval Medical and Scientific Views of Women." Ideas of witchcraft and the taboos on sexuality, especially as they influenced Hincmar in the ninth century, are in J. Devisse, *Hincmar, Archevêque de Rheims, 845–82*, vol. 1, pp. 369 ff.

Many examples of the twelfth-century elaboration of Anglo-Saxon history, including the story of Cynethryth, are contained in C. E. Wright, *The Cultivation of Saga in Anglo-Saxon England.* The growth of the romantic view in the twelfth century, especially in relation to the story of Bertrada and Philip, is discussed by G. Duby, *Medieval Marriage: Two Models from Twelfth-Century France*, especially pp. 35 ff. The story of Angelberga and Hucbald is dissected by G. Pocchettino, "L'Imperatrice Angelberga, 850–90," pp. 55 ff., though with little sympathy for Angelberga.

G. Frugoni, "L'iconografia del matrimonio e della coppia nel medioevo" discusses the low valuation of women in the context of the low valuation of marriage and sex by the medieval church; see especially pp. 933 ff. and 944–45. The link between the view of marriage and women is also made by P. Toubert, "La Théorie du mariage chez les moralistes carolingiens," who demonstrates ninth-century Carolingian attempts to reevaluate both.

Chapter 2

L. Mair, *Marriage*, is an excellent comparative study of all aspects of marriage, from the factors governing choice, through the rituals of the event, to the resulting family relationships. The considerations that affected the choice of all noble and royal wives in the central Middle Ages are discussed by G. Duby, *Medieval Marriage: Two Models from Twelfth-Century France*, especially chap. 1, and by the same author in his "Le Mariage dans la société du haut moyen âge."

The dynastic context of early medieval marriage is treated by K. Schmid, "Heirat, Familienfolge, Geschlechterbewußtsein," with particular reference to the Carolingian and Ottonian family settlements. He treats the Ottonian family settlement in more detail in his "Neue Quellen zum Verständnis des Adels im 10 Jahrhundert" and especially in "Die Thronfolge Ottos des Großen."

The essential starting point for any study of Carolingian brides and marriages is still S. Hellman, "Die Heiraten der Karolinger," discussing both individual matches and family policy. S. Konecny, "Die Frauen des karolingischen Königshauses: Die politische Bedeutung der Ehe und die Stellung der Frau in der frankischen Herrscherfamilie vom 7 bis zum 10 Jahrhundert," has extended his study, and in this context has much to add on the political circumstances of individual matches. For the earliest Carolingians she has not replaced E. Hlawitschka, "Die Vorfahren Karls des Großen." E. Ewig, "Studien zur merowingischen Dynastie," is an indispensable guide on this as on all aspects of the Merovingian dynasty.

On the Capetians see J. Dhondt, "Sept femmes et un trio de rois," eminently readable, and also M. Facinger, "A Study of Medieval Queenship: Capetian France, 987–1237." G. Duby, *Medieval Marriage*, chap. 2, has much to say on the factors governing the choices of Robert the Pious. On all the Capetians and the later Carolingians, the standard biographies in the Bibliotheque de l'Ecole des Hautes Etudes are still invaluable mines of information; see A. Eckel, *Charles le Simple*; P. Lauer, *Robert I et Raoul de Bourgogne rois de France, 923–936*; idem, *Le Règne de Louis IV d'Outremer*; F. Lot, *Les Derniers Carolingiens: Lothaire, Louis V, Charles de Lorraine, 954–991*; idem, *Etudes sur le règne de Hugues Capet et la fin du Xe siècle*; C. Pfister, *Etudes sur le règne de Robert I Pieux, 996–1031*.

I have discussed the English brides in my "King's Wife in Wessex," and also in "Charles the Bald, Judith and England"; the latter is specifically concerned with the context of the marriage of Judith and Æthelwulf and also considers the marriage alliances arising from the Viking invasions of the ninth and tenth centuries.

B. Kliman, "Women in Early English Literature, *Beowulf* to the *Ancrene Wisse*" treats the subject of women as peacemakers and the "active" role this gives their marriages in the early period. R. Schneider, *Königswahl und Königserhebung im Frühmittelalter: Untersuchungen zur Herrschaftsnachfolge bei den Langobarden und Merowingern*, discusses Merovingian and Lombard marriages with widows; the whole work is of relevance, but see especially pp. 246 ff. This important book also has much to add on the factors influencing the choice of Merovingian wives.

Full details of Clothar's marriages are in E. Ewig, "Studien zur merowingischen Dynastie"; those of Hugh receive further treatment in G. Fasoli, *I re d'Italia, 888–962*, and R. Poupardin, *Le Royaume de Provence sous les Carolingiens, 855–933*, especially pp. 223 ff.

The Supponides and their royal marriages are treated by E. Hlawitschka, *Franken, Alemannen, Bayern und Burgunder in Oberita-*

lien, 774–962, pp. 27, 299–309, and Bertilla especially by H. Keller, "Zur Struktur der Königsherrschaft im karolingischen und nachkarolingischen Italien," pp. 175 ff.

The elusive Mathilda, second wife of the Capetian Henry I, is tracked down by S. de Vajay, "Mathilde, reine de France inconnue."

Chapter 3

The literature on marriage continues to grow apace. L. Mair, *Marriage*, is a good starting point, and on medieval marriage in particular G. Duby, *Medieval Marriage*, provides a study of the tenth to twelfth centuries, with an especial interest in Capetian marriage and divorce. The essential reading is now *Il matrimonio nella società altomedievale*, the publication of the Spoleto conference on the topic held in 1976: on the topics covered in this chapter see especially G. Duby, "Le Mariage dans la société du haut moyen âge"; J. Gaudemet, "Le Legs du droit romain en matière matrimoniale"; P. Toubert, "La Théorie du mariage chez les moralistes carolingiens"; R. Manselli, "Il matrimonio nei penitenziali"; C. Vogel, "Les Rites de la celebration du mariage: Leur signification dans la formation du lien durant le haut moyen âge"; G. Fransen, "La Rupture du mariage"; P. Fedele, "Vedovanza e seconde nozze"; and C. Frugoni, "L'iconografia del matrimonio e della coppia nel medioevo." Vogel has not replaced K. Ritzer, *Le Mariage dans les eglises chrétiennes du Ier au XIe siècle*, which exhaustively traces the development of the rituals. G. H. Joyce, *Christian Marriage* is still a useful account in English, especially of the development of the Church's doctrinal position.

Polygamy, concubinage, serial monogamy, and marriage strategies in general, together with many other central questions, are discussed in a typically brilliant and thought-provoking way by J. Goody, *Production and Reproduction: A Comparative Study of the Domestic Domain*. For an anthropologist's view on the definition of marriage see E. Leach, "Polyandry, Inheritance and the Definition of Marriage." S. Konecny, "Die Frauen des karolingischen Königshauses," chap. 2, treats of forms of marriage in the early Middle

Ages and their role in royal marriage and strategy. J. A. Brundage, "Concubinage and Marriage in Medieval Canon Law," highlights the problems that later canonists had in distinguishing the two.

The divorce case of Lothar II has attracted much comment and discussion. There is a full and interesting discussion, especially of the politics of the affair, in S. Konecny, "Die Frauen des karolingischen Königshauses," chap. 7. The involvement of Hincmar is much debated. C-R. Brühl, "Hinkmariana II," interprets Hincmar's stand in a highly political fashion, and tends to see him as a tool of Charles the Bald's politics; I have rather followed J. Devisse, *Hincmar, Archevêque de Reims, 845–82*, who places the divorce in the context of the archbishop's thinking on marriage and suggests a more principled stand, though Devisse tends to make Hincmar too consistent. On detailed aspects of the case see L. Dupraz, "Deux preceptes de Lothaire II, 867 et 868, ou les vestiges diplomatiques d'un divorce manqué"; and G. F. Pölnitz-Kehr, "Kaiserin Angilberga: Ein Exkurs zur Diplomatik Kaiser Ludwigs II von Italien," suggesting that a retrospective dowry document was forged for Angelberga.

The clash between ecclesiastical views and secular needs is discussed in the works of Duby cited, in all the works on the Lothar affair, by S. Konecny in "Die Frauen des karolingischen Königshauses" for the whole ninth century, and specifically for the reign of Louis the Pious in her "Eherecht und Ehepolitik unter Ludwig dem Frommen." See also J. A. McNamara and S. Wemple, "Marriage and Divorce in the Frankish Kingdom."

Charlemagne's marital career is further discussed by S. Konecny, "Die Frauen des karolingischen Königshauses"; I have largely followed E. Ewig, "Studien zur merowingischen Dynastie," in my reconstruction of Chlothar's marriages. Robert the Pious's affairs are discussed by G. Duby, *Medieval Marriage*, and I have treated Eadwig's marriage and divorce further in my "King's Wife in Wessex." On Brunhild and Columbanus see G. Kurth, "La Reine Brunehaut," but especially the excellent reappraisal of Brunhild by J. Nelson, "Queens as Jezebels: The Careers of Brunhild and Balthild in Merovingian History." L. Levillain, "Etudes merovingiennes: La Charte de Clotilde, 10 mars 673," pp. 48 ff., discusses the eighth- and early ninth-century Carolingian women who are termed *reginae*.

On the children of Otto II and Theophanu see A. Hofmeister, "Studien zu Theophanu," with the corrections of O. Perst, "Zur Reihenfolge der Kinder Ottos II und der Theophano." The birth of Theophanu's children in nunneries is detailed in M. Uhlirz, "Studien über Theophano III: Die Interventionen der Kaiserin Theophano zugunsten der Nonnenklöster während der Regierungszeit Ottos II und ihre Bedeutung." K. F. Werner, "Die Nachkommen Karls des Großen bis um das Jahr 1000 (1–8 Generation)," provides a mine of detailed information on the marriages and families of the Carolingians and of the various ninth- and tenth-century families connected to them by blood. M. L. Bulst-Thiele, *Kaiserin Agnes*, has details of that empress' children.

On Charles the Bald's desire for children and the ecclesiastical measures he took to procure them see E. H. Kantorowicz, "The Carolingian King in the Bible of San Paolo fuori le Mura"; on tenth-century fertility cults, K. Schmid, "Heirat, Familienfolge, Geschlechterbewußtsein."

Chapter 4

On property and women see J. Goody, *Production and Reproduction*, and his "Inheritance, Property and Women: Some Comparative Considerations." Women and treasure in the Merovingian period are discussed by J. Nelson, "Queens as Jezebels: The Careers of Brunhild and Balthild in Merovingian History"; and R. Schneider, *Königswahl und Königserhebung im Frühmittelalter: Untersuchungen zur Herrschaftsnachfolge bei den Langobarden und Merowingern*; in the Carolingian period by J. Hyam, "Ermintrude and Richildis." I have discussed the property of tenth- and eleventh-century English queens in my "King's Wife in Wessex." M. Uhlirz, "Die rechtliche Stellung der Kaiserinwitwe Adelheid im deutschen und im italischen Reich," deals with the dowry of Adelaide and the problems it caused. Statements on the queen's estates in Italy are based largely on P. Darmstadter, *Das Reichsgut in der Lombardei und Piemont, 568–1250*, especially pp. 18 ff. and 33 ff., with further information on grants to Angelberga from G. Pochettino, "L'Imperatrice Angelberga, 850–90."

For courts as centers of learning and the queen's role in this regard see P. Riché, *Education and Culture in the Barbarian West*,

Sixth through Eighth Centuries; and R. R. Bezzola, *Les Origines et la formation de la littérature courtoise en occident, 500–1200*. On fostering and its functions, J. Goody, *Production and Reproduction*, and E. Goody, "Forms of Pro-Parenthood: The Sharing and Substitution of Parental Roles."

A fuller account of the reign of Louis the Pious and Judith's crises may be had in L. Halphen, *Charlemagne et l'empire Carolingien*. The intrigues surrounding the death of Charles the Fat are discussed by H. Keller, "Zum Sturz Karls III"; and the saga of Charles of Lorraine, Adalbero, and Emma may be followed in F. Lot, *Les derniers Carolingiens: Lothaire, Louis V, Charles de Lorraine, 954–991*.

Chapter 5

On Angelberga, see G. Pochettino, "L'Imperatrice Angelberga, 850–90," very informative but unsympathetic; C. E. Odegaard, "The Empress Angelberga," factual but uncritical; and a good reinterpretation of certain aspects of her career in S. Konecny, "Die Frauen des karolingischen Königshauses," chap. 8. On Æthelflæd see F. Wainwright, "Æthelflæd, Lady of the Mercians." In spite of her undoubted importance there is no full modern biography of Adelaide. On her early life see F. P. Wimmer, *Kaiserin Adelheid, Gemahlin Ottos I des Großen in ihrem Leben und Wirken von 931–973*; on her widowhood and landed power, M. Uhlirz, "Die rechtliche Stellung der Kaiserinwitwe Adelheid im deutschen und im italienischen Reich"; and on Verona and the events surrounding it, M. Lintzel, "Der Reichstag von Verona im Jahre 983." Her role and that of Theophanu in the early years of Otto III are highlighted by P. Kehr, "Zur Geschichte Ottos III." On Italian queens, especially Ageltrudis, Adelaide in Italy, and Willa, see G. Fasoli, *I re d'Italia, 888–962*. R. Poupardin, *Le Royaume de Provence sous les Carolingiens, 855–933*, has more on Ermengard, wife of Boso. On the tenth-century Carolingian and Capetian queens see in general J. Verdon, "Les Femmes et la politique en France au Xe siècle," and details in the biographies of their husbands and sons by Eckel, Lauer, and Lot. On the Byzantine empresses see L. Brehier, *Le Monde byzantin*.

On queens and ecclesiastical patronage F. Prinz, *Frühes Mönch-tum im Frankenreich: Kultur und Gesellschaft in Gallien, den Rhein-landen und Bayern am Beispiel der monastischen Entwicklung*, is a mine of information on the Merovingian period. Theudelinda and her ecclesiastical "policies" are discussed by G. P. Bognetti, "Santa Maria foris Portas di Castelseprio e la storia religiosa dei Longo-bardi." J. Nelson, "Queens as Jezebels: The Careers of Brunhild and Balthild in Merovingian History," discusses the religious pat-ronage, motives, and allies of Brunhild and Balthild; on the latter see E. Ewig, "Das Privileg des Bischofs Berthefrid von Amiens für Corbie von 664 und die Klosterpolitik der Königin Balthild." On the patronage of Burgundian queens see R. Poupardin, *Le Royaume de Bourgogne, 888–1038*, especially p. 158 ff. Tenth-century English queens are dealt with by M. A. Meyer, "Women and the Tenth-Century English Monastic Reform," and both tenth- and eleventh-century English queens by my "King's Wife in Wessex."

J. Schulenberg, "Sexism and the Celestial Gynaeceum from 500–1200," emphasizes the link between periods of conversion and re-form and the prominence of royal women, a point underlined by K. Leyser, *Rule and Conflict in an Early Medieval Society, Ottonian Saxony*, section 2.

On the making of queens and coronations see my "Charles the Bald, Judith and England." C-R. Brühl, "Fränkischer Krönungs-brauch und das Problem der Festkrönungen" has details of virtually all known ninth-century coronations and consecrations. E. H. Kan-torowicz, "The Carolingian King in the Bible of San Paolo fuori le Mura," demonstrates the link between Ermentrud's anointing and fertility; L. Levillain, "L'Avènement de la dynastie carolingienne et les origines de l'état pontifical," discusses the possible anointing of Bertha in the context of the Carolingian seizure of the crown. M. Fa-cinger, "A Study of Medieval Queenship: Capetian France, 987–1237," treats Capetian queen making, but does not delve into its tenth-century origins.

The *consors regni* formula has been much debated. C. G. Mor, "*Consors regni*: La regina nel diritto pubblico Italiano dei secoli IX–X," argued for the formal powers of queens so designated; T. Vogelsang, *Die Frau als Herscherrin im höhen Mittelalter*, seems to accept this, though he discusses the formula in largely a diplomatic context; the essential reinterpretation upon which statements in this chapter are largely based is that of P. Delogu, "*Consors regni*, un problemo carolingio."

References to the royal vestments of Merovingian queens are in R. Schneider, *Königswahl und Königserhebung im Frühmittelalter*, pp. 218 ff.; ibid., pp. 208 ff. on Theudelinda's crown. R. Deshman, "*Christus rex et magi reges*: Kingship and Christology in Ottonian and Anglo-Saxon Art," discusses the royal iconography of the tenth century, including that of Maria Regina, though reference must still be made to P. E. Schramm, *Die deutschen Kaiser und Könige in Bildern ihre Zeit*. Further details of Dunstan's career are in J. A. Robinson, *The Times of St. Dunstan*; the entries in the Reichenau confraternity book are discussed by L. Levillain, "Etudes merovingiennes: La Charte de Clotilde, 10 mars 673," appendix.

P. Toubert, *Les structures du Latium médiéval, le Latium méridional et la Sabine du IXe siècle á la fin du XIIe siècle*, pp. 749–68, demonstrates the powers over land enjoyed by women in some parts of Italy.

Chapter 6

Many of the details of deaths and ages at death for the Merovingians are derived from E. Ewig, "Studien zur merowingischen Dynastie"; for the Carolingians and their successors from K. Werner, "Die Nachkommen Karls des Großen bis um das Jahr 1000 (1–8 Generation)"; for the Ottonians from K. Leyser, *Rule and Conflict in an Early Medieval Society, Ottonian Saxony*, pp. 49 ff.

On Brunhild, G. Kurth, "La Reine Brunehaut" is still essential, an informative if romantically sympathetic account, but this must be read in conjunction with J. Nelson's excellent reappraisal in "Queens as Jezebels." There is discussion of Eadgifu in my "King's Wife in Wessex."

The essential comparative introduction to succession practices is J. Goody, *Succession to High Office*; I have discussed the question and its general relation to early medieval queens and power in my "Sons and Mothers: Family Politics in the Early Middle Ages." On the early period P. Grierson, "Election and Inheritance in Early Germanic Kingship," deals with the sixth century and before; and I. Wood, "Kings, Kingdoms and Consent," is full of illuminating insight for the sixth and seventh centuries. For the Merovingians reference should also be made to J. M. Wallace-Hadrill, *The Long-Haired Kings and Other Studies in Frankish History*; and on Merovingians and Lombards, R. Schneider, *Königswahl und Königserhebung im Frühmittelalter*, is now essential. For the Lombards this has largely replaced C. G. Mor, "La successione al trono nel diritto pubblico longobardo." On England D. Dumville, "The *Ætheling*: A Study in Anglo-Saxon Constitutional History" is necessary reading. See also A. Williams, "Some Notes and Considerations on Problems Connected with the English Royal Succession, 860–1066." In my "King's Wife in Wessex" I have discussed tenth- and eleventh-century English succession practice, especially in the effect it had on royal women.

On female regency in Italy and Merovingian Gaul, see R. Schneider, *Königswahl und Königserhebung im Frühmittelalter*, and further discussion in J. Nelson, "Queens as Jezebels." S. Konecny, "Die Frauen des karolingischen Königshauses," especially pp. 61 ff., suggests the continuation of Merovingian practices of female regency into the early Carolingian period.

On Mathilda and her preferences see M. Lintzel, "Königin Mathilde"; idem, "Die Mathildenviten und das Wahrheitsproblem in der Überlieferung der Ottonenzeit"; but especially his "*Heinricus natus in aula regali*: Miszellen zur Geschichte des zehnten Jahrhunderts nr. V." K. Schmid, "Die Thronfolge Ottos des Großen" is essential on all the Ottonian succession plans of the 920s and 930s and on their family repercussions. On Constance see the unsympathetic accounts of J. Dhondt, "Sept femmes et un trio de rois"; C. Pfister, *Etudes sur le règne de Robert I Pieux, 996–1031*, especially chap. 3.

There is detailed treatment of the events on the death of Clovis in 511 and Clotild's part in them in I. Wood, "Kings, Kingdoms and Consent." The maneuverings which preceded the anticipated death of Charles the Fat are dissected and explained by H. Keller, "Zum Sturz Karls III"; and on the attempt to gain the imperial crown for Louis the Blind and the Vision of Charles the Fat see E. Ewig, "Kaiser Lothars Urenkel, Ludwig von Vienne, der präsumtive Nachfolger Kaiser Karls III." J. Nelson, "Inauguration Rituals" has much to say on the making of a king and the arguments that could be put forward in the discussions surrounding his accession.

P. Kehr, "Zur Geschichte Ottos III" deals with the early years of the infant emperor and the support given to Adelaide and Theophanu; M. L. Bulst-Thiele, *Kaiserin Agnes*, discusses Agnes's regency and its clerical support. On the English Emma, see M. Campbell, "Emma, reine d'Angleterre, mère dénaturée ou femme vindicative?" but compare my "Sons and Mothers: Family Politics in the Early Middle Ages" and "The King's Wife in Wessex." For more detailed discussion of the succession dispute in England in 975 see D. J. V. Fisher, "The Anti-Monastic Reaction in the Reign of Edward the Martyr," and my "Reign of Æthelred II: A Study in the Limitations on Royal Policy and Action." The marriage of Judith and Æthelbald, and other marriages with royal widows, are treated in my "Charles the Bald, Judith and England"; W. Chaney, *The Cult of Kingship in Anglo-Saxon England*, pp. 26 ff. suggested the survival of matriliny in the marriage to stepmothers.

Angelberga receives detailed treatment at the unsympathetic hands of G. Pochettino and there is especial concern for the succession in S. Konecny, "Die Frauen des karolingischen Königshauses," chap. 8.

Chapter 7

On the early developments in female monasticism see F. Prinz, *Frühes Mönchtum im Frankenreich*; Marquis de Maillé, *Les Cryptes de Jouarre*; and J. Godfrey, "The Double Monastery in English History." J. Nicholson, "*Feminae gloriosae*: Women in the Age of Bede," surveys seventh-century Englishwomen and their religious activities. J. T. Schulenberg, "Sexism and the Celestial Gynaeceum from 500 to 1200," has interesting comments on female sanctity, and on "waves" of female saints. On nunneries and women in tenth-century Germany, with much wider implications, see the excellent study by K. Leyser, *Rule and Conflict in an Early Medieval Society, Ottonian Saxony*, chap. 6.

🜲 Bibliography

Abbreviations

B.A.R.   British Archaeological Reports

B.E.H.E.   Bibliothèque de l'Ecole des Hautes Etudes

E.H.R.   English Historical Review

Ep.KA.   Epistolae karolini aevi

F.S.I.   Fonti per la storia d'Italia

M.I.Ö.G.   Mitteilungen des Instituts für Österreichische Geschichtsforschung

MGH   Monumenta Germaniae historica

PL   Patrologia Latina

SS   Scriptores

SRG   Scriptores rerum germanicarum in usum scholarum

SS RM   Scriptores rerum merovingicarum

Primary Sources

Agobard. *Letters*. Ep.KA., vol. 3. Berlin, 1899.

———. *Libri duo pro filiis et contra Judith uxorem Ludovici Pii.* MGH SS 15. Hanover, 1887. Pp. 274–79.

Alcuin. *Letters*. MGH Ep.KA., vol. 2. Berlin, 1895.

Ambrose. *De Virginibus*. PL, vol. 16.

Bibliography

Anglo-Saxon Charters. Edited by A. J. Robertson. Cambridge,
    1956.
Anglo-Saxon Charters: An Annotated Handlist and Bibliography.
    Edited by P. H. Sawyer. London, 1968.
Anglo-Saxon Chronicle. Edited and translated by D. Whitelock,
    D. C. Douglas, and S. Tucker. London, 1965.
Anglo-Saxon Poetry. Translated by R. K. Gordon. London, 1954.
Anglo-Saxon Wills. Edited by D. Whitelock. Cambridge, 1930.
Anglo-Saxon Writs. Edited by F. Harmer. Manchester, 1952.
Annales de Flodoard. Edited by P. Lauer. Collection de Textes.
    Paris, 1905.
Annales mettenses priores. MGH SRG, vol. 12. Hanover, 1909.
Annales Quedlinburgenses. MGH SS 3. Hanover, 1839.
Annales regni Francorum. MGH SS 1. Hanover, 1895. Translated
    by B. W. Scholz as *Carolingian Chronicles.* Michigan, 1972.
Annales de Saint Bertin. Edited by F. Grat, J. Vielliard, and
    S. Clemencét. Paris, 1964.
Annals of Fulda. MGH SRG, vol. 4. Hanover, 1891.
Asser. *Life of King Alfred.* Edited by W. E. Stevenson. Oxford, 1904.
[Astronomer]. *Anonymous Life of Louis the Pious.* MGH SS 2.
    Hanover, 1929. Translated by A. Cabaniss as *Son of
    Charlemagne.* Syracuse, 1961.
Bede. *Ecclesiastical History of the English Nation.* Edited by
    C. Plummer. Oxford, 1896.
Benedict of Mont Soracte. *Il chronicon di Benedetto Monaco di S.
    Andrea del Soratte.* Edited by G. Zucchetti. F.S.I., vol. 55.
    Rome, 1920.
Beowulf. Edited by F. Klaeber. 3d ed. London, 1951.
Beowulf and Judith: Anglo-Saxon Poetic Records, vol. 4. Edited by
    E. von Kirk Dobbie. London, 1954.
Capitularia regum Francorum. Edited by A. Boretius. MGH.
    Hanover, 1883.
Cartularium Saxonicum. Edited by W. de Gray Birch. 3 vols. London, 1885–99.
Chronicle of Æthelweard. Edited and translated by A. Campbell.
    London, 1962.
Chronicle of Odoranus of Sens. Edited by R. H. Bautier. Paris,
    1973.

Claudius Pontificals. Edited by D. H. Turner. Henry Bradshaw Society, vol. 97 for 1964. London, 1971.

Codex diplomaticus aevi Saxonici. Edited by J. M. Kemble. 6 vols. London, 1839–48.

Coronatio Judithae Karoli II filiae, coronatio Hermintrudis Reginae. Legum sectio II. Edited by A. Boretius and V. Krause. MGH. Hanover, 1897.

Councils and Ecclesiastical Documents. Edited by A. W. Haddan and W. Stubbs. Vol. 3. Oxford, 1871.

Diplomata I (Louis the German, Karloman, Louis the Young). Edited by P. Kehr. MGH. Berlin, 1934.

Diplomata II (Charles III). Edited by P. Kehr. MGH. Berlin, 1937.

Diplomata Karolinorum III (Lothar I and II). Edited by T. Scheiffer. MGH. Berlin, 1966.

Diplomata regum ex stirpe Karolinorum IV (Zwentibold and Louis the Child). Edited by T. Scheiffer. MGH. Berlin, 1960.

Diplomatum regum et imperatorum Germaniae I (Conrad I, Henry I, Otto I). MGH. Hanover, 1879–84.

Diplomatum regum et imperatorum Germaniae II, part 1 (Otto II). MGH. Hanover, 1888.

I diplomi di Berengario I. Edited by L. Schiaparelli. F.S.I., vol. 35. Rome, 1903.

I diplomi di Guido e di Lamberto. Edited by L. Schiaparelli. F.S.I., vol. 36. Rome, 1906.

Eddius Stephanus. *Life of Bishop Wilfrid.* Edited and translated by B. Colgrave. Cambridge, 1927.

Edward, King and Martyr. Edited by C. E. Fell. Leeds Texts and Monographs, n.s. 3. Leeds, 1971.

Einhard. *Life of Charlemagne.* Edited by H. W. Garrod and R. B. Mowat. Oxford, 1925.

Encomium Emmae Reginae. Edited and translated by A. Campbell. Camden Series, vol. 72. London, 1949.

Epitome chronicorum Casinensium jussu Sanctissimi Stephani Papae II conscripta ab Anastasio seniore, sedis apostolicae bibliothecario. Rerum italicarum scriptores, vol. 2, pp. 345–70.

Ermoldus Nigellus. *In honorem Hludowici.* Poetae latini aevi carolini, vol. 2. MGH. Hanover, 1884.

Florence of Worcester. *Chronicon ex chronicis*. Edited by B.
  Thorpe. London, 1848–89.
Fredegar. *Fourth Book of the Chronicle of Fredegar*. Edited and
  translated by J. M. Wallace-Hadrill. London, 1960.
Fulbert of Chartres. *Letters*. PL, vol. 141.
Gaimar. *L'Estorie des Engles*. Edited by T. D. Hardy and C. T. Mar-
  tin. Rolls Series, 1885.
Gerbert. *Lettres*. Edited by J. Havet. Collection des textes. Paris,
  1889.
Gregory of Tours. *History of the Franks*. Edited and translated by
  O. M. Dalton. 2 vols. Oxford, 1971.
Helgaud of Fleury. *La Vie de Robert le Pieux*. Edited and translated
  by R. H. Bautier and G. Labory. Paris, 1965.
Hincmar. *De ordine Palatii*. Edited by A. Boretius. MGH Capit.,
  vol. 2. Hanover, 1883.
Hrabanus Maurus. *Expositio in librum Hester*. PL, vol. 109.
————. *Letters*. MGH Ep.KA., vol. 3. Berlin, 1899.
Hroswitha of Gandersheim. *Gesta Ottonis*. Edited by P. Winterfeld.
  MGH SRG. Berlin, 1965.
Jerome.*Contra Jovinianum*. PL, vol. 23.
Karolus Magna et Leo Papa. Poetae latini aevi carolini, vol. 1.
  MGH. Hanover, 1881.
Liber historiae Francorum. Edited and translated by B. S. Bach-
  rach. Lawrence, Kansas, 1973.
Life and Miracles of St. Wistan: Chronicon Abbatiae de Evesham.
  Edited by W. D. Macray. Rolls Series, 1863.
Life of King Edward Who Rests at Westminster. Edited and trans-
  lated by F. Barlow. London, 1962.
Life of Wala. Translated by A. Cabaniss as *Charlemagne's Cousins*.
  New York, 1967.
Liudprand of Cremona. *Works*. Translated by F. A. Wright. Lon-
  don, 1930.
Miracula Sancti Benedicti. Edited by E. de Certain. Paris, 1858.
Nithard. *Histoire des fils de Louis le Pieux*. Edited by P. Lauer.
  Paris, 1926.
Odilo of Cluny. [*Epitaph of Adelaide*] *Die Lebensbeschreibung der
  Kaiserin Adelheid von Abt Odilo von Cluny*. Edited by H.
  Paulhart. M.I.Ö.G., supplementary vol. 20, part 2. *Festschrift*

zur Jahrtausendfeier der Kaiserkrönung Ottos des Großen, part 2. Cologne, 1962.

Paul the Deacon. *History of the Lombards*. Translated by W. D. Foulke, edited and introduction by E. Peters. Philadelphia, 1974.

————. [*Poems*] *Die Gedichte des Paulus Diaconus*. Edited by K. Neff. Quellen und Untersuchungen zur lateinischen Philologie des Mittelalters, edited by L. Traube, vol. 3, part 4. Munich, 1908.

Ralph Glaber. *Historiarum libri quinque*. Edited by M. Prou. Paris, 1886.

Recueil des actes de Charles II le Chauve. Edited by G. Tessier. 3 vols. Paris, 1943–55.

Recueil des actes de Charles III le Simple roi de France. Edited by F. Lot and P. Lauer. Paris, 1940–49.

Recueil des actes de Louis IV roi de France, 936–54. Edited by P. Lauer. Paris, 1914.

Recueil des actes de Lothaire et de Louis V rois de France, 954–987. Edited by L. Halphen and F. Lot. Paris, 1908.

Regino of Prum. *Chronicon cum continuatione treverensi*. Edited by F. Kurze. MGH SRG. Hanover, 1890.

Richer. *Histoire de France, 888–995*. Edited and translated by R. Latouche. Paris, 1930 and 1937.

Sedulius Scottus. *Liber de rectoribus Christianis*. Edited by S. Hellmann. Quellen und Untersuchungen zur lateinischen Philologie des Mittelalters. Munich, 1906.

Tertullian. *De cultu feminarum*. PL, vol. 1.

Thegan. *Vita Hludowici*. MGH SS 2. Hanover, 1829.

Theodulf of Orleans. *Poems*. Poetae latini aevi carolini, vol. 1. MGH. Hanover, 1881.

Thietmar von Merseburg. *Chronicle*. Edited by R. Holtzmann, MGH SRG, n.s. 9. Berlin, 1935.

Venantius Fortunatus. *Opera poetica*. Auctorum antiquissimorum, vol. 4, part 1. MGH. Berlin, 1881.

La Vie de S. Wulfhilde par Goscelin de Cantorbéry. Edited by M. Esposito. Analecta Bollandiana, vol. 32. 1913.

Visio Caroli Grassi. MGH SS 10. Hanover, 1852. P. 458.

Visio cuiusdam mulieris pauperculae. Edited by Löwe Wattenbach-Levison. Deutschlands Geschichtsquellen im Mittelalter, Vorzeit und karolinger, vol. 3. Weimar, 1957.

Vita Dunstani Auctore B: Memorials of St. Dunstan. Edited by W. Stubbs. Rolls Series, 1874.

Vita Mahthildis reginae antiquior. Edited by R. Koepke. MGH SS 10. Hanover, 1852.

Vita Mahthildis reginae posterior. MGH SS 4. Hanover, 1841.

Vita Sanctae Balthildis. MGH SS RM II. Hanover, 1888.

Vita S. Radegundis liber I. Venantius Fortunatus. MGH SS RM II. Hanover, 1888.

Vita S. Radegundis liber II. Baudonivia. MGH SS RM II. Hanover, 1888.

Widukind. *Rerum gestarum Saxonicarum, libri tres.* Edited by H. Lohmann and P. Hirsch. MGH SRG. Hanover, 1935.

William of Malmesbury. *De gestis regum Anglorum.* Edited by W. Stubbs. Rolls Series, 1887.

Wipo. *The Deeds of Conrad II.* Edited and translated by T. E. Mommsen and K. F. Morrison. Imperial Lives and Letters of the Eleventh Century. New York, 1962.

Secondary Sources

Ackroyd, J. "Women in Feudal Japan." *Transactions of the Asiatic Society of Japan*, ser. 3, vol. 7 (November 1959): 31 –68.

Barlow, F. *Edward the Confessor.* London, 1970.

———. *The English Church, 1000–1066.* London, 1963.

Bezzola, R. R. *Les Origines et la formation de la littérature courtoise en occident, 500–1200*, vol. 1. B.E.H.E., vol. 226. Paris, 1958.

Bird, P. "Images of Women in the Old Testament." In *Religion and Sexism*, edited by R. R. Ruether. New York, 1974.

Bognetti, G. P. "Santa Maria foris Portas di Castelseprio e la storia religiosa dei Longobardi." In *L'eta longobarda*, vol. 2. Milan, 1966.

Brehier, L. *Le Monde byzantin*, vol. 2. Paris, 1949.

Brühl, C-R. "Fränkischer Krönungsbrauch und das Problem der Festkrönungen." *Historische Zeitschrift* 194 (1962): 265–326.

————. "Hinkmariana II. Hinkmar im Widerstreit von kanonischen Recht und Politik in Ehefragen." *Deutsches Archiv* 20 (1964): 55–77.

Brundage, J. A. "Concubinage and Marriage in Medieval Canon Law." *Journal of Medieval History* 1 (1975): 1–17.

Bullough, V. L. "Medieval Medical and Scientific Views of Women." *Viator* 4 (1973): 485–501.

Bulst-Thiele, M. L. *Kaiserin Agnes*. Beiträge zur Kulturgeschichte des Mittelalters und der Renaissance, vol. 52. Leipzig, 1933.

Büsing, A. "Mathilde, Gemahlin Heinrichs I." Ph.D. dissertation, University of Halle-Wittenberg, 1910.

Campbell, M. W. "Emma, reine d'Angleterre, mère dénaturée ou femme vindicative?" *Annales de Normandie* 23 (1973): 97–114.

————. "Queen Emma and Ælfgifu of Northampton, Canute the Great's Women." *Medieval Scandinavia* 4 (1971): 66–79.

Chaney, W. *The Cult of Kingship in Anglo-Saxon England*. Manchester, 1970.

Condanne, L. "Baudonivia, moniale de Sainte-Croix et biographe de S. Radegunde." In *Etudes merovingiennes*.

Cutler, K. E. "Edith, Queen of England, 1045–66." *Medieval Studies* 35 (1973): 222–31.

Darmstadter, P. *Das Reichsgut in der Lombardei und Piemont, 568–1250*. Strassburg, 1896.

Daudet, P. *Etudes sur l'histoire de la juridiction matrimoniale*. Les origines carolingiennes de la compétence exclusive de l'église. Paris, 1933.

Delaruelle, E. "Sainte Radegonde, son type de sainteté et la chrétienté de son temps." In *Etudes merovingiennes: Actes des journées de Poitiers, 1–3 May 1952*. Paris, 1953.

Delogu, P. "*Consors regni*, un problemo carolingio." *Bulletino dell'Istituto storico italiano per il medio evo et archivo muratoriano* 76 (1964): 47–98.

Deshman, R. "*Christus rex et magi reges*: Kingship and Christology in Ottonian and Anglo-Saxon Art." *Frühmittelalterliche Studien* 10 (1976): 367–405.

Devisse, J. *Hincmar, Archevêque de Reims, 845–82*, vol. 1. Geneva, 1975.

Dhondt, J. "Election et hérédité sous les Carolingiens et les premiers Capétiens." *Revue Belge de philologie et d'histoire* 18 (1939): 913–53.

———. "Sept femmes et un trio de rois." *Contributions à l'histoire economique et sociale*, vol. 3. Solvay, 1964–65.

Douglas, D. C. *William the Conqueror.* London, 1964.

Duby, G. "Le Mariage dans la société du haut moyen âge." *Il matrimonio, settimane di studio . . . Spoleto*, vol. 24. Spoleto, 1977.

———. *Medieval Marriage: Two Models from Twelfth-Century France.* Translated by E. Forster. Baltimore, 1978.

Dumville, D. "The Ætheling: A Study in Anglo-Saxon Constitutional History." In *Anglo-Saxon England*, edited by P. Clemoes. Vol. 8. Cambridge, 1979.

Dupraz, L. "Deux préceptes de Lothaire II, 867 et 868, ou les vestiges diplomatiques d'un divorce manqué." *Zeitschrift für schweizerische Kirchengeschichte* 19 (1965): 193–236.

Eckel, A. *Charles le Simple.* B.E.H.E., vol. 124. Paris, 1899.

Elze, R. "Die eiserne Krone in Monza." In *Herrschaftszeichen und Staatssymbolik*, edited by P. E. Schramm. Vol. 1, pp. 450–79.

Ewig, E. "Kaiser Lothars Urenkel, Ludwig von Vienne, der präsumtive Nachfolger Kaiser Karls III." In *Das erste Jahrtausend: Kultur und Kunst im werdenden Abendland an Rhein und Ruhr*, edited by V. Elbern. Vol. 1. Düsseldorf, 1962.

———. "Das Privileg des Bischofs Berthefrid von Amiens für Corbie von 664 und die Klosterpolitik der Königin Balthild." *Frankia* 1 (1973): 62–114.

———. "Studien zur merowingischen Dynastie." *Frühmittelalterliche Studien* 8 (1974): 15–59.

Facinger, "A Study of Medieval Queenship: Capetian France, 987–1237." *Studies in Medieval and Renaissance History* 5 (1968): 3–48.

Fasoli, G. *I re d'Italia, 888–962.* Florence, 1949.

Favre, E. *Eudes, comte de Paris et roi de France, 882–898.* B.E.H.E., vol. 99. Paris, 1893.

Fedele, P. "Vedovanze e seconde nozze." In *Il matrimonio, settimane di studio . . . Spoleto*, vol. 24. Spoleto, 1977.

Fell, C. E. "Edward, King and Martyr and the Anglo-Saxon Hagiographic Tradition." In *Ethelred the Unready: Papers from the Millenary Conference*, edited by D. Hill. B.A.R. vol. 59. Oxford, 1978.

Fisher, D. J. V. "The Anti-Monastic Reaction in the Reign of Edward the Martyr." *Cambridge Historical Journal* 10 (1952): 254 ff.

Fitzgerald, C. P. *The Empress Wu*. London, 1956.

Forde, D., and P. M. Kaberry, eds. *West African Kingdoms in the Nineteenth Century*. Oxford, 1967.

Fossier, R. "La Femme dans les sociétés occidentales." *Cahiers de civilisation médiévale*, vol. 20, nos. 2–3 (1977): 93–104.

Fransen, G. "La Rupture du mariage." In *Il matrimonio, settimane di studio . . . Spoleto*, vol. 24. Spoleto, 1977.

Freeman, E. A. *History of the Norman Conquest*, vols. 1 and 2. Oxford, 1877.

Frugoni, C. "L'iconografia del matrimonio e della coppia nel medioevo." In *Il matrimonio, settimane di studio . . . Spoleto*, vol. 24. Spoleto, 1977.

Ganshof, F. L. "Le Statut de la femme dans la monarchie Franque." *Recueils Jean Bodin* 12 (1962): 5–58.

Gaudemet, J. "Le Legs du droit romain en matière matrimoniale." *Il matrimonio, settimane di studio . . . Spoleto*, vol. 24. Spoleto, 1977.

Godfrey, J. "The Double Monastery in English History." *Ampleforth Journal* 79 (1974): 19–32.

Goody, E. "Forms of Pro-Parenthood: The Sharing and Substitution of Parental Roles." In *Kinship*, edited by J. Goody. London, 1971.

—————. "Legitimate and Illegitimate Aggression in a West African State." In *Witchcraft Confessions and Accusations*, edited by M. Douglas. London, 1970.

Goody, J. "Inheritance, Property and Women: Some Comparative Considerations." In *Family and Inheritance*, edited by J. Goody, J. Thirsk, and E. P. Thompson. Cambridge, 1976.

—————. *Production and Reproduction: A Comparative Study of the Domestic Domain*. Cambridge, 1976.

—————, ed. *Kinship*. London, 1971.

—————, ed. *Succession to High Office*. Cambridge, 1966.

Grierson, P. "Election and Inheritance in Early Germanic Kingship." *Cambridge Historical Journal* 7 (1941): 1–22.

Guillot, O. *Le Comte d'Anjou et son entourage au XIe siècle*. Paris, 1972.

Halphen, L. *Charlemagne et l'empire carolingien*. Paris, 1947.

Hamilton, B. "The House of Theophylact and the Promotion of the Religious Life among Women in Tenth-Century Rome." *Studia monastica* 12 (1970): 195–217.

Harris, G. "Furies, Witches and Mothers." In *The Character of Kinship*, edited by J. Goody. Cambridge, 1973.

Hellmann, S. "Die Heiraten der Karolinger." In *Ausgewählte Abhandlungen zur Historiographie und Geistesgeschichte des Mittelalters*, edited by H. Beumann. Darmstadt, 1961.

Herlihy, D. "Land, Family and Women in Continental Europe, 701–1200." *Traditio* 18 (1962): 89–120.

———. "Life Expectancies for Women in Medieval Society." In *The Role of Women in the Middle Ages*, edited by R. T. Morewedge. New York, 1975.

Hlawitschka, E. *Franken, Alemannen, Bayern und Burgunder in Oberitalien, 774–962*. Forschungen zur oberrheinischen Landesgeschichte, vol. 8. Freiburg im Breisgau, 1960.

———. "Die Vorfahren Karls des Großen." In *Karl der Große*, edited by W. Braunfels. Vol. 1. Düsseldorf, 1965.

Hodgkin, T. *Italy and her Invaders*, books 6–8. Oxford, 1892.

Hofmeister, A. "Studien zu Theophanu." In *Festschrift Edmund E. Stengel*. Münster, 1952.

Höhler, C. "St. Osyth and Aylesbury." *Records of Buckinghamshire* 18 (1966–70): 61–72.

Hyam, J. "Ermentrude and Richildis." In *Charles the Bald: Court and Kingdom*, edited by M. Gibson, J. Nelson, and D. Ganz. B.A.R. international series, vol. 101. Oxford, 1981.

Joyce, G. H. *Christian Marriage: An Historical and Doctrinal Study*. London, 1933.

Judd, E. "Women before the Conquest: A Study of Women in Anglo-Saxon England." *Papers in Women's Studies*. University of Michigan, n.d.

Kantorowicz, E. H. "The Carolingian King in the Bible of San Paolo fuori le Mura." In *Late Classical and Mediaeval Studies in Honor of A. M. Friend, Jr.*, edited by K. Weitzmann et al. Princeton, 1955.

———. *Laudes Regiae*. Berkeley, 1946.

Kehr, P. "Zur Geschichte Ottos III." *Historische Zeitschrift* 66 (1891): 385–443.

Keller, H. "Zum Sturz Karls III." *Deutsches Archiv* 22 (1966): 333–84.

————. "Zur Struktur der Königsherrschaft im karolingischen und nachkarolingischen Italien." *Quellen und Forschungen aus italienischen Archiven und Bibliotheken* 47 (1967): 123–223.

Klauser, R. *Der Heinrichs und Kunigunden Kult in mittelalterlichen Bistum Bamberg.* Bamberg, 1957.

Kliman, B. "Women in Early English Literature, *Beowulf* to the *Ancrene Wisse.*" *Nottingham Medieval Studies* 21 (1977): 32–49.

Körner, S. *The Battle of Hastings: England and Europe, 1035–66.* Bibliotheca historica Lundensis, vol. 14. Lund, 1964.

Konecny, S. "Eherecht und Ehepolitik unter Ludwig dem Frommen." M.I.Ö.G. 85 (1977): 1–21.

————. "Die Frauen des karolingischen Königshauses: Die politische Bedeutung der Ehe und die Stellung der Frau in der frankischen Herrscherfamilie vom 7 bis zum 10 Jahrhundert." Ph.D. Dissertation, University of Vienna, 1976.

Kurth, G. "Le Concile de Mâcon et l'âme des femmes." In *Etudes Franques*, vol. 1. Paris, 1919.

————. "La Reine Brunehaut." In *Etudes Franques*, vol. 1. Paris, 1919.

Lauer, P. *Le Règne de Louis IV d'Outremer.* B.E.H.E., vol. 127. Paris, 1900.

————. *Robert I et Raoul de Bourgogne rois de France, 923–936.* B.E.H.E., vol. 188. Paris, 1910.

Leach, E. R. "Polyandry, Inheritance and the Definition of Marriage." In *Kinship*, edited by J. Goody. London, 1971.

Lemarignier, J. F. *Le Gouvernement royal aux premiers temps Capétiens, 987–1108.* Paris, 1965.

Le Patourel, J. "The Norman Succession, 996–1135." E.H.R. 86 (1971): 225–50.

Levillain, L. "L'Avènement de la dynastie carolingienne et les origines de l'état pontifical." *Bibliotheque de l'Ecole des Chartres* 94 (1933): 225–95.

————. "Etudes merovingiennes: La Charte de Clotilde, 10 mars 673." *Bibliotheque de l'Ecole des Chartres* 105 (1944): 5–63.

Levison, W. *England and the Continent in the Eighth Century.* Oxford, 1946.

Leyser, K. *Rule and Conflict in an Early Medieval Society, Ottonian Saxony*. London, 1979.

Lintzel, M. "*Heinricus natus in aula regali*: Miszellen zur Geschichte des zehnten Jahrhunderts nr. V." In *Ausgewählte Schriften*, vol. 2. Berlin, 1961.

———. "Königin Mathilde." *Westfälische Lebensbilder*, ser. 5 (1937), pp. 161–75.

———. "Die Mathildenviten und das Wahrheitsproblem in der Überlieferung der Ottonenzeit." *Ausgewählte Schriften*, vol. 2. Berlin, 1961.

———. "Der Reichstag von Verona im Jahre 983." *Ausgewählte Schriften*, vol. 2. Berlin, 1961.

Lot, F. *Les Derniers Carolingiens: Lothaire, Louis V, Charles de Lorraine, 954–991*. B.E.H.E., vol. 87. Paris, 1891.

———. *Etudes sur le règne de Hugues Capet et la fin du Xe siècle*. B.E.H.E., vol. 147. Paris, 1903.

de Maillé, Marquise. *Les Cryptes de Jouarre*. Paris, 1971.

Mair, L. *African Kingdoms*. Oxford, 1977.

———. *Primitive Government*. London, 1964.

———. *Marriage*. London, 1971.

McLaughlin, E. C. "Equality of Souls, Inequality of Sexes: Woman in Medieval Theology." In *Religion and Sexism*, edited by R. R. Ruether. New York, 1974.

McNamara, J. A., and S. Wemple. "Marriage and Divorce in the Frankish Kingdom." In *Women in Medieval Society*, edited by S. M. Stuard. Pennsylvania, 1976.

———. "The Power of Women through the Family in Medieval Europe." In *Clio's Consciousness Raised*, edited by M. Hartmann and L. W. Banner. New York, 1974.

Manselli, R. "Il matrimonio nei penitenziali." In *Il matrimonio, settimane di studio . . . Spoleto*, vol. 24. Spoleto, 1977.

Il matrimonio nella societa altomedievale. Settimane di studio del centro Italiano de studi sull'alto medioevo, vol. 24. Spoleto, 1977.

Meyer, M. A. "Women and the Tenth-Century English Monastic Reform." *Revue benedictine* 87 (1977): 34–61.

Mor, C. G. "*Consors regni*: La regina nel diritto pubblico italiano dei secoli IX–X." *Archivio Giuridico*, ser. 6, vol. 4 (1948): 7–32.

————. "La successione al trono nel diritto pubblico longobardo."
In *Studi in onore di Federico Cammeo*, vol. 2. Padua, 1933.

Morris, I. *The World of the Shining Prince: Court Life in Ancient Japan*. London, 1964.

Nelson, J. "Inauguration Rituals." In *Early Medieval Kingship*, edited by P. H. Sawyer and I. Wood. Leeds, 1977.

————. "Queens as Jezebels: The Careers of Brunhild and Balthild in Merovingian History." In *Medieval Women*, edited by D. Baker. Oxford, 1978.

Nicholson, J. "*Feminae gloriosae*: Women in the Age of Bede." In *Medieval Women*, edited by D. Baker. Oxford, 1978.

Odegaard, C. E. "The Empress Engelberga." *Speculum* 26 (1951): 77–103.

Perst, O. "Zur Reihenfolge der Kinder Ottos II und der Theophano." *Deutsches Archiv* 14 (1958): 230–36.

Pfister, C. *Etudes sur le règne de Robert I Pieux, 996–1031*. B.E.H.E., vol. 64. Paris, 1885.

Pochettino, G. "L'Imperatrice Angelberga, 850–90," *Archivio storico Lombardo*, ser. 5, vol. 48 (1921): 39–149.

von Pölnitz-Kehr, G. F. "Kaiserin Angilberga: Ein Exkurs zur Diplomatik Kaiser Ludwigs II von Italien." *Historisches Jahrbuch* 60 (1940): 429–40.

Poole, R. L. "The Alpine Son-in-Law of Edward the Elder." In *Studies in Chronology and History*. Oxford, 1934.

Portmann, M-L. "Die Darstellung der Frau in der Geschichtsschreibung des früheren Mittelalters." Ph.D. Dissertation, University of Basel, 1958.

Poupardin, R. *Le Royaume de Bourgogne, 888–1038*. B.E.H.E., vol. 163. Paris, 1907.

————. *Le Royaume de Provence sous les Carolingiens, 855–933*. B.E.H.E., vol. 131. Paris, 1901.

Prinz, F. *Frühes Mönchtum im Frankenreich: Kultur und Gesellschaft in Gallien, den Rheinlanden und Bayern am Beispiel der monastischen Entwicklung*. Munich, 1965.

Prusak, B. P. "Woman: Seductive Siren and Source of Sin?" In *Religion and Sexism*, edited by R. R. Ruether. New York, 1974.

Richards, A. I. "African Kings and Their Royal Relatives." *Journal of the Royal Anthropological Institute* 91 (1961): 135–50.

Riché, P. *Education and Culture in the Barbarian West, Sixth through Eighth Centuries*, translated by J. J. Contreni. Columbia, 1976.

Ritzer, K. *Le Mariage dans les eglises chrétiennes du Ier au XIe siècle*. Lex orandi, vol. 45. Paris, 1970.

Robinson, J. A. *The Times of St. Dunstan*. Oxford, 1923.

Ruether, R. R. "Misogynism and Virginal Feminism in the Fathers of the Church." In *Religion and Sexism*, edited by R. R. Ruether. New York, 1974.

————, ed. *Religion and Sexism: Images of Women in the Jewish and Christian Traditions*. New York, 1974.

Schmid, K. "Heirat, Familienfolge, Geschlechterbewußtsein." *Il matrimonio, settimane di studio . . . Spoleto*, vol. 24. Spoleto, 1977.

————. "Die Thronfolge Ottos des Großen." *Königswahl und Thronfolge in ottonisch-frühdeutscher Zeit*, edited by E. Hlawitschka. Wege der Forschung, vol. 178. Darmstadt, 1971.

————. "Neue Quellen zum Verständnis des Adels im 10 Jahrhundert." In *Königswahl und Thronfolge in ottonisch-frühdeutscher Zeit*, edited by E. Hlawitschka. Wege der Forschung, vol. 178. Darmstadt, 1971.

Schneider, R. *Königswahl und Königserhebung im Frühmittelalter: Untersuchungen zur Herrschaftsnachfolge bei den Langobarden und Merowingern*. Monographien zur Geschichte des Mittelalters, vol. 3. Stuttgart, 1972.

Schnith, K. "*Regni et pacis inquietatrix*: Zur Rolle der Kaiserin Mathilde in der 'Anarchie.'" *Journal of Medieval History* 2 (1976): 135–57.

Schramm, P. E. *Die deutschen Kaiser und Könige in Bildern ihre Zeit*. Leipzig, 1928.

Schramm, P. E. *Herrschaftszeichen und Staatssymbolik*, vols. 1 and 2. Schriften der Monumenta Germaniae Historica, vol. 13 i/ii. Stuttgart, 1954–55.

Schramm, P. E. and F. Mütherich. *Denkmale der deutschen Könige und Kaiser*. Veröffentlichungen des Zentralinstituts für Kunstgeschichte in München. München, 1962.

Schulenberg, J. T. "Sexism and the Celestial Gynaeceum from 500 to 1200." *Journal of Medieval History* 4 (1978): 117–33.

Spromberg, H. "Judith, Königin von England Gräfin von Flandern." *Revue belge de philologie et d'histoire* 15 (1936): 397–428.

Stafford, P. A. "Charles the Bald, Judith and England." In *Charles the Bald*, edited by M. Gibson, J. Nelson, and D. Ganz. B.A.R. Oxford, 1981.

———. "The King's Wife in Wessex." *Past and Present*, no. 91 (1981), pp. 3–27.

———. "The Reign of Æthelred II: A Study in the Limitations on Royal Policy and Action." In *Ethelred the Unready: Papers from the Millenary Conference*, edited by D. Hill. B.A.R., vol. 59. Oxford, 1978.

———. "Sons and Mothers: Family Politics in the Early Middle Ages." In *Medieval Women*, edited by D. Baker. Oxford, 1978.

Stenton, D. M. *The English Woman in History*. London, 1957.

Stevenson, W. "An Alleged Son of Harold Harefoot." *English Historical Review* 28 (1913): 112–17.

Stranks, C. J. *St. Etheldreda, Queen and Abbess*. Ely, 1975.

Thirsk, J. "The Family." *Past and Present*, no. 27 (1964), pp. 116–22.

Toubert, P. *Les Structures du Latium médiéval, le Latium méridional et la Sabine du IXe siècle à la fin du XIIe siècle*. 2 vols. Rome, 1973.

———. "La Théorie du mariage chez les moralistes carolingiens." In *Il matrimonio, settimane di studio . . . Spoleto*, vol. 24. Spoleto, 1977.

Uhlirz, M. "Die rechtliche Stellung der Kaiserinwitwe Adelheid im deutschen und im italischen Reich." *Zeitschrift der Savigny-Stiftung für Rechtsgeschichte, germanistische Abteilung* 74 (1957): 85–97.

———. "Studien über Theophano, I & II: Die Herkunft der Kaiserin Theophano. Die beiden Lebensbeschreibungen des Abtes Gregor von Burtscheid." *Deutsches Archiv* 6 (1943): 442–74.

———. "Studien über Theophano III: Die Interventionen der Kaiserin Theophano zugunsten der Nonnenklöster während der Regierungszeit Ottos II und ihre Bedeutung." *Deutsches Archiv* 9 (1951): 122–35.

de Vajay, S. "Mathilde, reine de France inconnue." *Journal des Savants* (1971), pp. 241–60.

Verdon, J. "Les Femmes et la politique en France au Xe siècle." In *Economies et sociétés au moyen âge: Mélanges offerts à*

Edouard Perroy. Paris, 1973.

―――. "Les Sources de l'histoire de la femme en occident aux Xe-XIIIe siècles." *Cahiers de civilization médiévale* 20 (1977): 219–51.

Vogel, C. "Les Rites de la celebration du mariage: Leur signification dans la formation du lien durant le haut moyen âge." In *Il matrimonio, settimane di studio . . . Spoleto*, vol. 24. Spoleto, 1977.

Vogelsang, T. *Die Frau als Herrscherin im höhen Mittelalter*. Frankfurt, 1954.

Wainwright, F. "Æthelflæd, Lady of the Mercians." In *Scandinavian England: Collected Papers of F. Wainwright*, edited by H. P. R. Finberg. Chichester, 1975.

Wallace-Hadrill, J. M. "A Carolingian Renaissance Prince: The Emperor Charles the Bald." *Proceedings of the British Academy* 64 (1978): 155–84.

―――. *The Long-Haired Kings and Other Studies in Frankish History*. London, 1962.

Warner, M. *Alone of All Her Sex: The Myth and Cult of the Virgin Mary*. London, 1976.

―――. *The Dragon Empress: Life and Times of Tz'u Hsi, Empress Dowager of China*. London, 1972.

Werner, K. F. "Die Nachkommen Karls des Großen bis um das Jahr 1000 (1–8 Generation)." In *Karl der Große: Lebenswerk und Nachleben*, edited by W. Braunfels and P. E. Schramm. Vol. 4. Düsseldorf, 1967.

Williams, A. "Some Notes and Considerations on Problems Connected with the English Royal Succession, 860–1066." In *Proceedings of the Battle Conference on Anglo-Norman Studies*, edited by R. Allen Brown. Vol. 1. Ipswich, 1978.

Wimmer, F. P. *Kaiserin Adelheid, Gemahlin Ottos I des Großen in ihrem Leben und Wirken von 931–973*. Regensburg, 1897.

Wood, I. "Kings, Kingdoms and Consent." In *Early Medieval Kingship*, edited by P. H. Sawyer and I. N. Wood. Leeds, 1977.

Wright, C. E. *The Cultivation of Saga in Anglo-Saxon England*. London, 1939.

Genealogical Tables and Maps

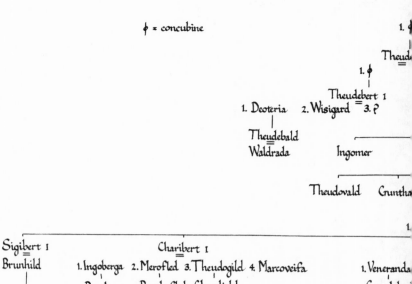

1. MER(
(order of mar

φ = concubine

1. (

Theud(

1. φ

Theudebert 1

1. Deoteria 2. Wisigard ⚌ 3. ?

Theudebald
Waldrada

Ingomer

Theudovald   Gruntha

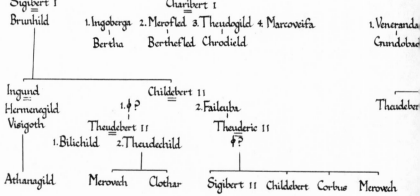

1.

Sigibert 1 ⚌
Brunhild

Charibert 1
1. Ingoberga 2. Merofled 3. Theudogild 4. Marcoveifa

1. Veneranda
Gundobac

Bertha   Berthefled Chrodield

Ingund ⚌
Hermenegild
Visigoth

Childebert 11 ⚌
1. φ ?

2. Faileuba

Theudeber

Theudebert 11
1. Bilichild 2. Theudechild

Theuderic 11
φ ?

Athanagild   Merovech   Clothar

Sigibert 11 Childebert Corbus Merovech

1.

Clothar 111
?

Clovis   Cl

Landechild   Audofled

Clotild   Theodoric Ostrogoth

     Amalasuntha

Childebert I   Clotild
Ultrogotha   Amalaric Visigoth

Chroteberga   Chrotesind

     Clothar I

2. Guntheuca   3. Arnegund   4. φ Chunsina   5. Radegund

...am   Gunther   Gundoald   Chramn

...l 3. Austrechild - Bobilla   Chalda

Chlodomer   Chlodoberga   Chlodichild

     Chilperic I

1. Audovera   2. Galswinth   3. Fredegund

Chlodovech   Basina   Samson   Chlodobert   ?   Rigunth   Theuderic   Clothar II
                            1. Berchtetrud
                            2. φ Sigihild
                            3. Haldetrud

Merovech   Charibert II
                            ?

     Dagobert I   Chilperic

2. Nantechild   3. φ ?   4. ? φ Ragnetrud   5. Vulfegund   6. Berchild

Clovis II   Sigibert III
Balthild   Himnechild

...ic III   Childeric II = Bilichild   Childebert   Dagobert II
...hild   Chilperic II/Daniel   ?

...ebert III   Clothar IV   son

...bert III

...deric IV

...deric III

ϕ = concubine

2. C
(order of mar

Drogo — 1. Plectrud
Grimoald

1. Chrotrud — 2. Bernhard

Carloman — Hiltrud
Drogo — Odilo of Bavaria
Tassilo

1. ϕ Himiltrud   2. dtr. of Desiderius   3. Hildegard   4. ϕ 5
Pepin the Hunchback   Charles Adelaide Rotrud Pepin of Italy   Lo
? ϕ 1.
Bernard

Alpais Arnulf Lothar I   Pepin I Rotrud Hildegard Loui
Ermengard   Ringart

Louis II   Lothar II Charles   Pepin II
Angelberga 1. Theutberga 2. ϕ Waldrada of Provence

Gisela Ermengard   Hugh Bertha
Boso of Vienne   1. Count of Arles 2. Margrave of Tuscany

Louis the Blind
Adelaide   Hugh of Vienne

1. Willa 2. Alda 3. Marozia 4. Bertha ϕ Wandelmoda ϕ Rotrud ϕ Pezola ϕ Stephania

Lothar
Adelaide

Carloman   Hildegard Ermengard Louis III   Gisela C
1. ϕ Liutswind 2. ϕ 1. ϕ 2. Liutgard   1.

Arnulf   Hugh Louis Hildegard   E
1. ϕ 2. ϕ 3. ϕ 4. Uota

Zwentibold Ellinrat Ratold Louis the Child

A

3. ♦
Childebrand

3. ? ♦ Swanhild
Grifo

emigius

Carloman   Gisela   Pepin
Gerberga

6. Liutgard   7. ♦ Madelgard   8. ♦ Gersvind   9. ♦ Regina   10. ♦ Adelind

Lothar Bertha Gisela Hildegard

2. Judith

Gisela
=
Eberhard,
Duke of Friulia

Berengar I
of Italy

1. Bertilla 2. Anna

Gisela

Berengar II
=
Willa

Charles the Bald
=
1. Ermentrud   2. Richildis

Rotrud

Gisela

Hildegard

Ermentrud

Lothar

Carloman

Charles

Louis
the Stammerer
=
Judith   1. Ansgard   2. Adelaide

1. Æthelwulf   Ermentrud   Charles the Simple
   of Wessex   Louis III   =
2. Æthelbald   Carloman   1. ♦   2. Frederun   3. Eadgifu
   of Wessex   Hildegard
3. Baldwin   Gisela
   of Flanders

Arnulf Drogo Roric Alpais   Louis IV
                          d'Outremer

dis   Ermentrud Frederun Adelaide Gisela Rotrud Hildegard   Gerberga

Lothar   Mathilda   Charles dtr. Louis Charles of Provence Henry
=   Conrad of Burgundy   Adelaide
2. Emma

. ♦

aard   Louis V   Bertha   Rudolf III
     Adelaide   1. Eudes of Blois 2. Robert the Pious

φ = concubine

1. Osburh...

Athelstan   Æthelbald   Æthelberht
               Judith

Æthelflæd   Edward the...
=
Æthelred,   1. φ Ecgwyna   2. Ælfflæ...
Lord of the Mercians
                 Athelstan   Eadgyth
Ælfwyn   =
                          Sihtric of York

Ælfweard	Edwin	Eadgifu	Æthelhild,	Eadgyth	Eadflæd,	Eadhild	Ælfgif...
		=	nun	=	nun	=	=
		Charles		Otto I		Hugh	Conrad
		the Simple				the Great	of Bu...

Eadwig   1. Æt...
=
Ælfgifu   Edw...

Athelstan	Ecgberht	Edmund Ironside		Eadwig		Abbess of Wherwell	
		=					Eadgyt...
		Ealdgyth	Eadred		Edgar		=
							Eadric of Merci...

Edmund   Edward the Exile

                  Godwine

Edgar the Ætheling   Harold II   Tostig

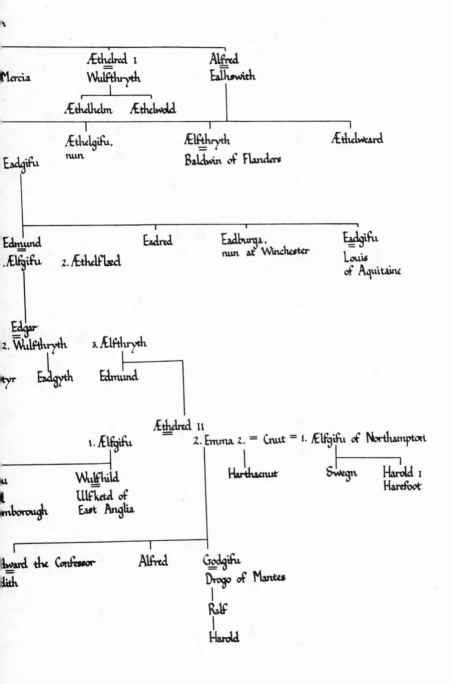

Mercia

Æthelred I = Wulfthryth   Alfred = Ealhswith

Æthelhelm   Æthelwold

Æthelgifu, nun   Ælfthryth = Baldwin of Flanders   Æthelweard

Eadgifu

Edmund = .Ælfgifu   2. Æthelflæd   Eadred   Eadburga, nun at Winchester   Eadgifu = Louis of Aquitaine

Edgar
2. Wulfthryth   3. Ælfthryth

tyr   Eadgyth   Edmund

Æthelred II

1. Ælfgifu = 2. Emma 2. = Cnut = 1. Ælfgifu of Northampton

u

l   Wulfhild = Ulfketd of East Anglia   Harthacnut   Swegn   Harold I Harefoot

mborough

ward the Confessor
dith   Alfred   Godgifu = Drogo of Mantes

Ralf

Harold

4. OTTONIAN ROYAL HOUSE

(not complete: order of marriage and children not always certain)

Henry the Fowler
=
1. Hatheburg   2. Mathilda

Thangmar

Otto I
=
1. ⊕ Slav captive   2. Eadgyth   3. Adelaide

William, Archbishop of Mainz

Liudolf   Liudgard

Henry   Brun

Mathilda, Abbess of Quedlinburg

Otto II
=
Theophanu

Gerberga
=
1. Gilbert, Duke of Lotharingia
2. Louis IV d'Outremer

Lothar   Mathilda
Emma   Conrad of Burgundy

Louis V

Hathui
=
Hugh the Great

Henry, Duke of Bavaria

Henry the Wrangler

Henry II
=
Cunigund

Bruno, Archbishop of Cologne

Hugh Capet
=
Adelaide

Bertha   Rudolf III of Burgundy

Robert the Pious
=
1. Suzanne/Rozala   2. Bertha of Blois   3. Constance

Bertha
=
1. Eudes of Blois   2. Robert the Pious

Sophia, Abbess of Gandersheim   Adelaide, Abbess of Quedlinburg   Mathilda   dtr. Otto III

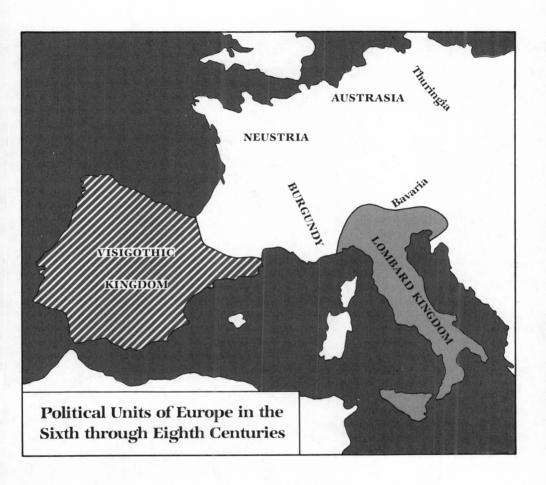

Political Units of Europe in the
Sixth through Eighth Centuries

235

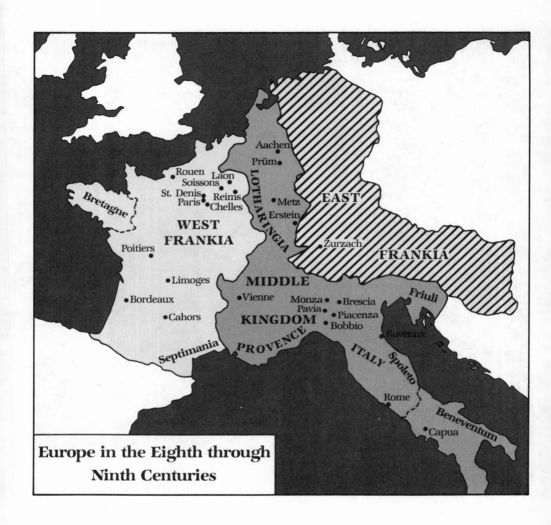

Aachen
Prüm
Rouen
Laon
Soissons
St. Denis
Reims
Paris
Chelles
Metz
Erstein
EAST
LOTHARINGIA
Bretagne
WEST
FRANKIA
Zurzach
FRANKIA
Poitiers
MIDDLE
Friuli
Limoges
Vienne
Monza
Brescia
Pavia
Piacenza
Bordeaux
KINGDOM
Bobbio
Cahors
Ravenna
Septimania
PROVENCE
ITALY
Spoleto
Rome
Beneventum
Capua

Europe in the Eighth through Ninth Centuries

236

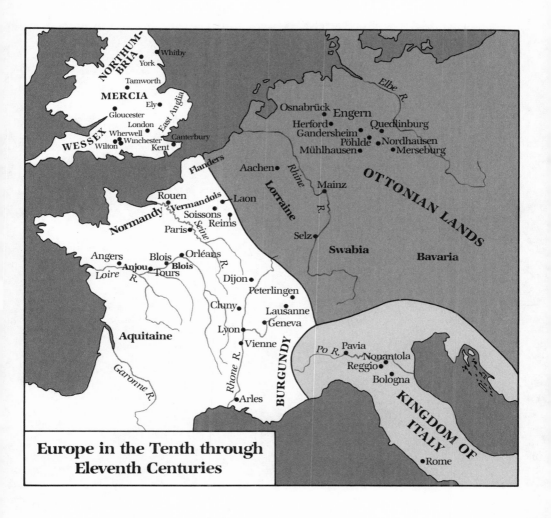

Europe in the Tenth through Eleventh Centuries

NORTHUM-
BRIA
Whitby
York
Tamworth
MERCIA
Ely
Gloucester
East Anglia
London
Wherwell
Winchester
Canterbury
WESSEX
Wilton
Kent

Osnabrück
Engern
Herford
Gandersheim
Quedlinburg
Pöhlde
Nordhausen
Mühlhausen
Merseburg
Elbe R.

Flanders
Aachen
Rhine R.
Mainz
OTTONIAN LANDS

Rouen
Vermandois
Laon
Lorraine
Soissons
Reims
Paris
Seine
Selz
Swabia
Bavaria

Angers
Blois
Orléans
Anjou
Blois
Loire R.
Tours
Dijon
Normandy

Aquitaine
Peterlingen
Cluny
Lausanne
Lyon
Geneva
Vienne
Rhône R.
BURGUNDY
Po R.
Pavia
Nonantola
Reggio
Bologna
KINGDOM OF ITALY
Garonne R.
Arles
Rome

237

Index

Index

Index

Death: age at, 143–45, 208; reasons for, 144–45, 184, 187; of the empress Adelaide, 184; of Mathilda (wife of Henry the Fowler), 184–85

Desiderius, 28, 47, 54, 60, 101, 177

Divorce, 79–86; of Louis and Angelberga, 17, 23, 75, 135; excuses used for, 17, 29, 74, 75, 81–84, 93, 180; of Lothar II, 29, 75–76, 83, 85, 135, 177, 203; of Edward the Confessor, 41, 76, 82, 179; as repudiation of alliance, 44; forced on kings, 44, 75, 93; common in sixth and seventh centuries, 79–80; Church views on, 80–81, 84–85, 86; of Robert the Pious, 83–85, 86, 97, 204; harder by tenth century, 88, 92

Doda, 69

Dowry: of Mathilda, 34; of Frederun, 37; of Rigunth, 58; importance of, in marriage, 62–63, 70; nunneries as, 101–2, 178–79; provided for queens, 101–5; inalienable, 103–4

Dunstan, archbishop of Canterbury, 16, 85, 91, 98, 124, 208; career of, 125–26; and Eadgifu, 148–49, 161

Dynastic struggle: effects on choice of wife, 41; effects on queens, 119, 132–33

Eadburh, 17–18, 177; as West Saxon hate-figure, 31, 134; accused of murder, 96; and treasure, 104–5

Eadgifu, wife of Charles the Simple: dowry of, 102; widowhood of, 110, 115; succession of son of, 164; remarriage of, 168–69, 180; burial of, 190

Eadgifu, wife of Edward the Elder, 74, 208; landgrants to, 103; and daughter-in-law, 111; and support for reform, 121, 124, 125–26; death of, 143, 144, 145; career of, 148–49; regent, 151; and succession, 157, 158–59, 161

Eadgyth, wife of Otto I, 6, 104; marriage and wooing of, 34–35, 56; birth of son of, 91; and relations with Mathilda, 110; and interventions in charters, 124; burial of, 189

Eadgyth, wife of Sihtric, 48

Eadred, 16, 125, 148. See also Succession disputes, on death of Eadred

Eadwig, 16, 144; marriage of, 16, 39, 44, 55, 204; divorce of, 75, 83, 125–26, 204;

and Eadgifu, 149, 157. See also Succession disputes, on death of Eadred

Eanfled, 44, 58, 89, 112–23, 120, 122

Ecclesiastics: queens and, 124–27, 161. See also Adalbero of Laon, Æthelwold, Dunstan, Liaisons

Ecgberht, 2, 18

Ecgfryth, 15, 74, 81–82, 87

Ecgwyna, concubine of Edward, 65, 70

Eddius, 15

Edgar, 55, 74, 112, 125, 144; accused of adultery, 16, 85, 91; wooing, 21–22, 32–33; and Eadgifu, 148–49, 157

Edith, 129; in Life of Edward, 4, 5–6, 23, 25, 28–29; marriage of, 39, 110; attempted divorce of, 41, 82, 179; education of, 54–55; accused of murder, 97; advances supporters, 98; and royal dignity, 101, 106, 107, 108; dowry of, 102; landholding of, 102–3; rears heirs, 112; nature of power of, 113–14; and succession, 162, 171; and Wilton, 179; burial of, 189

Edmund, 111, 125, 144, 148, 186

Edmund Ironside, 36–37, 40, 78

Education: and nunneries, 54, 181–82; of queens, 54–55; and court, 100; queen's responsibility for, 112–13, 166

Edward the Confessor, 4, 89, 106–7, 108, 110, 171, 179; marriage of, 39, 56; attempted divorce of, 41, 76, 82, 179; mother's actions for, 78, 164; mother's actions against, 157–58; provides for Edith, 166; and Emma, 166, 170; burial of, 189

Edward the Elder, 55, 74, 78, 141, 145, 148, 179; daughters' marriages, 41, 48; marriage of, probably incestuous, 43; and Æthelflæd, 173

Edward the Martyr, 79, 125, 133, 163

Edwin of Northumbria, 44, 89, 176

Ely, nunnery, 177, 178, 181, 190

Embroidery, 107

Emma, wife of Æthelred the Unready and Cnut, 3, 4, 5, 141, 151, 210; marriage to Cnut, 40, 49; as peacemaker, 45; marriage to Æthelred, 48, 110; followers at marriage, 58; attempts to gain succession for her sons, 72, 78, 105, 157–58, 161, 163, 164, 165; age of, at childbirth, 91; dowry of, 102; land granted to, 103;

Index

Index

Succession disputes (*continued*)
on death of Otto II, 141–42, 149–50, 160,
161; on death of Louis the Stammerer,
160; on death of Robert the Pious, 167–68
Succession to: Edward the Confessor, 5, 162,
171; Charles the Fat, 66, 95–96, 162–63,
172, 206, 209; to Lothar of West Frankia,
94–95, 167, 206; to Arnulf, 95; to Louis
II, 135–36, 171–73. *See also* Louis the
Pious
Supponides, 38–39, 136, 166, 202
Suzanne/Rozala, 42, 74, 83, 102, 176, 190
Swanhild: marriage of, 40, 44, 45; as concubine, 64, 128; and succession, 164, 179

Tertullian, 26
Theodahad, 137
Theoderic the Ostrogoth, ix, 89, 137
Theodora of Rome, 30, 138
Theodore, Archbishop, 15, 80
Theophanu, 1, 30, 115, 118, 136, 140, 141,
142; origins of, 1; Adelaide's dislike of, 9,
103, 110–11; marriage of, 48; children of,
88, 89, 90; dowry of, 102, 179; and Ade-
laide's dowry, 103; and treasure, 105;
anointed, 132; regency of, 139, 149–50,
154–55, 161, 210; death of, 144, 186;
burial of, 190
Theudebald, 51
Theudebert I, 51, 64
Theudebert II, 64, 67, 87, 146, 147, 187
Theudechild, 50, 73, 169, 180
Theudelinda, 33, 40, 49, 89, 110, 123, 129,
130, 161–62, 207
Theuderada, 138
Theuderic II, 64, 67, 128, 146, 147
Theutberga, 29, 39, 75–76, 83, 130, 177, 180
Tostig, 4, 5, 41, 97, 114
Tours, nunnery, 178
Towns: and queens, 101, 102, 117–20, 178
Treasure, 49–50, 104–6, 161, 166, 205

Ultrogotha, 31, 144, 175
Uncles and nephews, 154–55, 165, 167. *See
also* Charles of Lorraine, Liudolf
Uota, 66, 82, 95

Venantius Fortunatus, 6, 9–10, 11, 45, 175,
182
Vengeance: women as wreakers of, 11, 45–

46; against women, 176–77, 188. *See also*
Foreign wives, Murders
Vices: allegedly female, 20–25, 29
Vikings, 48–49, 202
Virago, 30
Vision of a Poor Woman, 162
Vision of Charles the Fat, 162–63
Vision of Wetto, 180
Vita Mahthildis reginae antiquior, 3, 28,
199
Vita Mahthildis reginae posterior, 3, 28,
199

Wærburh, 144
Wala, 19, 93
Walahfrid Strabo, 19, 25
Waldrada, Lombard princess, 40, 51, 52
Waldrada, Lothar II's concubine, 29, 70,
75–76, 130
Wandelmoda, 53
Wantage, 89
Wherwell, nunnery, 21, 25, 32, 76, 110,
124, 178, 179
Whitby, nunnery, 120, 122
Widows: Carolingian reception of, 18, 76,
177, 180; and own kin, 45, 53, 116, 166,
176–77; marriage of, 49–51, 51–54,
137–38, 168–70, 202; longevity and prev-
alence of, 143–46; sonless, and succes-
sion, 166, 171–73; remarriage of royal,
168–69, 210; vulnerability of, 174–77;
and nunneries, 177–82
Wigbod of Parma, 135, 166
Wilfrid, 15, 82, 87, 107, 112
Willa, wife of Berengar II, 54, 136, 206;
Liudprand on, 20, 24, 25; military role,
118, 119
Willa, wife of Rudolf of Burgundy, 52
Wilton, nunnery, 32, 54–55, 178–79, 180,
190
Wimborne, nunnery, 177
Winchester, 102, 105, 110, 161, 178
Wisigard, 51
Witchcraft, 29–30, 200
Wooing, 21–22, 32–34, 56–57
Wulfhilde, 32
Wulfthryth, 32, 74, 179, 180

Zurzach, nunnery, 88, 136, 179
Zwentibold, 50, 66

248